ISLANDS
OF PLACE AND SPACE

Arne Kruse on the island of Brattværet, Møre and Romsdal, his ancestral home.
Photo: Berit Sandnes, used with kind permission.

Arne Kruse at the replica of the runestone at Kuli, Møre and Romsdal.
Photo: Svein Olav Kruse, used with kind permission.

ISLANDS
OF PLACE AND SPACE

A Festschrift in Honour of
Arne Kruse

Edited by Christian Cooijmans

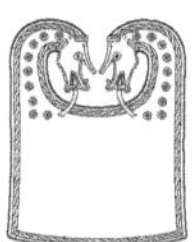

Published in Scotland by
The Scottish Society for Northern Studies
c/o Scandinavian Studies, School of Literatures, Languages and Cultures,
University of Edinburgh
50 George Square, Edinburgh EH8 9LH
www.ssns.org.uk

ISBN 978-1-3999-3523-4

Cover Image: Painting of a coastal scene at Veiholmen, Johan Berthelsen
Cover Design: Christian Cooijmans
Typesetting: Laura Kincaid (Ten Thousand)

The Scottish Society for Northern Studies is a registered charity (SC010647)

Contents

Scandinavian countries have long been among Scotland's closest partners. We share rich and diverse ties that have had a lasting impact on the fabric of our nation, from Shetland to Galloway. Woven through centuries of economic, cultural, and social exchanges, these links continue to nourish a sense of affinity and interdependency that stretches far beyond mere geographical proximity.

People and ideas have shuttled back and forth across the North Sea for millennia, from Viking longboats to today's digital means of communication. Collectively, they have fashioned a vast and yet still developing Scottish-Scandinavian heritage, where intangible cultural connections are as important as the bountiful tangible testimonies of our common history.

Spanning over three decades, Dr Kruse's work has brought a crucial contribution to our understanding of the Scandinavian elements of Scotland's identity. His research on place-names and onomastics has shown us that a tour of Scottish towns and Scottish islands is also very often a metaphorical journey through Scottish-Scandinavian history. He has mapped and celebrated the power and significance of linguistic connections, of which my own family and professional background makes me a committed supporter.

This festschrift is published 550 years after Orkney and Shetland left the Danish-Norwegian kingdom and became united with the rest of Scotland. In addition, 2022 has been designated as the Year of Scotland's Stories, to encourage our communities to share their tales and reflect on what nurtures our sense of place, history, and belonging. Dr Kruse's body of work and this festschrift stand in themselves as valued contributions to the celebrations for these anniversaries.

Both our history and our present-day international engagements show that Scotland's compass points firmly north. The Scottish Government is determined to build on existing connections and pursue ever closer collaboration with our Scandinavian neighbours around the many challenges and ambitions that we have in common. With similar population sizes, geographical features, and – crucially – similar outlooks, Scotland and Scandinavian countries continue to exchange knowledge and expertise in a wide range of sectors. To promote even greater cultural, trade, and policy cooperation, this year the Scottish Government opened an office in Copenhagen, whose remit encompasses all three Scandinavian countries.

It is a new and exciting chapter in the long history of Scottish-Scandinavian ties that Dr Kruse's research has helped us explore and appreciate. Thanks in no small measure to his work, we can cherish our rich Scandinavian legacies and look confidently north for our future journeys.

Takk skal du ha, Arne.

Angus Robertson
Cabinet Secretary for the Constitution,
External Affairs and Culture

Scottish Government
1 November 2022

Introduction

Christian Cooijmans
with Brigitte Guenier-Kruse

Wherefore my heart leaps within me,
My mind roves with the waves
Over the whale's domain, it wanders far and wide
Across the face of the earth, returns again to me
Eager and unsatisfied; the solitary bird screams,
Irresistible, urges my heart to the whale's way
Over the stretch of the sea.

– Anonymous, 'The Seafarer'.[1]

This festschrift, *Islands of Place and Space,* honours and celebrates the achievements of Dr Arne Kruse, who retired from the University of Edinburgh in 2021 after an accomplished scholarly career of over four decades as a researcher and educator. In doing

---

1. 'The Seafarer' is among a group of Old English poems found in the tenth-century Exeter Book (Exeter Cathedral Library, MS 3501, ff. 81v–83r). Although its precise date of composition is unknown, it is considered to have been handed down for at least several generations before being put to parchment. See Orton 2001: 213. The present translation is from 'The Seafarer': 118.

so, the volume pays tribute to an academic all-rounder, whose wide-ranging scholarship has carried him into the realms of onomastics, history, art history, archaeology, ethnography, and literature; encompassing the medieval period to the present day; and shining a light on Scandinavia, Scotland, the United States, and the myriad interfaces within, between, and beyond their respective physical and cultural boundaries.[2] As eclectic and broad-ranging as these interests and investigations have been, however, a shared thematic thread has always been apparent throughout Arne's academic work – one marked by seas and shorelines, by ships and sails, by tides and currents, and, above all, by islands and their inhabitants. As well as holms, skerries, stacks, and other stone and soil sites surrounded by water and wind, these have included peoples and communities as islands in their own right – be they travellers, immigrants, diasporas, or even outcasts – bound together by shared lives, languages, legacies, and lots.

But for all of their many-sidedness, Arne has made sure never to treat his research interests themselves as insular, consistently finding ways to connect and journey between them in a cross-disciplinary fashion, whilst offering new insights and perspectives along the way. In much the same manner, although himself born an islander, Arne is by no means a proverbial island unto himself, and is widely known and admired by colleagues and students, past and present, for his good-natured and generous demeanour, leading many to consider him not just as a lecturer, mentor, or co-worker, but as a friend – as is readily apparent from the many warm thoughts and testimonies shared throughout this volume.

Arne Dagfinn Kruse was born on 14 July 1954 to Johannes O. Kruse and Hanna Øien. Descended, on his father's side,

---

2. For an overview of Arne's publications, see the Bibliography at the end of the volume.

from a long lineage of fishermen from the island community of Brattværet, he himself grew up on nearby Smøla – part of the same seaswept archipelago in Møre and Romsdal.

Having moved to Kristiansund as a teenager, he pursued his first degree at the University of Trondheim, focusing on history, religion, and geography. Notwithstanding a two-year interruption to his studies – which was spent working on a fishing boat – Arne was granted his candidatus philologiae (cand.philol.) in 1983, having penned his thesis on the names of Smøla's fishing grounds.[3] In the years following his graduation, he found work as both a high school teacher in Rissa (Trøndelag) as well as a lecturer at the department of Norwegian Language, Literature, and Social Sciences at Lund University, to which he commuted from Copenhagen.

In 1985, Arne was awarded a Fulbright Visiting Scholar grant, allowing him to further develop his burgeoning academic pursuits as he made his way overseas to the University of Wisconsin-La Crosse, taking up a role as its first Fulbright scholar-in-residence.[4] Although originally appointed for a single academic session, his stay would eventually be extended into 1987, as he coordinated the ongoing establishment of UW-L's Norwegian Language and Culture Project (NLCP) – a collaborative programme which promoted research on Norwegian-American language and culture whilst supporting the university's Scandinavian Studies curriculum.[5] Under the auspices of the NLCP, Arne likewise carried out a detailed study of Norwegian place-names in western Wisconsin, a venture that helped to inspire multiple publications across several

---

3. Kruse 1983. His thesis was supervised by the late Nils Hallan.
4. Winrich 1986: 4.
5. Sutton and Kruse 1987. The authors would like to thank Arnstein Hjelde for furnishing this report.

decades.[6] It was also during this time that Arne met Brigitte Guenier – his future wife – who was then teaching French at UW-L on a visiting lectureship.

Following his stint in the United States, Arne returned to Norway, where he took up a position at the research centre of Møreforsking in Volda (1987–89), focusing his efforts on a pilot project to collect and organise the place-names of Møre and Romsdal alongside the late philologist Peter Hallaråker. In 1988, he also briefly held a position as assistant professor at Møre and Romsdal Distriksthøgskule (now University College Volda).[7] But it was in 1989 that he would apply to his career-defining position at the recently established Scandinavian Studies department of the University of Edinburgh, joining an academic community he would remain part of for thirty-two years.

As Edinburgh's first full-time lecturer in Norwegian – at a time when the university had become the only one in Scotland to offer Scandinavian Studies – Arne played an instrumental role in developing the department into the thriving centre of Nordic languages, cultures, and histories it remains today. Ever generous with his time and knowledge, Arne's teaching, mentorship, and supervision were marked by his dedication and good humour, whilst his versatile public engagement demonstrated a clear belief that there need not be a sharp divide between the academic and the layperson – a point he has accentuated himself.[8]

Arne's research continued unabatedly as well, even as his scholarship became increasingly focused on the place-names and settlement history of Scotland. Yet his appointment in Edinburgh would also allow him to revisit and reshape his

---

6. See, among others, Kruse 1991a; 1991b; 1996; 2007.
7. The authors are indebted to Geir Petter Hjorthol for providing these particular details.
8. Kruse 2000: 9.

Trondheim thesis into the monograph *Mål og méd. Målføre og médnamn frå Smøla,* which was published in 2000.[9] Arne was a founding member of the Hjaltland Network, a cross-disciplinary and cross-institutional research initiative to map Shetland's Viking past (2011–13), and has been a regular delegate for Scotland to the quadrennial Viking Congress, as well as numerous other international conferences. On top of his role at the university, he has likewise taken on various responsibilities within the Scottish Society for Northern Studies, assuming the general editorship of its journal, *Northern Studies,* from 1999 to 2006, and editing the well-received volume *Barra and Skye: Two Hebridean Perspectives* (2006). He eventually served as president of the Society between 2012 and 2015.

Having retired from his senior lectureship post in 2021, Arne continues to be affiliated with the University of Edinburgh as an honorary fellow. As well as maintaining his academic pursuits, he remains an avid outdoorsman, and enjoys boating, fishing, (hill)walking, and cycling. He and Brigitte divide their time between Edinburgh, the island of Veiholmen (Smøla), and the village of Crocy (Normandy). They have two sons, Erik Norvald and Philip Johan.

As a testament to Arne's broad-ranging research interests and influence, the fifteen contributions to this festschrift collectively cover a wide range of time, space, and fields of enquiry. Due to this diversity, any thematic division or delineation imposed on such a collection would be entirely arbitrary, and the editor has been defeated in his efforts to do so. Instead, these essays are presented in an order that roughly aligns them with Arne's own academic positions and interests over the course of his career. Apart from chapters III, XIII, and XV – which are of a more personal and anecdotal nature – all contributions to

---

9. Kruse 2000.

this volume have been peer-reviewed, and the editor wishes to acknowledge the fourteen anonymous reviewers who generously provided their time and expertise.

To begin with, harking back to Arne's own research at UW-L on language heritage, Arnstein Hjelde provides insights into the development of Minnesota-Norwegian dialects since the 1980s – observing the appearance of specific sounds that are otherwise absent from their European counterparts. Subsequently, Botolv Helleland, whom Arne also first met during his time in the United States, offers an overview of the widespread use of metaphors in the mountain names of western Norway. Berit Sandnes then characterises the methodology and legacy of the place-name collection project of the county of Møre and Romsdal (1985–95), which Arne actively contributed to during the latter half of the 1980s.

As one of Arne's earliest colleagues at the University of Edinburgh, Bjarne Thorup Thomsen then presents a consideration of Swedish author Selma Lagerlöf's perspectives on Norway, comparing two of her lesser-known works, published on either side of the dissolution of the union with Sweden in 1905. Afterwards, in reference to Arne's indefatigable championing of Nynorsk in Edinburgh, Guy Puzey highlights a prior sojourn of another Norwegian scholar, Aasmund Olavsson Vinje, to the Scottish capital, during which he authored the (presumed) first English-language essay on this new standard of the Norwegian language (1863).

In line with – and often drawing on – Arne's own long-standing and wide-ranging investigations into the Scandinavian presence in premodern Scotland, the subsequent chapters delve into aspects of the onomastic and linguistic legacy of these interactions.

First up is Alan Macniven, who (re)considers the presence and prevalence – as well as the associated implications – of the Old Norse (ON) topographic place-name element *dalr* in northern and western Scotland. This is followed by a brief note by Brian Smith on the potential whereabouts of the ON place-name *Þursasker*, as featured in *Orkneyinga saga* (c. 1200). Ryan Foster, in turn, examines the distribution of ON shieling (i.e. summer pasture) names in Caithness, pointing to a seemingly atypical distribution of the element *aergi*, in particular. Afterwards, Anke-Beate Stahl casts a light on the place-names of the island of Mingulay – in the Outer Hebrides – as well as the individuals and institutions who witnessed, collected, and recorded them over the years. Finally, Pavel Iosad considers the processes through which the Norse vernacular spoken in Scotland would have been replaced by Gaelic following the Viking Age.

Turning the focus briefly back to Norway itself, Peder Gammeltoft provides an analysis of the significance of two Viking Age place-name types, *bólstaðr* and *staðir*, drawing on data from the digital *Norske Gaardnavne* ('Norwegian Farm Names') database as well as cadastral and land-resource information – demonstrating their combined value for place-name research. Subsequently, in reference to Arne's own background as a fisherman, Linda Riddell assesses the development and downturn of the herring trade in Shetland during the latter part of the nineteenth century, highlighting its impact on local communities.

Arne's more recent work on early modern witchcraft, its persecution, and the associated parallels between Scotland and Scandinavia are likewise represented by two contributions. Liv Helene Willumsen paints a picture of Arne's interdisciplinary approach to language and landscape, illustrated by her experience of conducting fieldwork with Arne in connection to the North Berwick witchcraft trials. Andrew Jennings then provides a brief insight into the Old Norse terminology on magical practices inherited by the dialects of Orkney and Shetland.

Wrapping up this festschrift is a prose poem dedicated to Arne by Hilde Rognskog and Heidi Rognskog Mella, evoking a windswept journey 'home', to Norway, over land and sea, across islands of place and space. Collectively, these fifteen contributions represent a fitting tribute to Arne as a valued and versatile colleague, mentor, and friend, as well as a resourceful and committed researcher.

On a final note, the editor himself also wishes to extend his gratitude to Arne, whose unwavering support has been instrumental to his own academic ventures, and whose energy and enthusiasm remain an example to aspire to.

Bibliography

Exeter Cathedral Library, MS 3501, ff. 81v–83r.

Kruse, Arne. 1983. 'Médnamn frå Smøla'. Cand.philol. thesis. University of Trondheim.

———. 1991a. 'Norske stadnamn i Coon Valley, Wisconsin. Møte mellom to tradisjonar'. In Botolv Helleland (ed.), *Norsk språk i Amerika*. Oslo: Novus, 135–171.

———. 1991b. 'A Few Names in a Vast Land – Scandinavian Place-Names in the Midwest'. *Northern Studies* 28, 25–34.

———. 1996. 'Scandinavian-American Place-Names as Viewed from the Old World'. In P. Sture Ureland and Iain Clarkson (eds), *Language Contact across the North Atlantic*. Tübingen: Max Niemeyer Verlag, 255–268.

———. 2000. *Mål og méd. Målføre og médnamn frå Smøla*. Trondheim: Tapir Akademisk Forlag.

——— (ed.). 2006. *Barra and Skye: Two Hebridean Perspectives*. Edinburgh: Scottish Society for Northern Studies.

———. 2007. 'Fashion, Limitation and Nostalgia: Scandinavian Place-Names Abroad'. In Arne Kruse and Peter Graves (eds), *Images and*

Imaginations: Perspectives on Britain and Scandinavia. Edinburgh: Lockharton Press, 9–39.

Orton, Peter. 2001. 'To Be a Pilgrim: The Old English Seafarer and its Irish Affinities'. In Christian J. Kay and Louise M. Sylvester (eds), *Lexis and Texts in Early English*. Leiden: Brill, 213–223.

Sutton, Richard C. and Kruse, Arne. 1987. 'Norwegian Language and Culture Project: 1986–87 Annual Report'. University of Wisconsin-La Crosse.

'The Seafarer'. Kevin Crossley-Holland (trans.). In Bruce Mitchell (ed.), *The Battle of Maldon and Other Old English Poems*. 1966. London: Macmillan, 113–119.

Winrich, Mary Fran (ed.). 1986. 'Special Alumnus Campus Update'. *The Alumnus: University of Wisconsin-La Crosse*. Winter 1986, 1–11.

Tabula Gratulatoria

In addition to the contributors of this volume, the following colleagues, former students, and friends send their well wishes to Arne, and wish to distinguish him for his research achievements, his committed collegiality, and his selfless generosity.

Lesley Abrams
Gesine Argent
Susan Bainbrigge
John Baldwin
Andrew Barker
Colleen Batey
Karen Bek-Pedersen
Philip E. Bennett
Charlotte Berry
Gunilla Blom Thomsen
Laura Bradley
Stefan Brink
Elettra Carbone
Dana Caspi
Pernille Chapman
Lisa Collinson
Sarah Colvin
Barbara Crawford
Peter Davies
Peter Dayan
Véronique Desnain
Kari Dickson
Kirsti Dinnis
Clare Downham
Andrew Dugmore
Caitlin Ellis
Ersev Ersoy
Martine Foltier Pugh
Randi Forsgren Eden
Ian Fraser
James Fraser
Janet Garton
Howard Gaskill
Wen Ge
Ian Giles
William Gillies

John Gilmour
James Graham-Campbell
Peter Graves
David Griffiths
Terry Gunnell
Gunilla Halsius
Jesper Hansen
Stephen Harrison
Lars-Erik Hauge
Caroline Heycock
Dominic Hinde
Geir Petter Hjorthol
Jan Kristian Hognestad
Ida Hummel Vøllo
Hephzibah Israel
Ernst Håkon Jahr
Judith Jesch
Jenny Knudsen (née Heron)
Allan Juhl Kristensen
Tom Kristiansen
Fanney Kristmundsdottir
Will Lamb
Julie Larsen
Christina Lee
Huw Lewis
Ragnhild Ljosland
Helen Lundén
Tom Lundskær-Nielsen
Margaret A. (Maggie) Mackay
Maija McKinnon
Wilson McLeod
Davide Messina
Klaus Johan Myrvoll
David Albert Natvig
Claudia Nocentini
Pontus Odmalm

Ylva Olausson
Richard Oram
Steinvör Pálsson
Federica G. Pedriali
James K. Puchowski
Unni Puntervold Pereira
Rachel Rankin
Morag Redford
John Renwick
Anna Ritchie
Helen Robinson
Sabine Rolle
Lara Ryazanova-Clarke
Mona Røhne
Alex Sanmark
Marion Schmid
Irene Scobbie
Svavar Sigmundsson
Frank Stewart
Jakob Stougaard-Nielsen
Şebnem Susam-Saraeva
Ruairidh Tarvet
Simon Taylor
Barbara Tesio-Ryan
Claire Thomson
Anja Tröger
Joe Wade
Bill Webster
David Wedderburn
Marie Wells
Diana Whaley
Alex Woolf
Steve Yearley
Kathrin Zickermann

· I ·

Real-Time Sound Changes in a Minnesota-Norwegian Dialect between the 1980s and 2010s

Arnstein Hjelde

Background

Over the last decade, intensive fieldwork has been conducted under the leadership of Professor Janne Bondi Johannessen (1960–2020) to document the language of the last American Norwegian speakers as part of the so-called NorAmDiaSyn project. Recordings of Norwegian-American speakers have been collected, many of which have been transcribed, and constitute the backbone of the Corpus of American Nordic Speech (CANS).[1] This online corpus also includes various older recordings, such as some of Haugen's from the 1940s, Seip and Selmer's from 1931, and my own from the 1980s and 1990s. This corpus is searchable, and its existence has completely changed the research in this field.

Although research on this topic was sparse before 2010, around forty scholars have published more than one hundred articles in the last decade. I took part in most of Professor

---

1. Johannessen 2015.

Johanessen's field trips, and this work has also brought me back
to the places where I conducted field work for my study on
the Inntrøndelag dialect in America thirty-five years ago.[2] At
that time, Arne Kruse was the coordinator of the Norwegian
Language and Culture Project at the University of Wisconsin–
La Crosse, and when I arrived there on a scholarship in the
early fall of 1986, he introduced me to the field of Norwegian-
American studies and supported me in my work; he even
housed me for a year while I was criss-crossing the upper
Midwest looking for speakers of this particular dialect spoken
in Trøndelag.

As fieldwork among Norwegian-Americans in general – and
particularly the way they spoke the heritage language[3] – was
the theme of many of our numerous late-night conversations,
I find it very natural that this present chapter focuses more
on language data than linguistic theory. By comparing my
general findings from the 1980s – especially the data included
in CANS, integrating the last decade – I describe what has
happened to the Inntrøndelag dialect since Arne returned to
Europe some thirty-five years ago.

A great challenge for me during the 1980s was to find
speakers of this dialect, and I depended on contacts who could
guide me in the neighbourhood, introduce me to local speakers,
and direct me to new contacts in other communities.

Arne introduced me to Thor (see 'speakers, data, and
method' section below), my first contact in Wanamingo, and
the first one I recorded. From there, I was taken to Zumbrota
– a neighbouring town, both being in Goodhue County, MN

---

2. Hjelde 1992.
3. 'A language qualifies as a heritage language if it is a language spoken
at home or otherwise readily available to young children, and crucially
this language is not a dominant language of the larger (national) society'.
Rothman 2009: 156.

– then directed to Madison and Appleton in Lac qui Parle County, MN. These two areas on the Minnesota prairie were settled by emigrants from Stjørdalen, in the southern part of Inntrøndelag. The oldest of them is the settlement in Goodhue County in the eastern part of the state; the first settlers from Stjørdalen arrived here in the mid-1850s. This community served as a mother settlement for the one in Lac qui Parle County in western Minnesota, as many of those who emigrated in the 1870s first came to Goodhue County before continuing westwards to Lac qui Parle County, where they could claim land and settle down as farmers.

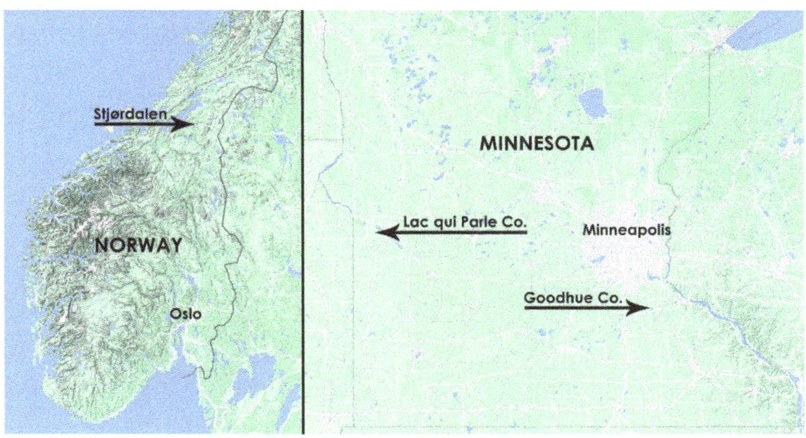

Figure 1: Maps illustrating the location of Stjørdalen in Norway, as well as Goodhue and Lac qui Parle Counties in Minnesota.

In 1987, I was able to record a total of fourteen speakers in these two communities; there were many more heritage speakers around, but only a fraction of them wanted to commit their voice on tape, or they found it more rewarding to spend the time working in the field rather than talking with me. At that time, I was sure that those I had found belonged to the last generation of heritage speakers and that Norwegian would be totally gone in a decade or so. However, I recently visited these two communities again, and, to my surprise, I found a new generation of Stjørdal Americans who still speak the heritage language. This opens exciting possibilities for comparing the language of the 1980s to that of the 2010s and thereby investigating cross-generational change over time.

Each recording in CANS typically lasts between one and two hours. The whole corpus contains about 750,000 tokens – or individual words – collected from around 250 speakers in nearly fifty different communities in the United States and Canada. This represents a tremendous opportunity to study many different aspects of the language, including syntax, lexicon, and code switching. However, when the number of speakers is limited – such as here, where corpus data from a very small group of individuals were used – it is sensible to study features that are frequently found in speech. Thus, the focus of this chapter is on phonology and the development of three different sounds in Stjørdal American (StAm) speech.

Benmamoun et al.[4] claim that, in heritage languages, 'phonological competence seems to be the best-preserved aspect of linguistic knowledge in heritage speakers', a statement supported by several other scholars.[5] However, 'best-preserved' does not mean that this competence is totally resistant to change – even if the sound system as a system per se seems to prove rather stable in language-contact situations, this does not mean that the realisation of the phonemes will not be altered. Therefore, we cannot totally rule out the possibility that the phoneme system might change over time – even if it is expected to be stable.

In the 1980s, I thought I could see tendencies towards several sound changes in StAm, and I found it reasonable to

---

4. Benmamoun et al. 2013: 136.
5. Westergaard and Kupich 2015: 470; Johannesen and Putnam 2020.

interpret these as a result of cross-linguistic influence (CLI) from English. In particular, three phonemes were affected: the high front rounded /y/ was sometimes realised as an unrounded [ɪ] or [i]; the apical vibrant /r/ was at times produced as a retroflex continuant [ɹ]; and the same could happen to the 'thick l', a retroflex flap, /ɽ/, which could also manifest as [ɹ]. There was, however, great individual variation in the use of these forms; for some heritage speakers, these innovations had become a frequent part of their repertoire, while others had hardly any of these changes at all.

The aim of this chapter is to look at how these tendencies of change, which I documented in the 1980s, evolved over time and across generations (or rather age-based cohorts idealised as generations). A question often addressed regarding changes in the language of heritage speakers is whether they are due to attrition or differential acquisition (previously referred to as 'incomplete acquisition') – that is, a change during an individual's lifespan caused by limited use of the language or never fully mastering a certain feature.[6] The latter might be the case for some of the speakers, as the typical story told by many of them was that Norwegian was the first language they learned but that as soon they started school around the age of six, they rapidly switched to English as their dominant language and they hardly speak Norwegian today.

The data used in this study are not suited for determining whether the changes were the result of decades of very limited use of the heritage language (attrition) or differential acquisition, when the feature in question is not (fully) acquired before the speaker changes their dominant language from the heritage language to the community language. However, by comparing the language of these two age groups, we can see which sounds

---

6. Cf. Montrul 2008.

are more stable and which are more prone to change across generations. Also included is data from a non-Inntrønder male individual who was recorded as a teenager in the 1940s and again when he was approaching ninety in 2017. By comparing the StAm data with the data from this particular heritage speaker, I hoped to get at least some indication of which sounds were more or less stable.

Speakers, data, and method

Seven StAm speakers were chosen for a more detailed study. All were born in the United States, and their ancestors came from the Stjørdal area in Trøndelag. They all had strong ties to farming – they grew up on farms, and as adults, they were either farmers or lived on farms. All of them grew up with Norwegian as a heritage language, as it was spoken at home and in the neighbourhood, and they encountered English when they started school. They were all of relatively advanced age, as the youngest were in their late seventies and the rest were in their eighties or early nineties when they were recorded. These were third- or fourth-generation immigrants; three of them came from Lac qui Parle County and four from Goodhue County. Two of them, Thor and Lloyd, were recorded in 1987, while the five others were recorded in the 2010s.

An obvious difference between these two cohort groups is that those recorded in the 1980s still had many Norwegian-speaking peers; thus, their heritage language was used almost on a daily basis. It must be said that the two from the 1980s included here were partly chosen for transcription in CANS due to their willingness and ease of speaking their heritage language. Furthermore, these two were confirmed in Norwegian and were, to some degree, able to master written Norwegian. Among those recorded during the 2010s, the language was only sporadically used – if at all. Even Iris and Olaf, a married couple, hardly used it between themselves.

The recordings from the 1980s and 2010s represent two different groups of speakers that can be idealised as different generations; the two speakers from the earliest recordings were born during the first decade of the twentieth century, while the speakers in the newer recordings were born in the mid-1920s or later. In fact, Thor and Iris are father and daughter.

Table 1: Background information on the speakers

Year recorded	Name[7]	County	Year of birth	Comment
1987	Thor	Goodhue	1908	Father of Iris
1987	Lloyd	Lac qui Parle	1905	
2011	Iris	Goodhue	1939	Married to Olaf
2011	Olaf	Goodhue	1935	Married to Iris
2012	Annie	Goodhue	1928	
2018	Morgan	Lac qui Parle	1924	
2018	Peter	Lac qui Parle	1926	
1948 2017	Mark	Rock Prairie, WI	1929	Recorded seventy years apart

When I conducted my first study on the material from the 1980s, I only transcribed parts in which the speech deviated

7. The names used in this chapter are pseudonyms; however, the fictive names correspond to participants' actual genders.

from the baseline. This enabled time to be saved during transcribing and left me with data documenting phonological and lexical influence from English. This provided insight into which structures in the participants' heritage language were prone to change and how many tokens there were, but I could not draw conclusions regarding the frequency of these changes. The CANS and transcriptions upon which this more recent study is based feature a phonetic transcription of the entire collection of recordings, thereby making it possible to conduct systematic searches of certain features, including the sounds studied in this chapter. Having access to data on their whole speech and not just selected stretches makes it possible to determine how common the changes are.

The recordings from the 1980s and 2010s were done in a similar way through semi-structured interviews or conversations between the heritage speaker and fieldworker. The conversations were organised to cover a set of topics, such as childhood and the 'old times', everyday life, ethnic traditions and celebrations, language use, contact with Norway, and so on. The aim was to encourage the interviewees to talk as freely as possible and put their focus more on the content rather than on how they said it (even though the latter is of greater interest in the present study).

The transcriptions are based on an impressionistic approach, as I – or other transcribers – base these on what is heard – or thought to be heard. This is not ideal for a study on phonetics. However, my own dialect, including its phonological system, is very similar to the one found in the Stjørdalen dialect; thus, I feel confident that I – at least in most cases – was able to spot any major deviations from the dialect as spoken in Norway.

Findings

Vowels

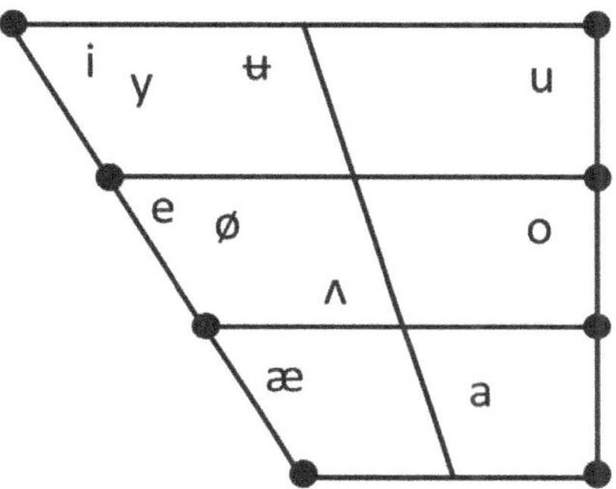

Figure 2: The vowels of the Stjørdalen dialect.

Unlike 'standard' Norwegian[8] (whatever that is), the traditional Stjørdal dialect has – like many other dialects in this region – ten vowels, namely /i, y, e, ø, æ, ʉ, ʌ, u, o, a/. In the contemporary Euro-Stjørdal dialect, one of these vowels, /ʌ/, has merged with /æ/, reducing the number of vowels to nine, which is in line with this 'standard'. This change has not taken place among the StAm speakers, as seen in Example 1; it is intact among virtually all the heritage speakers I found and recorded.

Example 1

(a)   fʌ:r   før   'earlier, before'
(b)   spʌ:r   spørre   'ask'
(c)   stʌ:r   større   'larger'

---

8. This includes the written standards, as well as many of today's dialects. At the same time, Norwegian has no officially standardised spoken variant. It is also worth noting that Trondheim is the 'city' for people in Stjørdalen, and the dialect here also has a system of nine vowels.

This does not mean that the sound system in this variety is not affected by tendencies towards change but that these changes follow a different path. The high fronted /y/, which is stable among speakers of this dialect in Norway, is a target for change in America. In the 1980s, I found that this phoneme showed tendencies towards being delabialised. Typically, the speakers could shift between a rounded (labialised) and unrounded (delabialised) pronunciation, but with individual variation, as some hardly had an unrounded variant, while among others, it was prevalent.

Example 2

(a)	bI:	*by*	'town'
(b)	dI:ʈ	*dyrt*	'expensive'
(c)	²tI:vende	*tjuande*	'twentieth'
(d)	²bIce	*byttar*	'change'
(e)	¹tIskera	*tyskararar*	'Germans'

In a study on Texas German, Pierce et al.[9] found that the use of rounded front vowels decreased over time. Moreover, in this variety, the vowels affected were /y/ and /ø/. They argued that markedness is a factor to consider when it comes to phonetic changes in language-contact situations. As Haspelmath[10] demonstrates, the notion of markedness is ambiguous and thus problematic. However, Pierce used this term for sounds that are cross-linguistically rare, and the hypothesis was that such sounds are more easily targeted for change than widespread cross-linguistic sounds are.[11] Based on Eikel's observations of Texas German that 'individual speakers are consistent: if a speaker

---

9. Pierce et al. 2015.
10. Haspelmath 2006.
11. Pierce et al. 2015: 124.

unrounds /y/, he invariably also unrounds /ø/,[12] paired with the assumption that /ø/ is more cross-linguistically rare (that is 'marked') than /y/,[13] these combined considerations suggest that /ø/ might be more prone to delabialisation than /y/. The present StAm data do not support such a general claim, as /ø/ remains unaffected, while /y/ is the target for delabialisation.

They also point to the German dialects involved, as front rounded vowels in many of these are even absent in the European variants. If it is not part of the baseline inventory, its absence is not surprising in a diaspora context.

The baseline is also an issue in Norwegian contexts, as there are dialects in Norway in which /y/ has been delabialised. This phenomenon is probably best known in Solør (south-eastern Norway), but we also find it in parts of Hallingdal, Sogn, Nordfjord, Romsdal, Møre, Trøndelag, and Senja, an island in northern Norway.[14]

Even if a rounded /y/ seems to have been re-established in most of these places today, delabialisation of /y/ was common during the era of emigration and could thus be a part of the baseline. This is also documented in old varieties of the dialect in Frosta, a neighbouring municipality to Stjørdalen. This trait has been imitated and ridiculed by others and is probably extinct today.[15]

Delabialisation of /y/ has never been reported in Stjørdalen, and it is likely that it would have been noted and remembered in the district, given the low status that it was assigned. However, we cannot totally rule out the possibility that a delabialised allophone was present in Stjørdalen around the time of emigration and that it was not salient enough to be mentioned, or perhaps not considered representative of the dialect. In such a scenario,

---

12. Eikel 1954: 28, quoted from Pierce et al. 2015.
13. Maddieson 2013.
14. Skjekkeland 1997: 48.
15. Dalen et al. 2008: 48.

the heritage speakers would have continued the change, while it would have been decommissioned in the homeland variety.[16]

In Norwegian, the two high-fronted vowels /y/ and /i/ are distinguished by the feature [+/- rounding], a feature not relevant for distinguishing vowel phonemes in American English (AmE). Thus, the likeliest explanation for the StAm tendency towards delabialisation is contact with AmE. Furthermore, the distinction between /y/ and /i/ is not a crucial one, as few words are distinguished by these two vowels, and any potential misunderstandings can normally be avoided through the context. That this delabialisation has happened in Norway – and not only in one dialect but in several different dialects that are independent from each other – demonstrates that the rounded /y/ is an easy target for change and that delabialisation of /y/ does not have a devastating effect on the vowel system.

Table 2: Delabialisation of y

		Delabialisation of y (%)
1987	Thor	0
1987	Lloyd	0
2011	Iris	2
2011	Olaf	86
2012	Annie	33
2018	Morgan	50
2018	Peter	45
1948	Mark 1	11
2017	Mark 2	12

---

16. This tendency of delabialisation of /y/ is found among most Norwegian American heritage speakers today, regardless of their dialect background, which strongly indicates that it is due to language contact.

While working on these data during the 1980s, I considered delabialisation of /y/ to be widespread in StAm, given that many of the speakers showed examples of such delabialisation. However, some of the speakers, such as Thor and Lloyd, did not show any such tendencies.

By contrast, we see that delabialisation of /y/ is quite common among the subsequent generation recorded in the 2010s. All of them show delabialisation of /y/, and for all except one, we see that this trait is very frequent, ranging from 33% to 86% of the tokens. The exception among this group of speakers is Iris, with only 2%. One interpretation of this is that this trait is stable at an individual level in the sense that once it is acquired, it does not change much over a lifespan. An argument for this is Iris' input – her father Thor does not have any delabialisation at all; thus, she was shielded from this change while acquiring the language, and input regarding this particular feature later in life did not affect it.

Her husband Olaf has a very high tendency to delabialise /y/ (in 86% of the instances), but this has not affected Iris. Mark's tendency to delabialise has not changed from eighteen to eighty-nine years of age, unlike some of the other phonological traits in his speech, which have changed. Of course, more data are required to establish a clearer picture of how this particular change happens over time and across generations, and such research should be possible, as we have access to several recordings of both individuals and parents–children recorded some thirty years apart.

Analysis of the data from the 1980s revealed that despite delabialisation of /y/, this phoneme did not merge with /i/, as there was still an articulatorily distinction between /i/, realised as [i], and the delabialised /y/, realised as [I].[17] This latter allo-

____

17. Hjelde 1996: 288–290.

phone was realised as more open and a bit further back than [i], but the main difference was still in the lips: while [i] was pronounced with tense lips, [I] was articulated with relaxed lips. My analysis at that time revealed that this was a case of reinterpretation of distinctive factors,[18] from [+/-rounding] to [+/-tense lips].[19]

At that time, I thought that delabialisation was a fairly new development among Norwegian-Americans, as it was not mentioned by Haugen in any of his numerous publications on the American-Norwegian language. However, when some of Einar Haugen's field notes (written by his assistant Magne Oftedal) emerged from basement storage at the University of Oslo a few years ago, we could see that the same delabialisation phenomenon was commented on regarding one speaker from Elroy, WI.[20] Oftedal, who was a trained phonetician, concluded – as I did – that delabialisation did not result in a merge with /i/ but a new allophone: [I]. The same phenomenon is described in some Norwegian dialects with iotacism, namely the previously mentioned Frosta dialect, where the distinction was kept even after delabialisation.[21] Most of the speakers in the 1980s data also had a rounded allophone in their repertoire, [y]; and [I] and [y] were in free variation, as seen in Example 3.

Example 3

(a)	bI:n – by:n	*byen*	'the town'
(b)	cI:r – cy:r	*kyr*	'cows'
(c)	mI: – my:	*mykje*	'much'

---

18. Weinreich 1953: 18.
19. Hjelde 1996: 289.
20. Oftedal 1948b.
21. Dalen 1985: 244.

All speakers from the 2010s still had a rounded allophone [y],
but now the delabialised element can be [i], in addition to
[I]. Thus, there are indications that this change is not purely
phonetic, but might also involve the phoneme system through
a merge of /i/ and /y/.

Consonants

The two Norwegian consonants that seem to be most prone
to influence from English are the rhotic /r/ and the so-called
thick l /ɽ/, both of which can have a realisation similar to that
of the American r, [ɹ].[22]

/r/

In Norwegian dialects, /r/ might be realised in several different
ways, but in the Stjørdalen dialect, like other eastern Norwegian
dialects, it is an alveolar vibrant [r] or tap [ɾ];[23] thus it is realised
in a different manner than in AmE, where it can be described
as a retroflex approximant [ɹ]. My 1980s data contain many
examples of the use of [ɹ] in an otherwise Norwegian context,
as shown in Example 4. This innovation is sometimes referred
to as r-approximation.[24]

---

22. The Oftedal field notes (1948c) comment on one person in Stoughton,
WI who sometimes pronounced /r/ as [l]; I also document the same
phenomenon in the speech of one individual in Vernon Co., WI. But this
realisation is so rare that it will not be commented on in this study, as none
of the speakers studied here have it. The Oftedal field notes also provide
insight into some of the challenges a fieldworker could be confronted with
seventy-five years ago, especially as parts of the transcriptions had to be done
simultaneously in the field. One of the speakers lacked his teeth, posing
considerable problem for the classification of dental consonants; another one
had such an oversized moustache that the articulation was very unclear and
hard for the fieldworker to plot.
23. In the transcription used here, I do not distinguish between the vibrant
and the tap; both are transcribed as [r], in opposition to the retroflex
approximant [ɹ].
24. Natvig 2021.

Example 4

(a)	ɹæt	*rett*	'correct'
(b)	¹ɹeːgel	*regel*	'rule'
(c)	spɹoːk	*språk*	'language'

Furthermore, what I found in the 1980s was that the [ɹ] allophone was in free variation with the 'traditional' vibrant/tap allophones [r], as seen in Example 5.

Example 5

(a)	oːr – oːɹ	*år*	'year'
(b)	¹læːvra – ¹læːvɹa	*levra*	'the liver'
(c)	²somor – ²somoɹ	*sommar*	'summer'

As discussed above, the method of transcribing only sequences of speech that showed deviation from the baseline was good enough if the purpose was to document that this kind of deviation existed and to get an idea of how widespread it was. However, it could not reveal how frequent such deviations were when compared to the apical pronunciation. My data from that time contained numerous examples of [ɹ] used in an otherwise Norwegian context, but we should also keep in mind that /r/ is among the most frequent phonemes in speech. I had numerous examples of [ɹ], but [r] was still by and large the dominant realisation of /r/. So [ɹ] was relatively less frequent than I thought it was; at least, that is what the data used for this chapter indicate.

Table 3: The use of ɹ for r

		ɹ for r (%)
1987	Thor	1
1987	Lloyd	0
2011	Iris	1
2011	Olaf	0
2012	Annie	5
2018	Morgan	6
2018	Peter	1
1948	Mark 1	1
2017	Mark 2	1

Table 3 shows that all but two speakers have [ɹ] in their repertoire but that it is not very frequent, and it is difficult to see a
clear pattern showing that this trait is more widespread among
the younger generation. Peter, Olaf, and Iris show the same
usage pattern as Thor and Lloyd. While Annie and Morgan
are the two 'super users' of [ɹ] among the investigated speakers,
their tendency to use [ɹ] for /r/ is still fairly low – only about
one token for every twenty instances. Therefore, even for these
two, [r] is the dominant realisation of this phoneme. Mark
does not show any increase in the use of [ɹ] between 1948 and
2017; it is stable at one token for every one hundred instances.

This r-approximation affects the realisation of the phoneme
/r/, but that does not change the phoneme inventory per se.
The same tendencies towards change of the realisation of /r/
was also documented in a study on speakers from Coon Valley

and Westby, WI.[25] Here, all American-born speakers showed r-approximation, but only to a limited extent; the vibrant [r] was still by far the most common realisation of this phoneme.

There is, however, one position where the use of [ɹ] has become more widespread between the 1980s and today, and that is in positions together with retroflex consonants. The Old Norse consonant combinations *rl*, *rn*, *rd*, *rt*, and *rs* have, in many Norwegian dialects, been assimilated to a retroflex *ŋ*, *l*, *ṭ*, *ḍ* and *ʃ*.[26] These retroflexes might be a part of the root or stem, as in Example 5, but we also see that this retroflexion is productive, both in relation to word inflection (Example 6d–f) and across word boundaries (Example 6g–h).

Example 6

(a)	øŋ̩		*ørn*		eagle
(b)	²æːɭe		*ærleg*		honest
(c)	¹æʈer		*ert*		pies
(d)	hør	*høyre*	høḍ	*høyrde (pret)*	heard
(e)	sʉːr	*sur*	sʉːʈ	*surt (neu)*	sour
(f)	raːr	*rar*	raː ʈ	*rart (neu)*	strange
(g)	ʃeːr dʉ	ʃeː ɖʉ	*ser du?*	'see you?'	Do you see?
(h)	fer ¹liːte	fe ¹ɭiːte	*for lite*	'for little'	too little

AmE also has retroflex consonants, such as the allophones of alveolar /n, l, t, d/ ([ŋ, ɭ, ʈ, ḍ]), but normally these do not appear alone as a single segment, as in Norwegian; they are found in combination with the rhotic ɹ, as in [ɹŋ, ɹɭ, ɹʈ, ɹḍ]. As we see in Table 4, this distributive pattern from AmE is spreading among many of the 'younger' speakers of heritage Norwegian.

---

25. Natvig 2021.

26. This assimilation is found in eastern and northern dialects in Norway but not in the western part of the country.

We see that, in the 1980s, Thor and Lloyd have few instances of ɹ in positions before retroflex consonants, while we find it frequently used in such positions by Peter, Morgan, and especially Annie in the 2010s. These observations are in line with Natvig's findings from Wisconsin, where he observed the insertion of [ɹ] in front of retroflex consonants to expand from the 1940s until today.[27] Our data also indicate that the tendency to use [ɹ] in this position might change at an individual level, as Mark more than doubled his tendency to use [ɹ] in combination with retroflex consonants over a span of about seventy years.

Table 4: The use of ɹ + retroflex

		ɹ + retroflex (%)
1987	Thor	1
1987	Lloyd	0
2011	Iris	2
2011	Olaf	0
2012	Annie	29
2018	Morgan	15
2018	Peter	16
1948	Mark 1	10
2017	Mark 2	23

The Thick l

The last sound discussed here is the so-called thick l (ɭ). This consonant is not found in all varieties of Norwegian, and within

---

27. Natvig 2021.

dialectology, it is one of the fundamental characteristics used to divide Norwegian dialects into two main groups: east and west Norwegian. The thick l is typical among east Norwegian dialects, to which the Stjørdalen dialect belongs, while west Norwegian dialects lack this sound.

The thick l is classified as a retroflex flap and has two historical origins. One is the result of the assimilation of the Old Norse consonant group *rð*, while the other originates from the Old Norse *l* in certain environments or positions. Although I do not describe the distribution of [ɽ] when originating from Old Norse *l* in detail, I provide the following general sketch: it is often found in internal and final positions after long vowels (except i:, ei, and rarely after e:, y:, or øy; cf. Examples 7a–c). Furthermore, we find it in clusters with certain consonants (such as k, g, p, b, m and v; cf. Examples 7d–f).[28] However, as Sandøy points out, today it is impossible to identify absolute rules for when the Old Norse *l* is rendered as a thick l, as there will always be exceptions.

Example 7

(a)	sta:ɽ	*stal*	stole
(b)	pɽu:g	*plog* (noun)	plough
(c)	hø:ɽ	*hol*	hole
(d)	²kɽase	*klasse*	class
(e)	bɽu:	*blod*	blood
(f)	kæɽv	*kalv*	calf

In the 1980s recordings, the most common realisation of this phoneme is as [ɽ], a retroflex flap. However, a new retroflex allophone was also introduced to the repertoire of most of the

---

28. Sandøy 1985: 185.

speakers at that time. This one was not a flap but a retroflex approximant [ɹ], and as far as I am able to judge, similar to the American r (Example 8).

Example 8

(a)   bɹa: *blad*   'magazine/
                                         newspaper'
(b)   bu:ɹ   *bord*   'table'
(c)   ²gæ:ɹi   *gale*   'wrong'
(d)   pɹas   *plass*   'place'
(e)   pɹøy   *pløye* (inf.)   'plough'

This change was obviously not a new development in the 1980s. This phenomenon is commented on in the Oftedal field notes from Haugen's study, and between Argyle and Wiota in southern Wisconsin, the thick l is reported to be replaced by such an approximant. Magne Oftedal, as Haugen's assistant, writes:

> Thick l has for the most part lost its flap and is very similar to English r. Still, I think that I can often hear a difference and in such cases I have used the common symbol l for this variant without the flap. In some cases, I can clearly hear the flap and put a point under ɬ. But often do I hear English r for thick l. The flap seems to be especially common in consonant groups, and it is possible that these two or three sound types are in combinatorial variation.[29]

In my data from the 1980s, the allophone [ɹ] was in free variation with the flapped allophone [ɽ], as seen in Example 9.

---

29. Oftedal 1948a. Author's translation.

Example 9

(a)	²gæːʈi	²gæːɹi	*gale*	'wrong'
(b)	²gameʈ	²gameɹ	*gammal*	'old'
(c)	pʈøy	pɹøy	*pløye*	'plough'
(d)	²pʈasa	²pɹasa	*plassar*	'places'

In his publications, Einar Haugen also comments on the fact that the thick l might be pronounced as [ɹ]. When he describes how AmE /ɹ/ is rendered in loanwords, he finds that 'the sound is commonly imported in loanwords, especially in dialects having ɽ[30] already, with which it is often confused',[31] In a 1938 article, he comments on the same, as for one speaker's thick l, 'the slap is entirely lacking so that his [r̩] and [l̩] are indistinguishable'.[32] Thus, this cannot be a new development in the American-Norwegian language; it is a process that at least goes back to the 1930s and probably even earlier.

In the data upon which this chapter is based, we get a rather good indication that the approximant allophone was common in the 1980s (Table 5). We see from the recordings of Lloyd that, in four out of ten instances, he produces a continuant, and this realisation is also found in the speech of Thor, even if it is quite rare in his repertoire. Among the young generation recorded in the 2010s, we see that the continuant is very frequent; for four of these five StAm speakers, it is the dominant allophone, and for the fifth speaker, it represents nearly half of the instances. We also see that the tendency to replace the flap with an approximant might change dramatically over a lifespan. For Mark, as a teenager, the ratio between approximant and flapped allophones was about 1:15; seventy years later, the ratio had changed to 1:1.

---

30. Haugen's notation of the thick l.
31. Haugen 1969: 435.
32. Haugen 1938: 66.

Table 5: Realisation of the thick l as ɹ

		ɹ for ɽ (%)
1987	Thor	3
1987	Lloyd	41
2011	Iris	98
2011	Olaf	92
2012	Annie	69
2018	Morgan	74
2018	Peter	45
1948	Mark 1	6
2017	Mark 2	50

It is obvious that the thick l is rather prone for change in realisation among the StAm speakers, and I think there are several reasons for this.

One obvious reason is related to articulation. Flapping is common for intervocalic t and d after a stressed vowel in AmE, but it is not a distinctive feature as it is in the Stjørdalen dialect. And the way from a [ɽ] to [ɹ] is fairly short, as the tongue's starting position for the [ɽ] is very similar to how it is raised when pronouncing [ɹ]. Thus, by eliminating the flap element in the pronunciation of [ɽ], we are left with a retroflex approximant – an [ɹ].

Furthermore, even if it is common to consider thick l as a phoneme in Norwegian, it is hard to find minimal pairs, and dialects lacking these sounds fill the slot with /r/ when the historical origin is *rð*, or with /l/ when that is the origin. The fact that the thick l is not carrying much 'distinctive force' might also make it more vulnerable to change.

Finally, we can be sure that the older generation was exposed to Norwegian varieties without the thick l. In Goodhue County, there was a significant group from western Norway, and Thor, for example, utilised the negation particle /ice/, *ikkje*, which we find in that part of Norway, instead of the Stjørdalen /ic/, which we would expect. Thus, dialect contact might also play a role here. The older generation also had some experience with a more literary language, both written and spoken. In writing, Norwegian is not codified with a letter denoting the thick l, and this sound was probably lacking in the educated speech of the clergymen.

Discussion and concluding remarks

There have been changes in the Norwegian sound system on both sides of the Atlantic, but these changes have followed different paths and have been motivated by different factors.

The Stjørdalen dialect of today has lost the phoneme /ʌ/, and it is reasonable to assume that this change, at least in part, is due to pressure from urban speech and proximity to the regional centre of Trondheim, as well as influence from the written standard. In America, influence from English plays an important role, and cross-linguistic influence can, to a great extent, explain the changes we observe for /y/, /r/, and /ʈ/. However, these three phonemes also seem somewhat fragile in a Norwegian setting.

We know that /y/ was delabialised in several Norwegian dialects, and that these areas are independent, scattered pockets around the country with great distances between them. Thus, this delabialisation can hardly be explained by dialect contact and spread from one area to another; the likeliest explanation is that these changes constitute independent developments in these areas. When such delabialisation occurs in several places, this should strongly indicate that y is prone to delabialisation even in a fairly stable monolingual setting; and when exposed to intense contact with a language lacking the rounded /y/, it is not a great surprise that we find this kind of delabialisation.

Likewise, /r/ is pronounced differently depending on the dialect, and in parts of Norway, this rhotic is also a sound prone to change. In western areas of the country, we find that the old apical thrill is losing terrain to a uvular or velar fricative [R]; it is assumed that this sound came to Bergen and Kristiansand around 1800, expanded rapidly during the last century, and continues to do so.[33] One of the explanations given for this is that the apical vibrant is 'difficult' to articulate and among the last sounds a child masters; thus, it is prone to replacement by a less complex realisation.[34] It is fair to assume that the same mechanism might work when the vibrant or tap r shows a tendency to be replaced by an approximant among Norwegian Americans.

Regarding the thick l, the situation is somewhat different, as this phoneme is found in only some Norwegian dialects. Even though this feature seems to be fairly stable inside its isogloss borders, the number of words distinguished by this phoneme is small.

The point here is that none of these three sounds are found in all the 'Old World' Norwegian dialects; there are varieties

---

33. Skjekkeland 1997: 89–90.
34. Fintoft et al. 1983: 42–44. They examine the spoken language of four-year-old Norwegian children and show that among speakers of dialects with apical [r], there is a high proportion of children who show deviations from the target apical pronunciation, while this is not the case among speakers of dialects with the uvular/velar pronunciation [R].

lacking one or more of these dialectal traits. The most surprising aspect of our findings is that, perhaps, the overall low tendency for [ɹ] to replace [r] and that the approximant does not show any clear and strong tendency to increase over generations. This conflicts with the general impression Norwegians have of how Norwegian Americans speak. When Norwegian Americans are caricatured in Norway, the /r/ is often an approximant, and even Norwegian scholars might claim that Norwegian Americans are quite quick to adopt this pronunciation.[35] All Norwegian Americans have the approximant in their speech, since it is commonly found in AmE loanwords, but as we see, the approximation of [r] to [ɹ] is not very common, and the increase over generations is moderate.

Table 6: The use (in percentages) of i for y; ɹ for r; ɹ + retroflex for a 'bare' retroflex; and ɹ for ʈ.

		i for y (%)	ɹ for r (%)	ɹ + retroflex(%)	ɹ for ʈ (%)
1987	Thor	0	1	1	3
1987	Lloyd	0	0	0	41
2011	Iris	2	1	2	98
2011	Olaf	86	0	0	92
2012	Annie	33	5	29	69
2018	Morgan	50	6	15	74
2018	Peter	45	1	16	45
1948	Mark 1	11	1	10	6
2017	Mark 2	12	1	23	50

35. Torp 2007: 35.

The only position where the approximant is expanding across generations is in a junction with a retroflex, where the segmented rhotic + retroflex is replacing a bare retroflex. This was especially frequent among some of the speakers from the 2010s, while it was rare among the oldest group. A somewhat similar, though more extreme, pattern was found for delabialisation of /y/; it was not present among the oldest cohort of speakers but very common among the youngest speakers. The most widespread change was the approximation of the thick l, the only change we documented among all the speakers, and the most frequent realisation of /ɽ/ for four out of five of those recorded in the 2010s.

If we contrast these findings with the data on Mark, who was recorded as a teenager, we see that in his speech when approaching ninety, the distribution of two of the features are extremely stable: /y/, and /r/ in a non-retroflexed environment. Segmentation of Norwegian retroflexes to /ɹ/ + retroflex shows a growing tendency from one out of ten instances to about every fourth instance. The most prominent change is related to the thick l, where the realisation as an approximant [ɹ] raises from 6% to 50%. We know that this particular speaker had spoken hardly any Norwegian during the fifty years before he was recorded in 2017; thus, the most reasonable explanation for this increase in the use of [ɹ] is attrition.

In my view, attrition is also the main explanation for the changes we found among the speakers from the 2010s. We know that those recorded in the 1980s grew up in a Norwegian-speaking community where the language had been passed on over several generations, with only some minor tendencies towards language change. At that time, many of them still used the language on a regular basis. The massive changes have occurred among the speakers recorded in the 2010s, those who have typically not spoken much Norwegian over the last few decades. Frequency of use has been shown to be an important factor in language attrition, and that seems to be the main difference between the speakers recorded in the 2010s and 1980s.

StAm is a moribund heritage language, as the limited number of speakers today are of advanced age and the last generation to have mastered it. It has been argued that this kind of heritage language is likely to show accelerated language decay, leading to reduced complexity.[36] In this study, it was found that even if tendencies towards variation in pronunciation of the examined phonemes are observed among the older generation, this accelerates among the young cohort. But still, the core structure of the StAm phoneme inventory is maintained and the status for these three targeted sounds in StAm varies across dialects in Norway as well. One could argue that despite the variations highlighted, these findings neither contradict nor challenge the previously mentioned claim of Benmamoun et al.[37] that phonological competence is a very well-preserved aspect of a heritage language.

The research reported in this chapter was partially supported by the Research Council of Norway. Project 301114, 'Norwegian across the Americas'.

Bibliography

Benmamoun, Elabbas et al. 2013. 'Heritage Languages and Their Speakers: Opportunities and Challenges for Linguistics'. *Theoretical Linguistics* 39:3–4, 129–181.

Bousquette, Joshua and Putnam, Michael T. 2020. 'Redefining Language Death: Evidence from Moribund Grammars'. *Language Learning* 70:S1, 188–225.

---

36. See Bousquette and Putnam 2020 for a discussion and references on this matter.
37. Benmamoun et al. 2013: 136.

Dalen, Arnold. 1985. *Skognamålet: ein fonologisk analyse.* Oslo: Novus forlag.

Dalen, Arnold et al. 2008. *Trøndersk språkhistorie: Språkforhold i ein region.* Trondheim: Tapir akademisk forlag.

Eikel, Fred Jr. 1954. 'The New Braunfels German Dialect'. PhD thesis. Johns Hopkins University.

Fintoft, Knut et al. 1983. *4 år: en undersøkelse av normalspråket hos norske 4-åringer.* Trondheim: Universitetet i Trondheim.

Haspelmath, Martin. 2006. 'Against Markedness (and What to Replace It with)'. *Journal of Linguistics* 42:1, 25–70.

Haugen, Einar. 1938. 'Phonological Shifting in American Norwegian'. *Language* 14:112–120.

———. 1969. *The Norwegian Language in America: A Study in Bilingual Behavior* (2nd ed.). Bloomington: University of Indiana Press.

Hjelde, Arnstein. 1992. *Trøndsk talemål i Amerika.* Trondheim: Tapir akademisk forlag.

———. 1996. 'Some Phonological Changes in a Norwegian Dialect in America'. In P.S. Ureland and I. Clarkson (eds), *Language Contact across the North Atlantic.* Tübingen: Max Niemeyer, 283–295.

Johannessen, Janne B. 2015. 'The Corpus of American Norwegian Speech (CANS)'. In B. Megyesi (ed.), *Proceedings of the 20th Nordic Conference of Computational Linguistics.* Linköping: Linköping University Electronic Press, 297–300.

Johannesen, Janne B. and Putnam, Michael T. 2020. 'Heritage Germanic Languages in North America'. In Michael T. Putnam and B. Richard Page (eds), *The Cambridge Handbook of Germanic Linguistics.* Cambridge: Cambridge University Press, 783–806.

Lie, Sven. 1993. *Kontrastiv grammatikk: med norsk i sentrum.* Oslo: Novus.

Maddieson, Ian. 2013. 'Front Rounded Vowels'. In Matthew S. Dryer and Martin Haspelmath (eds), *The World Atlas of Language Structures Online.* Leipzig: Max Planck Institute for Evolutionary Anthropology, http://wals.info/chapter/11. Accessed 21 March 2022.

Montrul, Silvina. 2008. *Incomplete Acquisition in Bilingualism: Re-Examining the Age Factor.* Amsterdam: John Benjamins Publishing.

Natvig, David. 2021. 'Variation and Stability of American Norwegian /r/ in Contact'. In *Linguistic Approaches to Bilingualism*, https://doi.org/10.1075/lab.20085.nat. Accessed 21 March 2022.

Oftedal, Magne. 1948a. 'Questionnaire: Informant 3C1. Argyle, Wisconsin'. Field notes. http://tekstlab.uio.no/norskiamerika/opptak/haugen.html. Accessed 21 March 2022.

———. 1948b. 'Questionnaire: Informant 13N4. Elroy, Wisconsin'. Field notes. http://tekstlab.uio.no/norskiamerika/opptak/haugen.html. Accessed 21 March 2022.

———. 1948c. Field notes. Manuscript. http://tekstlab.uio.no/media/lydogbilde/amerikanorsk/einar_haugen/Informantbeskrivelser-fra-Oftedal. Accessed 21 March 2022.

Pierce, Marc et al. 2015. 'The History of Front Rounded Vowels in New Braunfels German'. In Janne B. Johannessen and Joseph C. Salmons (eds), *German Heritage Languages in North America. Acquisition, Attrition and Change*. Amsterdam, John Benjamins Publishing Company, 117–131.

Rothman J. 2009. 'Understanding the Nature and Outcomes of Early Bilingualism: Romance Languages as Heritage Languages'. *International Journal of Bilingualism* 13:2, 155–163.

Sandøy, Helge. 1985. *Norsk dialektkunnskap*. Oslo: Novus forlag.

Skjekkeland, Martin. 1997. *Dei Norske Dialektane: Tradisjonelle Særdrag i Jamføring med Skriftmåla*. Kristiansand: Høyskoleforlaget.

Torp, Arne. 2007. *R: ei urokråke i språket*. Oslo: Samlaget.

Weinreich, Uriel. 1953. *Languages in Contact: Findings and Problems*. The Hague: Mouton & Co.

Westergaard, Marit and Kupich, Tanja. 2015. 'Stable and Vulnerable Domains in German Heritage Languages'. *Oslo Studies in Language* 11(2):503–526.

· II ·

Metaphors in Mountain Names
with Particular Reference to Western Norway

Botolv Helleland

Introduction

In the summer of 1985, I toured as a lecturer in the American Midwest with Anne Svanevik from the University of Oslo and Hans Eyvind Næss from the State Archives in Stavanger.[1] We visited a number of Sons of Norway lodges. In Norskedalen, we met Arne Kruse. He had already collected Norwegian-rooted field names in Coon Valley, Wisconsin, and later he generously submitted audio-tape recordings of the material to the Norwegian Place-Names Archive.

The following year, I organised a conference in Oslo entitled 'Norwegian language in America', with Arne contributing a lecture on Norwegian place-names in Coon Valley. I had the pleasure of editing the proceedings, which were published in 1991.[2] I have met Arne several times since, both in Norway and in Scotland, such as when he was one of the key speakers at the 25th International Congress of Onomastic Sciences in

---

1. My theme was 'Place-names on the Hardangervidda'.
2. Helleland 1991.

Glasgow (25–29 August 2014). I feel proud to be counted among his friends.

In August 2011, I participated as a Norwegian representative in a session of the United Nations Group of Experts on Geographical Names (UNGEGN). One evening, as I crossed Times Square, I became aware of a sizeable electronic screen showing the rock of *Trolltunga* ('the troll tongue') in Odda, Hardanger. I felt at home right away, as this rock is situated near my own place of birth.

This is not the only world-famous mountain name in Norway. In the county of Rogaland, to the south of Hardanger, we find another famous cliff bearing the name of *Preikestolen* ('the pulpit'). Its international reputation increased considerably after featuring in the film *Mission: Impossible – Fallout* (2018), in which it is scaled by Tom Cruise's character.

On the national level, however, another name has been even more focused upon. On the evening of 5 September 2019, the attention of many Norwegians was directed towards the municipality of Rauma in Romsdal, western Norway – a district familiar to Arne Kruse. That night, a large part of the rock *Veslemannen* ('the little man') came crashing down, accompanied by a loud rumbling and a cloud of dust. Although it was almost dark, it was possible to observe the drama on television. A threat which had been a daily concern for years was now more or less eliminated. The few families that used to live on the farm beneath *Veslemannen* had been evacuated several times, and now they were allowed to move back to their homes, hopefully on a more permanent basis. *Veslemannen* is a part of a larger mountain named *Mannen*, and thus the names are semantically related.

Figure 1: *Trolltunga* ('the troll tongue'), in Tyssedal, Hardanger.
Photo: Trolltunga Studios, used with permission.

These names are not unique examples of words for a person used in Norwegian place-names. At *Norgeskart.no*, it is possible to get access to the Mapping Authority's central place-names register (SSR), and when searching 'Mannen', more than fifty occurrences of this name pop up. Similar examples are *Bispen* ('the bishop') and *Presten* ('the priest'), both of which are represented more than a dozen times in names referring to mountains or other kinds of natural features.

In some cases, 'pair' names are used for two neighbouring features, for instance *Kongen* ('the king') and *Dronninga* ('the queen') – not unexpectedly, *Kongen* is used for the larger of the two. *Skrott* in Kvam and in Jondal is related to Old Norse *skratti* (m., 'troll'), and close to Skrott we find *Glynt*, cf. *glunt* (m., 'small boy'). According to Øystein Frøysadal, the latter name should be seen in relation to the bigger mountain Skrott.[3] A glance at the Norwegian landscape of place-names will reveal a multitude of comparisons or metaphors used in the naming of natural features.

Mountain names: general remarks

In an introductory chapter to the *Norsk stadnamnleksikon*,[4] I have outlined some aspects regarding the typology of Norwegian mountain names. The term 'mountain names' (also 'hill names', 'names of elevations') may be used in two ways – either for names referring to mountains and hills, or names containing words or word elements for such features. The first approach is based on a topographic point of view, whereas the latter is based on a linguistic one. For example, the name *Solbjørg* (meaning 'sunny mountain ridge') refers to a summer farm and not to a mountain, but lexically it relates to a mountain name. Originally, the name was given to the nearby mountain, but as its denotatum was transferred to the pastures and the summer

---

3. Frøysadal 1968: 75.
4. Helleland 1997: 49–53.

farm below, the mountain itself was renamed *Solbjørgryggen* ('the Solbjørg ridge'). A similar transition of denotatum applies to many, if not most, summer farms and settlements in Norway.

In a mountainous country like Norway, it is likely that names referring to hills and mountains are abounding, and so is the number of words used for describing various shapes of mountains – both topographical words and metaphors. Apparently, those coining the names had a number of topographic words at their disposal in reference to peaks and heights, whilst their ability to distinguish between minor nuances of these features would have been highly specialised.

Some words describe more or less the same feature, such as *noll* (m.) and *nott* (m., 'small rounded rock'); others may reflect minor nuances in shape and dimension, for instance *nip* (f.) and *nup* (m., 'protruding rock'), the latter referring to a larger type of feature than the former one. In the mountainous area of the western part of Hardangervidda, about sixty different words for convex features like peaks and heights have been found in place-names.[5]

Unsurprisingly, the relatively high number of words used in mountain names is small compared to the variety of words that can occur in Norwegian place-names at all. According to an electronic list of generics established on the basis of more than 200 master's theses at Norwegian universities, more than 3,500 different words are used in place-name formation, most of them as generics, including words used in metaphorical names. This vast topographical vocabulary includes many groups of words which dictionaries treat as synonyms.[6]

The terms were not all used simultaneously, as the naming process must have taken place over centuries. We have reason

---

5. Frøysadal 1968; Helleland 1970: 25.
6. Gelling 1984: 7.

to believe that most names of minor mountains have come into being after 1500, since the population decline after the Black Death led to a partial breach of the oral trading of place-names. However, it is believed that numerous names date back to the Middle Ages and even pre-Christian times, as, for instance, the mountain name of *Siggjo* on the island of Bømlo, derived from the same root as Old Norse *séa* ('to see'). This mountain is visible from a long distance on the west Norwegian coast. Along the coast, we find a number of ancient island names, originally motivated by a dominating mountain on each island – for instance, *Alden* in Askvoll, related to the Latin *altus* ('high'),[7] and *Huglo* in Stord, related to the German *Hügel* ('hill').[8]

Most mountain names, with the exception of metaphorical names, are compounds. According to some studies of locally collected place-names, the percentage of simplex names – such as *Hovden* ('the hill') – varies between ten and twenty.[9] That means that a majority of the name stock consists of compounds, such as *Grjothovden*, where the generic *-hovden* defines the feature type and the specific *Grjot-* ('stony area') provides further information about the characteristics of this particular *hovden* or mountain. In many cases, the specific is another place-name, as in *Seksehovden*, 'the hill at (the farm of) Sekse'. Chronologically, that means that the mountain name is younger than the name used as a specific.

Metaphorical names

In addition to a large number of words describing natural features, those coining the names also had the possibility to

---

7. Sandnes and Stemshaug 1997: 68.
8. Ibid.: 226.
9. Cf. Helleland 1970: 184.

bring in all kinds of terms through comparison. Topographical features that are particularly striking or characteristic tend to evoke notions of things or figures in the nominators' mental universe. In Scandinavia, the term *samanlikningsnamn* ('comparative names') is widely used, being defined as *appellativ betegnelse der har fået stednavnefunktion på grund af det betegnede fænomens lighed med lokaliteten* ('an appellative designation that has been given a place-name function due to the similarity of the designation phenomenon with the locality').[10] However, the terms 'metaphorical names' and 'associative names'[11] are now more commonly used. According to the *Oxford English Dictionary*, a 'metaphor' is a 'figure of speech in which a name or descriptive word or phrase is transferred to an object or action different from, but analogous to, that to which it is literally applicable'.[12]

As in other countries, metaphorical place-names are an important part of the place-name inventory in Norway. These kind of names have special interest, since they provide new insight into the way people are thinking in terms of their mental references. In the international onomastic literature, we find numerous parallels to the names discussed in this chapter.[13]

It is not unexpected that metaphorical names occur to a particular degree when it comes to mountain names. Any shape or figure in the mental universe of man may be used metaphorically in naming a natural feature, including words for tools, artefacts, animals, persons, parts of animals and persons, and so on. Even names given after other places may be motivated

---

10. Christensen and Kousgård Sørensen 1972: 230.

11. Zilliacus 2002: 216.

12. 'Metaphor, n.', *OED Online*, www.oed.com/view/Entry/117328. Accessed 11 June 2022.

13. See, for instance, the various relevant articles in the international handbook *Name Studies* (Eichler et al. 1996) and Šrámek 2004 for a more theoretical approach.

through a kind of comparison, such as *Sibir* (Siberia) for a locality which is felt as distant, cold, or isolated; and during and in the aftermath of the Six-Day War in 1967, *Golanhøgda* ('the Golan height') was given to elevations in several places in Norway, referring to the Golan Heights in Syria/Israel.

Some words, like *nakke* (m., 'neck, neck-shaped natural feature') and *skalle* (m., 'skull, skull-shaped natural feature'), are so frequently used in some areas that they have become part of the topographic vocabulary. Even *såte* (f., 'haystack'), as in *Såta*, may sometimes be recognised as a topographic designation. At first, such words may have been used as metaphors, but over the years, they have developed into topographic terms and should be considered as such. There may, however, be regional and individual differences to which degree they are accepted as topographic descriptions, and some users may still see the metaphorical element as predominant – although names like *Skuta* ('the ship') and *Geiteryggen* ('the goat back') are clearly to be considered as metaphors.

I suggest the following grouping of metaphors used as place-names:

1. Anthropomorphic beings
2. Animals
3. Body parts of anthropomorphic beings and animals
4. Buildings, furniture, tools, etc.
5. Metaphors as specifics in compound names
6. Metaphorical names with a place-name as first element

Anthropomorphic beings

As mentioned above, persons in various capacities may be represented metaphorically in mountain names. *Kongen* ('the king'), *Dronninga* ('the queen'), *Prinsen* ('the prince'), *Bispen* ('the bishop'), *Homannen* ('the tax collector'), *Presten* ('the priest'), *Prestkona* ('the priest's wife'), *Klokkaren* ('the church servant'), *Bakaren* ('the baker'), *Bonden* ('the farmer'), *Mannen* ('the man'), and *Kjerringa* ('the (old) woman') are examples from various local areas. Even representatives from the fairy-tale world like *Trollet* ('the troll'), *Risen* ('the giant'), and *Gygra* – also *Gjura* – ('the female giant') are found.

The metaphorical background of such names does not solely refer to the shape of the named feature, as it is difficult to decide if a rock resembles a church servant or a baker. It is also reasonable to think that the position and social role of the occupation in question are reflected in the naming. Through such names, those coining and using them (i.e. ordinary people) could – in a more or less humorous way – vent their frustrations with people of higher ranks.

Not all of the names reflecting persons are provided as comparisons. In some cases, the names may be motivated by ownership or because something happened to said person on the spot. This is probably the case for some of the names of *Skomakaren* ('the shoemaker'), which, according to SSR, is registered sixteen times, but only one of them in reference to a hill.

Domestic and wild animals

A number of domestic and wild animals are used metaphorically in mountain names. SSR lists the most popular one (on a nationwide basis) as *Hesten*, the definite form of *hest* (m., 'horse'), with ninety-five occurrences, almost all of which refer to mountains and hills. The indefinite form *Hest* comes up with twenty hits. Generally speaking, the indefinite form is considered to be the older one.

Of the approximately ninety occurrences of *Oksen/Uksen* – the definite form of *okse/ukse* (m., 'oxen') – only twenty refer to mountains. *Kua* ('the cow') and *Kalven* ('the calf') are found four and three times as mountain names, respectively. *Geita* ('the goat') is registered about ten times as a mountain name, whereas *Bukken* ('he-goat' or 'billy goat') is used as a mountain or hill name six times out of twenty in total. Another word for he-goat is Old Norse *hafr* (m.), which is the basis for two occurrences of the mountain name *Havren* (Høyanger and Vik in Sogn).

According to SSR, *Sauen* ('the sheep') and *Veren* ('the ram') are each found only twice as hill names. *Grisen* ('the pig') is found twelve times, but only twice as a mountain name. The male pig, *galte* (m., 'hog'), is entered approximately 150 times as *Galten* in SSR, mostly referring to skerries and shallow (dangerous) waters.[14] Only about 10% of the places named *Galten* are used for mountain-like features. The female pig, *purke* (f., 'sow'), occurs three or four times in the form of *Purka* as a mountain name.

The most dominant wild animal reflected in place-names is *bjørn* (m., 'bear'), most often as a specific in compounds, for instance *Bjørneheia*, composed of *bjørn* (m.) and *hei* (f., 'heath, height'), probably reflecting observation of this animal. As a simplex, it may be used metaphorically, as in *Bjørn* or in dialectal forms as *Bjønn* or *Bjødn*. *Varg* (m., 'wolf') is used in the peak name *Vargen* in Hardangervidda. Another word for the same animal, *skrubb* (m.), is used in the plural form *Skrubbane*, referring to some stones which may be compared with a pack of wolves.

Simle (f., 'female reindeer') is used in *Simla* to describe a big stone in Hardangervidda, while *rev* (m., 'fox') and *hare* (m., 'hare') are found in several names as *Reven* and *Haren*. Bird names like *kråke* (f., 'crow') and *ugle* (f., 'owl') are represented only in a couple of hill names as *Kråka* and *Ugla*, but they are very frequent as names of minor features like skerries and brooks (burns), often with reference to the sound of these birds.

---

14. Cf. Hovda 1978.

Figure 2: The mountain *Oksen* ('the ox'), situated at the inner part of the
Hardangerfjord. Photo: Johannes Sekse, used with permission.

Body parts of anthropomorphic beings and animals
We encounter a number of metaphorical mountain names
referring to body parts and limbs of anthropomorphic beings
and animals – including *Aksla/Oksla* ('the shoulder'), which
is used several hundred times nationwide for mountains and
rocks. One of the most famous uses of this word is *Aksla* in
Ålesund. *Nasa/Nosi* ('the nose') is also frequently used for
mountains. A plural form *Nasene* is also found several times in
mountain names.

Some names are seemingly coined in a masculine context,
such as *Kuntulven*, which contains the dialectal word *kuntulv*
(m., 'clitoris'). The name refers to a rather modest but salient
peak in the Hardangervidda. Another vivid imagination has
given rise to *Fansklørne* ('the devil's claws'), which refers to
some idiosyncratic stripes on a rock side.

The name *Hårteigen*, which refers to a characteristic
mountain peak in the middle of the Hardangervidda, has been
interpreted in several ways,[15] but to my mind, the resemblance

---

15. Bjorvand 2017: 27.

to the upper part of a skull is so striking that it must have motivated the name. In plain text, we can understand the name as 'the part of the head where hair grows', the first element being Old Norse *hár* (n., 'hair') and the second being *teigr* (m., 'limited area, field').

Figure 3: Hårteigen in the Hardangervidda.
Photo: Johannes Sekse, used with permission.

The horse's nose, *mule* (m., 'muzzle'), is frequently used in names of promontories, but also as a mountain name, as in *Mulen* in Ullensvang. In *Månene* ('the manes'), another body part of the horse is represented. *Spenane* ('the teats'), referring to two rising spikes on a mountain, is presumably compared to a goat's teats (if not the nipples of a woman). The well-known mountain name *Blåmanen* in Bergen is composed of *blå* ('blue') and *man* (f., 'mane') – *man* is a variant of *mån* (f.), from Old Norse *mǫn* (f.). Earlier it was misunderstood as 'the blue man (male person)'.

The abovementioned *Geitaryggen* ('goat back') in Hardangervidda is composed of two elements combined into one concept, which is more precise than the two words separately. Another example of this sort is *Ulvskjaft* ('wolf's jaw') in Ullensvang, referring to a rock which looks like a jaw. *Hanakamb* ('cock's comb') and *Hanakne* ('cock's knee') are found in a couple of names in western Norway.

Buildings, furniture, tools, etc.

A frequent mountain name referring to a building is *Kyrkja*, the definite form of *kyrkje* (f., 'church'). A wide mountain ridge in the Hardangervidda is named *Låven*, 'the (main part of a) barn'. In Ullensvang, we find *Bygningen* – cf. *bygning* (m. 'building') – as the name of a steep mountainside which has obviously been compared with the front side of a building. Another steep mountain seems to have been associated with an attic or loft, as its name is simply *Loft*. A related meaning is found in the rock name *Rot*, likewise in Ullensvang – cf. Old Norse *rót*, n., 'the space below the roof (a house)'.

A number of natural features have been named after comparisons with objects in daily life, like *Båten* ('the boat'), being a hill-spur, and *Kamben* ('the comb'), being a mountain ridge. Another mountain-spur is called *Hudnen*, from *hun* ('the slab'), with reference to its shape. In the proximity of a summer farm in Hardangervidda, we find *Holken*, from *holk* (m., 'the wooden tub'), referring to a rounded hill. A wooden box to carry various types of food is known as *laup* (n.) in the local dialect, and this word is used in the definite form *Laupen* with reference to a rounded hill.

There are several examples of compound designations in which the first element specifies the content of the last element. At a certain point on a mountain path in Ullensvang, it is possible to see a group of big stones called *Høylassi* ('the hay loads'). Another hill in the same area is named *Smørstampen* ('the butter tub').

Among names that refer to furniture, we can also include compounds like *Gygrastolen* ('the giantess' chair'), referring to a depression in a mountainside, and *Bispestolen* ('the bishop's chair'), referring to a chair-like rock. Another example is *Skomakarstolen* ('the shoemakers' chair'), referring to a rock which has been compared with the working chair of a cobbler. In these names, the metaphor is based on the meaning of the compound. The first element specifies or modifies the kind of chair that is used as a metaphor.

Metaphors as specifics in compound names
In a number of names, the metaphorical element is combined with a topographical generic, such as *Flautenuten*, where the first element is *flaute* (f., 'crossbar on a timber sledge'), composed with *nut* (m., 'mountain'). Other examples include *Kistenuten*, where the first element is *kiste* (f., 'chest, coffin'), and *Oksenuten*, where the first element is *okse* (m., 'ox'). Such names may occur as variants of the simplexes *Bjørn*, *Kista*, and *Oksen*. It should also be noted that not all the names of the type *Oksenuten* or *Kistenuten* are to be considered metaphors; the specifics *Okse-* or *Kiste-* may instead refer to various circumstances related to an ox or to a coffin without any metaphorical reference.

Metaphorical names with a place-name as first element
In some names, the metaphorical content is modified by an adjective, such as Øvsta Oksli, 'the upper shoulder', or by another place-name, such as *Hengstrynet*, 'the nose at (the summer farm of) Heng'.

Conclusion

In this chapter, only a small selection of the metaphorical mountain names in western Norway have been touched upon. Nonetheless, the provided examples should be sufficient to illustrate the vivid imagination of those naming them. Place-names are, first and foremost, addresses – both through their linguistic content and through the features and figures they represent. They are also a source for the study of local language, history, topography, cultural history, social history, and psychology. Metaphorical place-names contribute particularly to the three last aspects. Many traces of people's mental lives are left in the place-name inventory, and not least in metaphorical names.

Bibliography

Bjorvand, Harald. 2017. 'Hårteigen'. In Lars-Erik Edlund and Elzbieta Strzelecka (eds), *Mellannorrland i centrum. Språkliga och historiska studier tillägnade professor Eva Nyman*. Umeå: Kungl. Skytteanska Samfundet, 27–31.

Christensen, Vibeke and Kousgård Sørensen, John. 1972. *Stednavneforskning 1. Afgrænsning. Terminologi. Metode. Datering*. Copenhagen: Universitetsforlaget i København.

Eichler, Ernst et al. (eds). 1996. *Name Studies: An International Handbook of Onomastics*. Volume 2. Berlin: Walter de Gruyter.

Frøysadal, Øystein. 1968. 'Fjellnamn i Hordaland og Sogn og Fjordane'. In Jørn Sandnes and Per Tylden (eds), *Namn i fjellet*. Oslo: Det Norske Samlaget, 70–88.

Gelling, Margaret. 1984. *Place-Names in the Landscape. The Geographical Roots of Britain's Place-Names*. London: J.M. Dent.

Helleland, Botolv. 1970. 'Noko om stadnamn frå Hardangervidda Vest'. Master's thesis. University of Oslo.

——— (ed.). 1991. *Norsk språk i Amerika – Norwegian Language in America*. Oslo: Novus.

———. 1997. 'Fjellnamn'. In Jørn Sandnes and Ola Stemshaug (eds), *Norsk stadnamnleksikon*. Fourth edition. Oslo: Det Norske Samlaget, 49–53.

Hovda, Per. 1978 [1941]. 'Okse, galt, hund og andre dyrenemne skjernamn'. In Ingeborg Hoff et al. (eds), *Frå hav til hei. Heidersskrift til Per Hovda på 70-årsdagen 17. oktober 1978*. Oslo, Bergen, and Tromsø: Universitetsforlaget,. 7–20.

Sandnes, Jørn and Ola Stemshaug (eds). 1997. *Norsk stadnamnleksikon*. Fourth edition. Oslo: Det Norske Samlaget.

Šrámek, Rudolf. 2004. 'Etymologie und Deutung in der Namenkunde'. In Andrea Brendler and Silvio Brendler (eds), *Namenarten und ihre Erforschung. Ein Lehrbuch für das Studium der Onomastik*. Hamburg: Baar, 93–106.

Zilliacus, Kurt. 2002. *Forska i namn*. Helsinki: Svenska literatursällskapet i Finland.

· III ·

The Place-Name Collection Project in Møre and Romsdal, Norway

Berit Sandnes

Introduction

Place-name studies have been a common thread throughout Arne Kruse's career, beginning with his master's thesis of 1983, which dealt with names on fishing grounds and bearings used by fishermen in Smøla in Norway. The thesis allowed him to combine his interest for place-names and dialect with his personal experiences of coastal fishing. Names of fishing grounds and bearings are rarely written down (though a few private collections exist). Rather, the names belong to an oral tradition specific to local fishermen, and Arne learned them from the people who used them in their trade.

Thus, Arne had a relevant background for the place-name collection project in his home county, Møre and Romsdal, on the west coast of Norway. The project was formally closed in 1995, but the finishing work continued. The project was organised by the University College in Volda, with the college's Peter Hallaråker as project leader throughout. It ran from 1985 to 1995, with Arne working as a researcher 1987–89, and was funded by the Møre and Romsdal county council, the Norwegian Mapping Authority in Møre and Romsdal, and the Arts Council of Norway.

The aim of the project was to collect as many place-names as possible, and the pivotal choice of method was to let non-professional locals do the collection. A total of about 200,000 place-names were collected. These names, with relevant information, were analysed by researchers and digitised. They are now easily accessible to the public in the county atlas.[1]

There is a considerable interest in place-name collection in Scotland these days, which is expressed in a number of local collections as well as published volumes such as *The Place-Names of Fife* series.[2] For this reason, a presentation of the county project and the methodology chosen may be of interest to a Scottish audience.

Hallaråker outlines the four steps of the project: 1) collection of place-names, carried out by local collectors, 2) scientific analysis of the collected material, 3) digitisation, and 4) publication.[3]

Collection by local place-name collectors

This was a crowd-sourcing project in the sense that the collection depended on local collectors in all thirty-eight municipalities of the county, with no formal training in place-name research. All collectors received basic training in the form of an introductory course, arranged by the project leader and the researchers Arne Kruse and Tor Erik Jenstad. The course included some theoretical background and guidelines as to which place-names and what information to include. The focus, however, was on practical work and instructions on how to carry out the actual

1. *Fylkesatlas Vestland*, https://www.fylkesatlas.no/stadnamn_alle. Accessed 4 July 2022.
2. Taylor and Márkus 2006-2013.
3. Hallaråker 1989: 49.

collection. Courses were arranged in all the municipalities, and a local coordinator was appointed.

The basis for the collection was the printed 1:5,000 map series. Each of the maps are identified by a place-name and a code. All place-name lists and recordings were organised by map sheet and marked with map name and code. The place-names lists were in standardised forms, to ensure that the required information was included for every place-name. Names already recorded on the maps were to be included in the collection, and each collector was responsible for a specific area in which they would collect as many names as possible. Equipped with map sheets, name lists, and tape recorders, they were ready to start.

STADNAMNLISTE NR 2, av 12 — Paul Øksenvåg f. 1921

KOMMUNE (NR OG NAMN) 1554 AVERØY — INFORMANT Petrine Alvheim — FØDSELSÅR 4.1924

KARTVERK OG KARTBLAD ØKSENVÅG BH 119-5-1 — OPPSKRIVAR Tove Skaret — OPPSKR.ÅR 1992

R	KART-RUTE	STADNAMN (med dialektskrift)	FONEMSKRIFT (Blir utfylt av prosjektleiinga)	KASSETT OPPTAK (x)	PREP (i, på)	STAD, LOKALITETSTYPE a) Kva slags stad, lokalitet b) Bruk av staden, no og før c) Tradisjon, andre namn
11	B3	Øksenvågskjæra / Øksenvågsjæra	/"øks*nvåg,s-x:ra/		utpå	N 152 små skjær
12	B3	Rumpbuketa / Rompboketa	/"romp,oktal/		uti	N 173 lita bukt
13	B3	Vasshaugneset / Vasshågnese	/"vashåg,nese/		bortpå	N 163 lite nes, ikke vegitasjon.
14	B3,4	Litlvasshaugen / Litjvasshåjin	/"litvas,hå:jiN/		oppå	N 118 haug m/lyng
15	B3	Storbrynnen / Storbrynn -brønn(...)	/"sto:r,bryN/		borti	N 203 liten vasspytt. K 182
16	B3,4	Storvasshaugen / Storvasshåjin	/"sto:rvas,hå:jiN/		oppå	N 118 haug m/lyng
17		Tallet 17 er gått ut.				
18	B4	Været OK	/'være/		nedi	K 113 bosted, før fiskebrygge
19	B4	Alvåre / Blvoret	/"ål£,vå:re/			utsiktspunkt for å se om båtene kom seg heim. Lyng K 118
20	B4	Tuvå / Tuva	/"tu:vå/			liten haug N 118 står hus der.

Figure 1: Part of place-name list two of twelve for the map Øksenvåg BH 119-5-1 in Averøy. Standardised form, phonemic spelling, and nature or culture code has been added by the project team. All other entries by the collectors.

The heading for each name list would include name and number of the map, the municipality (*kommune*), name of informant and year of birth, name of collector, and year of collection (see Figure 1). The collected names were given sequential numbers for each map and a grid reference (column 1 and 2). After that, the place-names were entered into the list (column 3, *stadnamn*).

Finding a suitable written form could be quite a challenge, since it was basically an oral collection and many of the names had never been rendered in writing before. The instruction was to spell the place-names in a rough dialect form with common letters, as close to the pronunciation as possible. The phonemic spelling (*fonemskrift*) was not to be filled in; this was left to the project leaders. The collectors filled in the preposition (*prep*) used with the name and the locality type (*stad, lokalitetstype*). In addition to locality type (a), the final column could be used for additional information, e.g. present and former use of the place (b), traditions, and older names (c). In the printed maps corresponding to the name lists, the location of the place-name was indicated only by a number, placed centrally in the object.

In spite of the structured outline, the actual organisation would vary. Many collectors would interview local informants, whereas some would only collect names they knew personally. Occasionally, the lists and maps were sent from house to house. Some collectors would record the names as they were collected. Quite often, however, the name lists were completed first and then the lists were recorded.

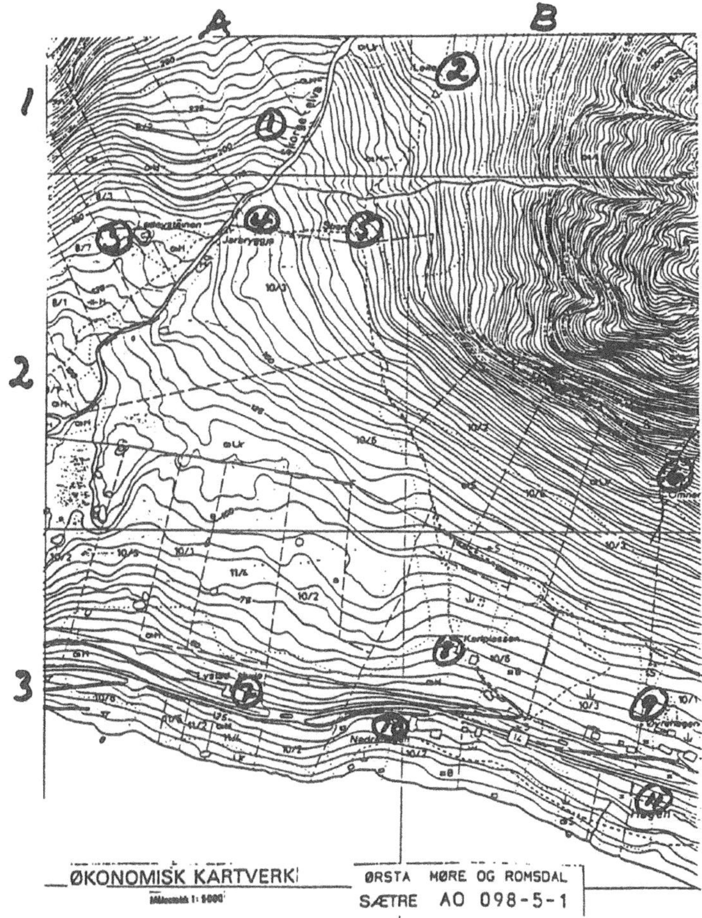

Figure 2: Part of map with place-name numbers,
Sætre map no. AO 098-5-1, Ørsta municipality.

Scientific analysis

The local collections resulted in a large number of handwritten
name lists with corresponding annotated maps and tapes containing the sound recordings. This material was handed over
to the project team for processing, who would check that all
necessary information had been included.

Standardisation of the written form of the place-names, as well as their simplified phonemic transcription, was left to the researchers. The pronunciation was recorded and thus safeguarded, but written forms were still necessary for databases and mapping, as well as scientific analysis. Standardised forms facilitate the searching, recognition, and comparison of names and name elements.

Even when standardised place-name forms in the project had no official status, the researchers adhered to the main principles of the Norwegian Place-Name Law of 1990.[4] According to that law, place-names should be standardised on the basis of the traditional local form, using the spelling principles of the Norwegian language. If place-names contain lexical words, these should normally be spelled according to the standard spelling. Regional forms are allowed to some extent. In Figure 1, all names have an additional form written above the line, which is the suggested standardised form. All these names are compounded of common words in the lexicon, so the standardisation is quite straightforward. When place-name elements are opaque, the pronunciation is the only guideline.

Phonemic spelling (column 4) was also left to the researchers. Even though some collectors complained that there were not enough letters in the alphabet to render the place-names adequately, an introduction to phonemic writing was not seen as a realistic part of the training for the collectors.[5] However, it is true that the dialects have a number of phonemes that do not have counterparts in the standard alphabet. In addition, a number of the major dialect dividing lines in Norwegian cross Møre and Romsdal, so the dialects differ greatly within the county.

---

4. 'Lov om stadnamn (stadnamnlova)', *Lovdata*, https://lovdata.no/lov/1990-05-18-11. Accessed 12 September 2022.
5. Hallaråker 1995: 201.

A simplified phonemic transcription system was established for the project, primarily based on the twenty-nine standard letters of the Norwegian alphabet, using small and capital letters. The approach was systematic in the way that capital vowels signify open vowels and capital consonants symbolise palatal letters. In addition, a few special signs found on standard keyboards were used, such as '9' for the velar nasal (*ng*) and '$' for the palatal fricative (*sj/sh*). When all columns of the place-name lists were filled in, these were digitised by student assistants.

Prior to filling in the phonemic spelling in the name lists, members of the project team established phoneme catalogues for every municipality, the idea being that the local dialect forms a phonemic and morphologic system of its own. The phoneme catalogues included a phoneme inventory, phonological rules (e.g. *v* is pronounced *f* in front of a *t*), and morphosyntactic rules. Traditionally, the phoneme inventory of the southern dialects include a 'double set' of vowels — closed and open — whereas the northern dialects have a wide range of consonants, including a set of palatals. A typical morphosyntactic feature is the change from velar to palatal when the definite article is added, as in *haug* – *haujen* ('mound – the mound'). This is reflected in no. 13 and 14 in Figure 1: collector's form *-håjin*, standardised form *-haugen*, and phonemic spelling -håjiN (N indicating palatal). The advantage of phonemic spelling is that it refers to an abstract system, rather than absolute values. Phonetic spelling can never be fully precise.

Table 1: Adapted version of the information for the place-name Litlvasshaugen after the scientific analysis.

Place-name: Litlvasshaugen	
Number	14
Standardised form	Litlvasshaugen
Collector's form	Litjvasshåjin
Phonemic spelling	/"liHvas,hå:jiN/
Municipality number	1554
Municipality name	Averøy
Map number	
Additional info	
Map name	BH 11951
Square	Øksenvåg
Tape nr	B3, 4
Informant	Paul Øksenvåg, Petrine Alvheim
Collector	Tove Skaret
Preposition	oppå
Locality type	

Problems and perspectives

Although the collection can be considered a success, the project team was well aware of potential problems. The main challenge in a project involving such a large number of collectors with no linguistic training is to make sure that the collection is carried out in a systematic manner and in a uniform way in all municipalities, ensuring that the material is suitable for scientific study. To deal with this, as we have seen, all collectors received basic training, and important instructions were repeated. The place-name lists were standardised to make sure the required information was included. Finally, all the municipalities signed a contract with the county's research institution, Møreforsking, in which they obliged to follow these instructions. Hallaråker concludes that the collection is systematic on the whole, and that the information provided about the place-names is reliable.[6] This means that the desired standard was achieved. The highest-quality output originated in municipalities where the local project coordinator had a linguistic background.

The map-sheet approach ensures systematic registration, but there are potential drawbacks. As Hallaråker points out, the discrepancy between social and cultural units and printed maps caused problems when collectors were mainly interested in collecting names from their own neighbourhood.[7] Norway does not have rural villages in the traditional sense, but rather groups of farms, which are often the result of the division of one original settlement. Many collectors were mainly interested in collecting names from their own estate or neighbourhood, and in some cases, they would cut up and glue together maps so that they would cover their area of interest.

The collection in the 1980s and 1990s was based on printed maps. New digital tools can certainly simplify parts of a collection process, and everyday smartphones can now be used to find coordinates as well as record the pronunciation of place-names. But even in a digital world, maps or grid systems are required to get an overview of an area, so traditional tools are hardly out of the game.

Publication and use of the material

There is always a danger that collections are stored in a closed archive, out of reach of the public. In the early years of the

6. Hallaråker 1995: 117.
7. Hallaråker 2003: 11.

project, the project leader envisaged place-name publications for the individual municipalities as well as a place-name lexicon for the county.[8] This has not been realised. What has been manifested instead is a digital publication, which makes the material more easily accessible for the public. Digitising the material is a continuous process, carried out by the county archive of Møre and Romsdal, in cooperation with its counterpart in Sogn and Fjordane. The place-names are georeferenced, and by clicking the name in the map, access is provided to a fact sheet similar to the one in Figure 3.

Hallaråker had a fourfold aim for the project: cultural, practical, scientific, and pedagogic.[9] The former means safeguarding the place-names for the future, which has certainly been accomplished. In addition to names already mapped, the collection includes a wealth of previously unrecorded names, such as field names and names of minor topographical features.

The collection is also of practical use. Road addresses have recently become mandatory for all inhabited houses in Norway. This meant that a large number of addresses had to be established, and many municipalities used the collection to find material for suitable road names. The collection is also useful for the Norwegian Mapping Authority, which is responsible for the registration of official place-names. The localisation of a place-name is easily checked on the county atlas website, and the pronunciation is invaluable for the standardisation. As seen above, place-name law prescribes that the spelling should be based on the local pronunciation.

The collected material has hardly been used for scientific purposes to the extent that the project team envisaged. This is partly due to the decline of place-name studies in Norwegian

---

8. Hallaråker 1989: 51–52.
9. Ibid.: 47.

universities, which is not to be discussed here. The collection preserves valuable material, but the value of the collection would be significantly enhanced if the place-names were interpreted. This does not necessarily imply printed publications. Instead, interpretations of place-names or place-name elements could be published digitally, the obvious advantages being is that digital material is easy to improve upon and open to everyone. The raw material is certainly available and waiting for further utilisation.[10]

Bibliography

Fylkesatlas Vestland. https://www.fylkesatlas.no/stadnamn_alle. Accessed 4 July 2022.

Hallaråker, Peter. 1989. 'Metodiske problem i samband med innsamling av stadnamn i Møre og Romsdal'. In P. Hallaråker et al. (eds), *Stadnamn i kystkulturen.* NORNA-rapporter 41. Uppsala: NORNA-förlaget, 47–62.

———. 1995. *Stadnamn i Møre og Romsdal. Innsamling, teori, metode og formidling.* Forskningsrapport 8. Volda: Høgskolen i Volda, Møreforsking Volda.

———. 2003. *Stadnamnarkivet og stadnamndatabasen for Møre og Romsdal.* Forskingsrapport 54. Volda: Høgskolen i Volda, Møreforsking Volda.

'Lov om stadnamn (stadnamnlova)'. *Lovdata.* https://lovdata.no/lov/1990-05-18-11. Accessed 12 September 2022.

Taylor, Simon and Márkus, Gilbert. 2006-2013. *The Place-Names of Fife.* 5 vols. Donington: Shaun Tyas.

---

10. Tor Erik Jenstad, Arne Kruse's colleague as a researcher, has provided information and notes to this contribution.

$$\cdot \text{IV} \cdot$$

Lagerlöf on the Border with Norway

Bjarne Thorup Thomsen

Swedish author Selma Lagerlöf is strongly associated with the region of Värmland, which borders on Norway. While more recent research has justifiably critiqued a tendency of traditional Lagerlöf scholarship to overstate in confining ways the regional dimensions of the author's work and perceived persona, instead promoting nation-orientated and transnational perspectives on her work and its impact, the role of Värmland in Lagerlöf's life and writing is nevertheless manifest.[1] In light of the proximity to the border with Norway that was a geographical fact of a considerable part of Lagerlöf's life, Norwegian literary historian Francis Bull, in his essay 'Selma Lagerlöf og Norge' ('Selma Lagerlöf and Norway'), expresses surprise that the author had little personal experience of the neighbouring country:

> *Besynderlig må det virke på en nordmann å oppdage at Selma Lagerlöf praktisk talt ikke kjente Norge av selvsyn. […] Å ta en tur til Norge skulle ha vært lett og nærliggende for henne, men det skjedde ikke ofte.*[2]

1. For a comprehensive study of the history of the critical reception of Lagerlöf's literary work and public persona, see Nordlund 2005.
2. Bull 1958: 59.

> It is peculiar for a Norwegian to realise that Selma Lagerlöf
> did practically not know Norway first-hand. [...] Taking a
> trip to Norway would have seemed easy and an obvious thing
> for her to do, but it seldom happened.[3]

The two recorded occasions on which Lagerlöf did visit Norway
were in the summer of 1902 (southern Norway including Larvik)
and the summer of 1904. The second occasion is of particular literary interest because it is bound up with a journey of discovery
to northern Sweden which the author undertook in preparation
for her famous nation-defining travelogue, school textbook, and
fantasy for children *Nils Holgerssons underbara resa genom Sverige*
(*Nils Holgersson's Wonderful Journey through Sweden*), which was
published in two volumes in 1906 and 1907. Lagerlöf's sphere of
interest during this northbound journey did clearly not exclude
Norway, since she visited both Narvik, travelling on the final
stretch of the so-called iron-ore railway line between Sweden
and Norway, opened as recently as 1903, and also Trondheim.
However, Lagerlöf never seems to have visited Norway after the
dissolution of the union with Sweden in 1905.

The fact that Lagerlöf's actual encounters with Norway were
limited should not lead to an assumption of a lack of appreciation
of Norwegian culture, nature, or indeed geopolitics on her part.
Francis Bull quotes Lagerlöf's assessment of the Norwegians
as the most aesthetically gifted of the Scandinavian peoples.
He cites, furthermore, Lagerlöf's expression of privilege in
having lived in an era when Europe's foremost authors wrote
in a language, i.e. Norwegian, which she could access without
translation, and in which they explored conditions that resem-
bled closely those in her own country.[4]

---

3. All translations into English are the author's.
4. Bull 1958: 56.

Writers such as Bjørnstjerne Bjørnson and Henrik Ibsen had a profound influence on Lagerlöf's work. Obvious cases in point are the novels *Jerusalem* (1901–02), inspired by Bjørnson's peasant tales, and *Bannlyst* (*Banished*, 1918), inspired by Ibsen's drama *Fruen fra havet* (*The Lady from the Sea*). Both novels testify to Lagerlöf's indebtedness to her Norwegian predecessors with regard to both the topographical and psychological dimensions of her writing.

As for Lagerlöf's perspectives on the geopolitical relationship between Norway and Sweden and on the Norwegian national question, we shall now turn our attention to a comparison of two lesser-known texts by the author: one from shortly before the dissolution of the union, and the other published almost thirty years later, depicting a visit to the borderland. Our discussion will aim to demonstrate, firstly, Lagerlöf's keen interest in a continuum and close bond between the two countries; secondly, through context, her support for Norwegian independence; and thirdly, her ambivalent appreciation of the post-unionistic border demarcation itself. My hope is that the topics of topography, nation, travel, and Scandinavian connections will resonate with my friend and colleague Arne Kruse's broader scholarly interests.

Countries baked together

In 1959, Lagerlöf scholar Erland Lagerroth published a hitherto unknown Lagerlöf manuscript which he had discovered in the archives of the Royal Library in Stockholm.[5] There is a strong likelihood that the short manuscript, which is entitled 'Läsebok. Brödlimpa' ('Textbook. Bread Loaf'), was planned

____

5. Lagerlöf 1959.

as a chapter of *Nils Holgersson*. More recently, Ulla-Britta Lagerroth, likewise an authority on Lagerlöf, goes as far as contending that the manuscript text was intended as the overall introduction to *Nils Holgersson*.[6] What, then, are the contents of a chapter with such a prominent presumed role, and why was the chapter omitted?

The chapter offers an allegory of the geological genesis and development of the peninsula of Norway and Sweden, asserting an almost organic affinity between the countries. Using imagery linked to a domestic sphere of production, the manuscript conceives of the countries as the result of God's not entirely successful attempt at baking bread. Due to too much yeast in the dough, two loaves have accidentally grown together, *den ena en smula ofvanför den andra*[7] ('one a little above the other'), without, however, losing their distinctiveness: *den ena hade blifvit hög och smal och den andra bred och platt*[8] ('one had become high and narrow, the other wide and flat'). A dominant topographical focus of the text is placed on the shared and combining 'borderland terrain' of the two loaves: *längs efter sammanväxningen hade de sprungit upp i en hög ås*[9] ('along the area that had grown together they [the loaves] had formed a high ridge'). Ultimately, the manuscript text maintains that the connection between the loaves/countries is so strong that separation seems impossible *utan att förstöra dem båda två*[10] ('without destroying both of them').

Erland Lagerroth terms the manuscript the 'fifth gospel'[11] of *Nils Holgersson*, based on the argument that it offers a more extensive topographical and geological conspectus than

---

6. Lagerroth 2000: 141.
7. Lagerlöf 1959: 557.
8. Ibid.: 558.
9. Ibid.
10. Ibid.: 557.
11. Lagerroth 1959: 560.

anything found in the published version of the travel adventure, which operates on regional levels and, principally, on a Swedish national level.[12] He dates the origin of the manuscript as being prior to the spring of 1905.[13]

As for a persuasive hypothesis on the rationale behind the omission of the manuscript, we need to turn to Ulla-Britta Lagerroth, who argues that the dissolution of the union between Norway and Sweden in the autumn of 1905, a year or so after the presumed conception of the manuscript text and a year before the publication of the first volume of *Nils Holgersson*, rendered the emphasis of the chapter on the common ground between the two countries outdated and overtaken by developments in national politics and binational relations.[14] The geopolitical conditions underpinning the textbook project had changed decisively.

While this posited connection between the dissolution of the union and the omission of the introductory chapter is a convincing one, it does not necessarily follow that the rediscovered manuscript reads as an endorsement and essentialisation of the unionistic relationship. A safer interpretation would be that the manuscript, rather than offering a geopolitical position, aimed to provide a pedagogical and imaginative account of the factual phenomenon of the ties between the two countries as they pertained to c. 1904.

Furthermore, the common ground between the countries, which the manuscript metaphorises, should not necessarily be read through the narrower lens of unionism. While respecting the Nordic nation states, Lagerlöf was a strong believer

---

12. For an in-depth study of the spatial design of *Nils Holgersson*, see Thorup Thomsen 2007.
13. Lagerroth 1959: 561.
14. Lagerroth 2000: 141.

in Scandinavianism and Nordism.[15] Such beliefs and, more broadly, an interest in cross-border continua and transnational interfaces that informs much of Lagerlöf's writing may be reflected in the manuscript.

Finally, Lagerlöf's stance on Norwegian independence, as it was substantiated just a year or so after the assumed conception of the manuscript, is difficult to square with a reading of the manuscript as a unionistic endorsement. In the beginning of March 1905, Lagerlöf was approached by her publisher Karl Otto Bonnier, who invited her to sign a planned public petition calling for Sweden, through generosity, to attempt to keep Norway within the union. Lagerlöf, however, immediately declined the invitation in a letter to Bonnier dated 7 March 1905, and instead forcefully advocated Norwegian independence:

Jag är [...] *sedan åratal tillbaka af den åsikten att Norge bör få bli ett eget rike. Att få se det gamla norska kungadömet återupprättadt och bevittna ett helt folks jubel öfver att åter få räknas med bland själfständiga stater har länge varit en af mina drömmar.*[16]

I have [...] for a number of years been of the opinion that Norway should be allowed to become a nation of its own. To see the resurrection of the old Norwegian kingdom and to witness the jubilation of an entire people at again being counted among the independent states have long been one of my dreams.

She went on to argue that the discontinuation of *denna pinsamma union*[17] ('this embarrassing union') would be beneficial for the national renewal of both countries and for their future co-existence:

15. For a wide-ranging exploration of Nordism in Lagerlöf, see Lagerroth 2000.
16. Lagerlöf 1969: 28.
17. Ibid.

Och till sist skulle vi verkligen komma att bli riktiga vänner, så som vi känna oss gentemot danskarna[18] ('And finally we would become real friends in the same way as we feel towards the Danes'). She concluded that she saw no other solution than separation.

The author's argumentation appears to have persuaded the powerful publisher to perform a U-turn, since the petition Bonnier eventually published in July 1905 – signed by a sizeable segment of the Swedish cultural elite – contained clear echoes of Lagerlöf's stance: it requested the Swedish parliament to initiate the ending of a union which, instead of its aim of drawing the two nations closer, had only served to distance them from each other.[19]

Hard or soft border

When Lagerlöf revisited the topics of the border with Norway and the topographical relationship between Norway and Sweden some thirty years on, in an essay entitled 'Värmländsk naturskönhet' ('The Natural Beauty of Värmland') published in the collection *Höst* (*Autumn*) in 1933,[20] some noteworthy differences are observable compared with the 'Bread Loaf' manuscript. Firstly, more emphasis is now placed on (landscape) *difference* between the two nations; and secondly, the representation of the border itself has become considerably more potentiated. When confronted with the post-unionistic 'hard' borderline between the countries, Lagerlöf expresses a range of responses and mixed feelings, articulating senses of serenity, stillness, mystique, and nostalgia – possibly even an implicit longing for a future 'softening' of the border.

18. Ibid.
19. The petition is reproduced between pp. 104-105 of Bonnier 1956.
20. Lagerlöf 1933.

A common denominator between the two texts considered in this chapter is the device, recurring in Lagerlöf, of approaching landscape as something constructed or consciously created. In the 'Bread Loaf' manuscript, the creation process was, as we saw, both divine and humorously domestic. In the Värmland essay, the process is artistic as well as architectural. While the former text asserted a transnational continuum as the result of the creation, the creative outcome in the latter text is best summed up in terms of discontinuity between the two nations, which may read as a recognition of their new, fully separate statuses.

The Värmland essay likens nature to a pictorial artist who has Värmland *uppsatt på staffliet*[21] ('placed on the easel') but has abandoned the painting in mid-process, rendering the landscape incomplete. This notion of being unfinished or lacking is reinforced in architectural terms in a subsequent passage which, notably, adds a national comparative axis that posits the Norwegian topography as a benchmark of natural beauty and the spectacular, which the Swedish topography seems unable to live up to: When nature *skapade allt det storartade och förunderligt sköna väster om Kölen*[22] ('created all the magnificent and marvellously beautiful to the west of Kölen', i.e. on the Norwegian side of the mountain range), it exhausted itself and had thus tired when it was time to tackle Värmland. It had intended *något i norsk väg*[23] ('something in a Norwegian vein') with *branta, himlastormande bergåsar*[24] ('steep mountain slopes yearning for the sky') and had, in fact, like a competent architect, made *en fin grundritning*[25] ('a fine foundation drawing'), but never built it beyond the base.

---

21. Ibid.: 101.
22. Ibid.: 102.
23. Ibid.
24. Ibid.
25. Ibid.

For the purposes of the present discussion, it is observable that, in addition to paying tribute to Norwegian nature, a primary message communicated in this passage is the stipulation of a much more finite border between the eastern and western topographies – and hence the two nations – than was conveyed in the 'Bread Loaf' text. This reading is, we shall argue by way of finishing, borne out by the continuation and conclusion of the Värmland essay.[26]

In the essay, Lagerlöf performs in elegant ways a form of touristic sightseeing in her home region. Her means of transport is a chauffeur-driven automobile, signalling both modernity and the elevated status the author acquired in later life. The destination of the concluding and most ambitious car journey depicted in the essay is Värmland's north-western part, Östmark, and in particular the very borderline between Sweden and Norway. As the essay reaches this end point, it seems to pit – is our argument – conflicting notions of the national border against each other. The culmination of the text could be characterised as a meditation on the phenomenology and temporality of the borderland. What meets the gaze of the author (who operates throughout the essay as an eyewitness to landscape phenomena) is a deserted and static no man's land dominated by a finite, humanly constructed incision between the nations: *Nu var vi alltså vid resans mål, men var hade vi riksgränsen? Jo; på andra sidan sjön såg man en bred, kalhuggen fåra*[27] ('Now we had reached the destination of our journey, but where was the national border? Ah yes, on the other side of the lake one saw a broad deforested furrow'). This sight evokes

---

26. It should be added that the essay goes on to complicate its view of Värmland's topography by demonstrating the near magical ability of the landscape to change, surprise, and confound expectations. This, however, does not form part of the focus of the present discussion.
27. Ibid.: 112.

a mixture of responses in the narrator: a sense of solemnity, a perception of the borderland as a serene resting place (with connotations of death) for the nation, a feeling, even, that the border is also of a spiritual nature as a demarcation between a real and a supernatural sphere. The main opposition, however, seems to be between the current finality of the border and the borderland's historic role as a vibrant cross-over and transition zone:

> *Det var väl just därför, att här var så stilla och fridsamt, som jag måste tänka på de mängder av olika människor, som fordom hade dragit förbi på en sådan plats. Här hade det rört sig, allt detta gränsfolket, som aldrig kan hålla sig lugnt kvar i eget land, utan jämt lockas över till grannens.*[28]

I suppose it was precisely because it was so still and peaceful here that I had to think of the multitude of different people who had passed through this area in bygone days. Here they had moved about, all these border people who can never remain calmly in their own country but are always enticed to go across to the neighbouring country.

The narrator goes on to enumerate how pilgrims and soldiers, spies and smugglers, traders and jesters, poor people and rich people frequented and traversed the borderland in earlier times – a dynamism and diversity now consigned to history.

It would not seem valid or politically meaningful to interpret Lagerlöf's registration of a decline in transnational, multifaceted cross-border exchange and traffic as an advocacy of a return to a unionistic type of relationship between Norway and Sweden. More plausibly, the emphasis on the past vibrancy

---

28. Ibid.: 113.

of the borderland reads as a blueprint for a prospective further softening of the relationship between the nations after a degree of post-unionistic distancing.[29] Interestingly, what seems to be Lagerlöf's preferred notion of an open and dynamic borderland between Norway and Sweden as well as the ambiguities we have identified in her depiction of the border itself can be aligned with current trends in border studies that emphasise the 'thick', extended, porous, and uncertain character of national borders.[30]

Bibliography

Agier, Michel. 2016. *Borderlands. Towards an Anthropology of the Cosmopolitan Condition*. David Fernbach (trans.). Cambridge: Polity Press.

Bonnier, Karl Otto. 1956. *Bonniers. En bokhandlarefamilj. Anteckningar ur gamla papper och ur minnet*, vol. V: *Firman Albert Bonnier under det nya seklet*. Stockholm: Albert Bonniers förlag.

Bull, Francis. 1958. 'Selma Lagerlöf og Norge'. *Lagerlöfstudier*, 47–64.

Lagerlöf, Selma. 1933. 'Värmländsk naturskönhet'. In *Höst. Berättelser och tal*. Stockholm: Albert Bonniers förlag, 101–116.

———. 1959. 'Brödlimpa. Ett okänt Nils-Holgersson-kapitel'. Erland Lagerroth (ed.). *Bonniers Litterära Magasin* 28:7, 557–559.

———. 1969. *Brev*, vol. II: 1903–1940. Ying Toijer-Nilsson (ed.). Lund: Selma Lagerlöf-sällskapet, Gleerups förlag.

Lagerroth, Erland. 1959. 'Geologiskt brödbak. En kommentar till Selma Lagerlöfs berättelse'. *Bonniers Litterära Magasin* 28:7, 560–562.

---

29. Cf. Lagerlöf's view, quoted above, that it may take some time after the dissolution of the union before the Norwegian and the Swedish people become 'real' friends.

30. These trends may be exemplified by French anthropologist Michel Agier's study entitled *Borderlands*. See in particular 2016: 15–36. Agier asserts the uncertainty of any border between nations: 'an uncertainty that is simultaneously temporal, spatial and social. The repeated drawing of the border reaffirms, if need be, its non-natural character, as its social inscription is inversely proportional to its natural self-evidence' (2016: 22).

Lagerroth, Ulla-Britta. 2000. 'Nordism i Selma Lagerlöfs liv och författarskap'. *Nordisk tidskrift för vetenskap, konst och industri* 76:2, 129–146.

Nordlund, Anna. 2005. *Selma Lagerlöfs underbara resa genom den svenska litteraturhistorien 1891–1996*. Stockholm/Stehag: Brutus Östlings Bokförlag Symposion.

Thorup Thomsen, Bjarne. 2007. *Lagerlöfs litterære landvinding*. Amsterdam: Amsterdam Contributions to Scandinavian Studies, University of Amsterdam.

· V ·

Ein målmann dristar seg ut:
Aasmund Olavsson Vinje in Edinburgh and the Emerging Nynorsk World View

Guy Puzey

Introduction

Arne Kruse's contributions to promoting Norwegian language and culture in the wider world have been of enormous value to cultural relations between Norway and other countries. This is especially true of cultural contacts between Norway and Scotland, his adopted home. On a more personal level, Arne's work has also been of life-changing significance for generations of students, including his passion for raising the profile of Nynorsk, the lesser-used of the two official written standards of Norwegian, and Arne's first written language. It is no coincidence that many advocates of Nynorsk have emerged from his classes, and my first real immersion in Nynorsk was back in 2003–04, with Arne's second-year literature classes on the extraordinary novel *Fuglane* (1957) by Tarjei Vesaas.

In giving many in Edinburgh their first encounter with Nynorsk, Arne has followed in the footsteps of writer Aasmund Olavsson Vinje (1818–70), one of the language's earliest users. In 1862–63, this linguistic and cultural pioneer had an extended stay in the Scottish capital, even venturing to the university that would one day be Arne's workplace, apparently for the opening of the winter session by the Principal, Sir David Brewster.[1] Vinje wrote of this event: 'There was hissing, and shouting, and throwing of peas and herrings, and waving of hats and sticks, producing on all sides of me a noise that was deafening. [...] I was thankful when I escaped from the meeting with unbroken bones'.[2]

While in Edinburgh, Vinje wrote *A Norseman's Views of Britain and the British* (1863). In addition to the material promised in its title, the book included probably the first essay-length account in English about the emerging cultural and linguistic movement later known as Nynorsk. In this text, Vinje wrote:

> Away in the wild district of Möre – a district of islands, fiords, and mountains – there lived a young man who [...] had applied himself with wonderful energy to the task of self-culture. He perused, and to some purpose, all the works which that poor region could supply to him. The libraries of the captain and the clergyman he speedily exhausted.[3]

Had Vinje lived a century or more later, he could well have been describing the young Arne Kruse growing up on the islands of Nordmøre, but he was instead writing about the man from Sunnmøre who had laid the groundwork for this new standard of Norwegian, Ivar Aasen (1813–96). Vinje's essay about the language is an unassuming milestone for the international profile of Nynorsk, appearing as an appendix in the book he wrote in Edinburgh. Over the last century and a half, *A Norseman's Views of Britain and the British* has been largely

---

1. *The Scotsman* 1862: 4.
2. Vinje 1863a: 22.
3. Ibid.: 3 (appendix).

forgotten by an Anglophone readership, and it is only recently that the significance of the appendix has been re-evaluated in Norway and first translated into Norwegian.[4]

Over eighty years ago, Sigmund Skard called for this book to be studied from a broader historical perspective.[5] This chapter is intended as one step in that process. The aim is to explore how Vinje's book, even though it was first written in English, contributed to an emerging world view that would come to characterise the Nynorsk movement.

In terms of methodology, this chapter will not provide an exhaustive account of the many topics covered in Vinje's book, which could be characterised as a culture-critical manifesto with satirical elements, blended with travel literature, and a sprinkling of Bakhtinian grotesque realism.[6] Due to the focus on shaping a world view, many of the references will be to the earlier, more general parts of Vinje's book. These are the sections that best illustrate his positioning *vis-à-vis* the subject matter.

Later sections of the book continue in a critical vein, arguably with increasing intensity, as Vinje highlights the social inequalities he witnessed, with discussion ranging from social class, the aristocracy, land ownership, and the power of capital to matters such as literature, agriculture, education, the press, political parties, religion, architecture, the legal profession, and some intriguing metaphors involving drainage. Peter Fjågesund points to Vinje's perspectives on a global power, coming from a representative of a more peripheral European viewpoint, being interesting in their own right.[7] At the same time, Vinje was entering into a greater European debate.[8] Meanwhile, his critical views of British society

---

4. Grepstad 2018; Vinje 2018.
5. Skard 1939a: 336.
6. Solberg 1992: 46; Fjågesund 2021: 289.
7. Ibid.
8. Ibid.: 317.

gave him new perspectives on social developments in Norway too.[9] From this network of viewpoints and gazes, a counter-hegemonic tendency with a particular relationship to power and authority acquires a clearer focus, a tendency that would become a defining feature of the Nynorsk movement as it developed.[10] This chapter therefore seeks to show how Vinje's travels abroad informed and reflected the ideological foundations of the Nynorsk movement.

After outlining the context of Vinje's international journey, and the aims of his time spent in Edinburgh, I will move on to compare Vinje's approach to travel with that of another renowned Scandinavian writer, a contemporary of Vinje, who wrote about his own travels in what Vinje called *Bretland*, namely Hans Christian Andersen. This comparison will shed further light on what was distinctive about Vinje's methods, which is also of relevance for the further discussion of how Vinje's book was received in reviews of the time. As will be seen, Vinje's views and the ways in which he took account of contemporary power structures may not have won him many admirers among Victorian journalists on the western shores of the North Sea. He clearly sought to distance himself from the Anglomania that he claimed 'pervades every country' and described as 'a disease'.[11] One fairly typical London review of the book claimed of Vinje's stay that 'most of that time he seems to have devoted himself to picking as many holes as possible in our coat'.[12] For another reviewer in Liverpool, meanwhile, the book was 'obviously the production of an acute and intelligent observer'.[13]

Although I believe there is a discernible current tying in with longer-term ideologies in the Nynorsk movement, certain

---

9. Skard 1939b: 434.
10. Puzey 2011.
11. Vinje 1863a: 91.
12. *The Standard* 1863: 2.
13. *The Albion* 1863: 6.

other elements of Vinje's thought that will be mentioned are extremely antiquated. Some other aspects of the book may seem overly scholarly from a modern perspective, with obscure and antiquated references, but many aspects of the satire and social criticism are still relevant.[14]

Background and itinerary for Vinje's international expedition

Aasmund Olavsson Vinje was one of the very first writers to make active use of Landsmål, the language that would later become known as Nynorsk. In 1853, Ivar Aasen published his *Prøver af Landsmaalet i Norge*, providing a template for a modern written standard of Norwegian based on the common denominator elements he had earlier sought to identify among spoken Norwegian dialects through his grammar (1848) and dictionary (1850). In 1858, Vinje began the publication of the newspaper *Dølen*, marking the debut of Landsmål in the press and giving the language a significant boost. *Dølen* translates as 'the dalesman' – in other words a person from a dale, glen, or valley. Vinje described his journalistic mission in the very first lines of the foreword to the first issue:

> *Dølen var i lang Tid ein vanvyrd Mann; men, Gud ske Lov, no er den Tid snart ute, og han dristar seg hermed ut i By og Bygd. Han vilde gjerne tala med Folk om Eit og Annat, som ligg honom på Hjartat; men han veit ikki ret, hvad Maal han skal mæla. Han kunde nok tala dansk, det er ikki for det; men han vilde no helst vera norsk, som han er født.*[15]

---

14. Solberg 1992: 44.
15. [Vinje] 1858: 1.

The dalesman was, for a long time, an object of disdain; but now, thank God, that time is almost over, so out he ventures through town and country. He would dearly like to talk with people about various things that concern him; but he is not sure exactly which language to speak. He could of course speak Danish if it comes to that; but he would really prefer to be Norwegian, as he was born.

The language as Vinje wrote it could be idiosyncratic, as he felt his way further forward along the path laid out by Aasen to define and expand this new standard of Norwegian. As Vinje later wrote, his spelling, neologisms, and reintroduction of words with a basis in Old Norse could leave his readers 'at times sorely puzzled'.[16] Even those first lines of *Dølen* given above featured a footnote to the word *ikki*, clarifying that *ki udtales kji* ('*ki* is pronounced *kji*').[17] Besides contributing to the corpus planning in the early development of Nynorsk, Vinje is well known for his work as a lyricist and the general role he played in advancing Norwegian journalism.

It was a major journalistic expedition that brought Vinje to Edinburgh. In June 1860, he applied to a government travel-grant scheme for the arts and sciences administered by the Royal Frederick University of Christiania (now the University of Oslo). Vinje's application for 400 speciedaler was to support a journey with the following purpose, as proposed by Vinje:

[...] *for under en Reise i det nordlige England og navnlig Skotland at gjøre sig bekjendt med de derværende comunale Indretninger og Retstilstande med stadigt Hensyn til Traditioner og Folkeliv.*[18]

---

16. Vinje 1863a: 4 (appendix).
17. [Vinje] 1858: 1.
18. Vinje 1969: 112 (letter 57, 16 June 1860).

[...] by travelling to northern England, and especially to Scotland, to investigate the local civic infrastructure and legislative situation with consistent reference to traditions and everyday life.

The university's appointed committee granted Vinje the funding. Bjørnstjerne Bjørnson and Henrik Ibsen were among the other applicants for a bursary, although their applications were initially turned down. The newspaper *Aftenbladet* protested, pointing to its former editor Bjørnson's international renown and doubting Vinje's qualifications, suggesting sarcastically that he might as well be sent to Scotland to learn the bagpipes.[19] The government intervened, so Bjørnson was awarded 500 speciedaler for travel to Italy, and Vinje was awarded 250, while Ibsen remained empty-handed.[20] In 1862, Vinje was awarded a supplementary grant of 100 speciedaler from the Royal Norwegian Society of Sciences and Letters, followed by a further 80 in 1863.[21] He was also supported with contributions from friends and contacts in Norway.[22]

Vinje's motivations for crossing the North Sea and for what he would write about may, in fact, be surmised from the first sentence in that first leader article in *Dølen*, which was effectively what might today be called a mission statement, as this dalesman sought to venture forth into the world. Now the dalesman would venture further than Norwegian town and country, heading out into the wider world. He wished to learn something on his travels, make comparisons between conditions in England and Scotland on the one hand and Scandinavia on the other. He also seems to have thought that

---

19. *Aftenbladet* 1860: [2].
20. Halvorsen 1885: 13; Vesaas 2001: 262–263.
21. Vinje 1969: 130, 144.
22. Djupedal 1968: 29–30.

this journey may give him indications of future political and economic developments to come in the rest of Europe.

Figure 1: Vinje photographed by Adolphe Anjoux, 270 rue Saint-Honoré, Paris, 1863. Public domain.

He would try to see the reality he encountered through his characteristic *tvisyn* (dual vision), a way of seeing things from contrasting perspectives, of taking life seriously but also seeing its humorous side, in an ironic fashion. According to Vinje, those who can use this type of vision *sjaa med eit Augnekast liksom Retta og Vranga paa Livsens Vev, soleides at me lettare kunna liksom graata med det eine Augat og læ med det andre* ('somehow see both sides of life's tapestry in one glance, as if we can more easily cry with one eye and laugh with the other').[23] This also fits well with a conception of truth that Vinje claimed to have discerned in the work of Meïr Aron Goldschmidt and that had appealed to him: *Sandheden er ikke noget Fixt og Færdigt, men en Proces, noget Flydende* ('Truth is not something fixed or finished, but a process, something fluid').[24] In any case, the contradictions and disparities that Vinje would encounter had the potential to show both sides of a complex social and political tapestry.

Many of Vinje's contemporaries in Scandinavian literature and art travelled further south in Europe, drawn by the civilisations of classical antiquity and the heritage of the Renaissance to places such as Italy. For Vinje, Rome stood out as a former empire, but he was clearly intrigued instead by the prospect of visiting an empire near the apex of its development. He already foresaw the decline of the British Empire when he wrote of this as a law of nature:

> Will theories, the results of which in other nations lie before us in history fail to produce their natural consequences in Britain? The laws of nature are generally steadfast, and it would be a hazardous policy to trust to a suspension of these laws for the aversion of a gigantic catastrophe.[25]

---

23. Vinje 1861: 28.
24. [Vinje] 1851: col. 58.
25. Vinje 1863a: 46.

In the published Norwegian translation, this passage is more specific, questioning a suspension of these laws *for Englands Skuld* ('for England's sake').[26]

Vinje's mention of *navnlig Skotland* ('especially Scotland') in his original application shows a clear desire to pay particular attention to this country, although the official announcement of Vinje's funding was less geographically specific than in the application, mentioning merely *en Reise i England og Skotland* ('a journey to England and Scotland').[27] Vinje's preferred destinations were stated in various ways in other letters: to his father, for instance, he once wrote of travelling *beint til Skotland* ('straight to Scotland'), while to Georg Sibbern, the Norwegian Prime Minister in Stockholm, he described his impending *engelske Reise* ('English journey').[28] Shortly before he left, he wrote of undertaking *en Reise i Skotland og det nordlige Engelland* ('a journey to Scotland and the north of England').[29] Some reasons for his special interest in Scotland were explained further in his original application:

> *Det er historisk bekjendt, at Nordmændene i gamle Dage stode i stadig Forbindelse med England og især Skotland med tilliggende Øer, og at mange af dem nedsatte sig der. [...] Sproget er i den Grad ligt vort Folkemaal, at en Skotlænder og en norsk Fjeldbonde strax forstaa hinanden.*[30]

It is well known historically that Norwegians in ancient times were in constant connection with England and especially Scotland with its adjacent islands, and that many of

---

26. Vinje 1873: 52.
27. Djupedal 1968: 28–29.
28. Vinje 1969: 122 (letter 63, 26 August 1861), 128 (letter 68, 11 May 1862).
29. Ibid.: 129 (letter 70, 12 May 1862).
30. Ibid.: 112 (letter 57, 16 June 1860).

them settled there. [...] The language [there] is so similar to our popular spoken language that a Scot and a Norwegian mountain farmer would immediately understand each other.

Vinje's argument would appear to be that the further north you come in England and Scotland, the stronger the connections are with Norway. To some extent that is true, but it is quite an exaggeration to suggest that the average Scot and a Norwegian mountain farmer would immediately understand each other's language. This notion may hold a little more water if applied solely to Orkney and Shetland, where the Scandinavian language Norn was spoken possibly until the 1700s.[31] Even that was some considerable time before Vinje wrote his application, though, and Vinje will most likely have heard three other main languages being spoken in Scotland: English, Gaelic, and Scots.

Vinje wanted to learn English, the majority language of the countries he intended to visit, so in September 1861 he went to Vågå, where an Englishman named Eardley John Blackwell (1832–66) would help him. Blackwell was a mountaineer who had settled in Vågå several years earlier.[32] Vinje and Blackwell initially got on well together, but they appear to have fallen out, perhaps because Vinje had fallen in love with Blackwell's sister-in-law, and when Blackwell found out, he is said to have threatened to shoot Vinje.[33] The host is also reported to have been enraged by Vinje's characterisation of politics in Blackwell's homeland as *pelande roten* ('quite rotten').[34] Vinje left Vågå somewhat abruptly in February 1862 and returned to Christiania.[35]

---

31. Knooihuizen 2005; Barnes 2010.
32. Schiötz 1986: 19.
33. Vislie 1890: 179.
34. 'Hugleik' 1912; Mo 1969: 12.
35. Vinje 1969: 122.

His journey finally began in June 1862 as Vinje set forth on board the steamer *Lindesnæs*, which was also carrying 250 students and academics to a pan-Scandinavian congress. Vinje accompanied them via Malmö and Lund to Copenhagen, before continuing to Hamburg, from whence he sailed on the steamer *John Bull* to London.[36] According to Olav Midttun, Vinje arrived in London in July 1862.[37] He would go on to spend almost a year in Britain, but it seems that he left England fairly early on, arriving in Scotland in any case before the end of September.[38] He then seems to have been mainly based in Edinburgh for around nine months, until 12 June 1863. On the way home he called in London and Paris, returning to Norway on 19 July 1863.[39]

While in Edinburgh, Vinje stayed in the New Town, at 22 Dundas Street, as a lodger of Mary Mackenzie, wife of the solicitor David M. Mackenzie, and her sister (see Figure 2).[40] Apart from an apparently quite intense dislike of Mr Mackenzie, Vinje was extremely happy in Dundas Street. To the linguist Hans Ross, Vinje wrote of Mrs Mackenzie and her sister: *Det er sanne Kvendfolk baade tvo* ('They are both real ladies').[41] The husband was, according to Vinje, often drunk and selfish, with Vinje even expressing a hope that Mr Mackenzie would soon

36. Vesaas 2001: 279–282.
37. Midttun 1960: 81.
38. Vesaas 2001: 288.
39. Ibid.: 301–302.
40. Post Office 1862: 206; Vesaas 2001: 289. According to the 1861 census, Mary Mackenzie and her sister Eliza McIver (a banker's wife) were born in Ireland in c. 1814 and 1816, respectively. Marriage records show that David Monypenny Mackenzie (born 1814) married Mary Doherty in June 1844 at St Cuthbert's in Edinburgh, while Eliza Doherty married John McIver (of City Bank, Glasgow) in August 1843 at Coleraine. Curiously, the Mackenzies already had an earlier Norwegian boarder staying with them on the census date in April 1861, the agricultural chemist (Hans) Anton Rosing (1828–67).
41. Vinje 1969: 135 (letter 72, 26 November 1862).

die. He felt pity for Mrs Mackenzie and wrote of his desire to take her with him back to Norway.[42]

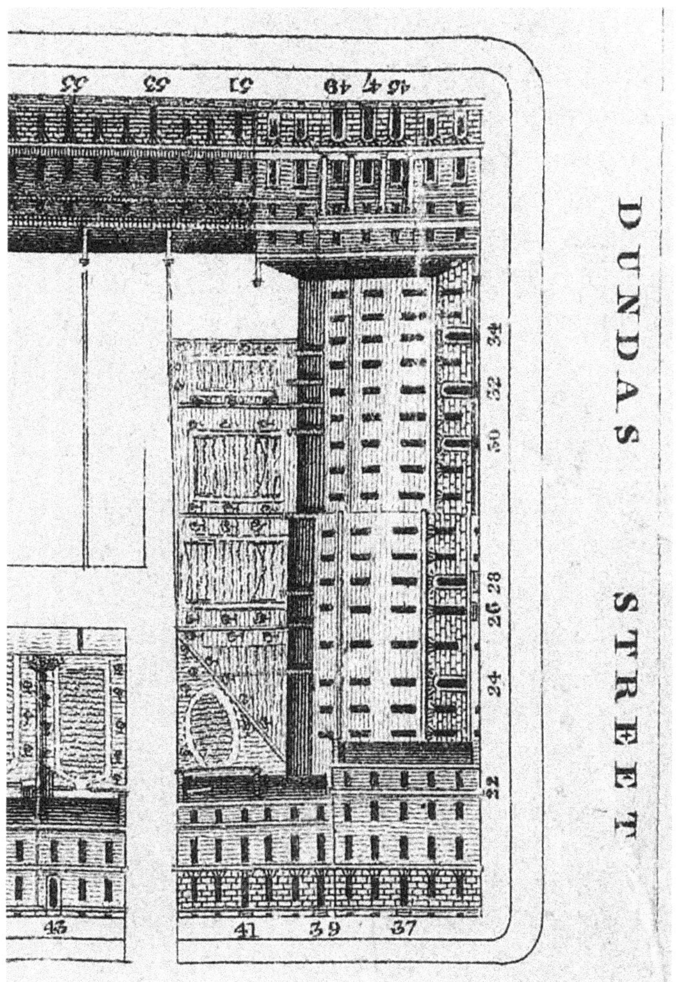

Figure 2: Vinje lodged at 22 Dundas Street, shown in this excerpt from Robert Kirkwood's 'Plan & Elevation of the New Town of Edinburgh' (1819). His tutor John Caven's address at number 32 can also be seen. The name of the street is now a focus of ongoing controversy in relation to the name's colonial links, and its namesake in Toronto is already due to be renamed.[43]
Reproduced with permission of the WS Society.

42. Ibid.
43. Dewar 2020; Draaisma 2021; Mullen 2021.

A Norseman's Views

A Norseman's Views of Britain and the British was published in Edinburgh in late May 1863, roughly a fortnight before Vinje left Scotland.[44] It comprised sixteen chapters styled as 'letters' written in English and addressed to Johan Sebastian Welhaven (1807–73), a well-known poet and professor of philosophy. Vinje claimed that the choice of format and distinguished addressee was because *Britain* [sic] *er et Land for Titler* ('Britain is a land of titles'), although Welhaven was actually Vinje's third choice.[45] Welhaven agreed to his name being used after Carl Arnoldus Müller (Vice-President of the Royal Norwegian Society of Sciences and Letters) had turned down the offer and Marcus Jacob Monrad, another professor of philosophy, had not responded to Vinje's request.[46] Vinje also wrote some extended articles in Norwegian for *Dølen* about his time in Britain, but his book was much more comprehensive.

The book was written with help from Vinje's English tutor in Edinburgh, John Caven (1826–1914) of 32 Dundas Street.[47] As Vinje wrote: 'My task of wrestling with a foreign language was, perhaps, equally difficult with his of mastering foreign views'.[48] Caven, educated in Edinburgh and Rome, later emigrated to Prince Edward Island, and on his death was described as Charlottetown's 'most highly cultured citizen – one whose

---

44. *The Scotsman* 1863: 4.
45. Vinje 1969: 147 (letter 77, 27 April 1863).
46. Ibid.; Vesaas 2001: 292.
47. Post Office 1862: 137; Vinje 1969: 135 (letter 72, 26 November 1862), 145 (letter 75, 9 February 1863).
48. Vinje 1863a: [i].

ability was proved as teacher, lecturer, editor, poet and singer'.[49] Vinje was not the only illustrious author whose craft was influenced by Caven, as among his students at Charlottetown's Prince of Wales College was L.M. Montgomery, creator of *Anne of Green Gables*. She later recalled that 'if one wanted, one could learn a good deal from him', and 'there was a certain tang about "Old Caven", as we irreverently called him behind his back, that one could not forget'.[50]

Vinje was keen to translate the book into Norwegian himself, writing to publisher Jørgen Wright Cappelen: *Stakkars Norske Publicum som skal læse Dølemaal eller Engelsk, dersom det ellers har nogen Lyst til at læse mig* ('The poor Norwegian readers who will have to read the dalesman's language or English if they have any desire to read my work').[51] He started on the translation task but would not complete it in his lifetime.[52] The remainder was translated by Halfdan Halvorsen, with the result published as *Bretland og Britarne* (lit. *Britain and the British*) in 1873, three years after Vinje's death.

Olav Vesaas points out that the Norwegian title is quite misleading in that it overlooks the centrality in the books of this particular Norwegian's views and reactions to the places he visited.[53] This is indeed true, and there are other curiosities within the titles in both languages.

The word *Norseman* is primarily used in English to describe the Scandinavians of ancient or medieval times, especially the Viking Age. *Norwegian* is more geographically specific, and also much more widely used (see Figure 3), but by using *Norseman*, Vinje may be characterising himself as a particular kind of

---

49. *Charlottetown Guardian* 1914: 3.
50. Montgomery MacDonald 1927: 30–31.
51. Vinje 1969: 150 (letter 79, 3 June 1863).
52. Vinje 1873: v.
53. Vesaas 2001: 293.

Norwegian: one sailing in the wake of the Vikings and walking in their footsteps. Not only was Victorian society obsessed with titles; a romantic image of the Vikings was also prevalent at that time. By choosing to describe himself as a Norseman, Vinje may have also been tapping into a self-characterisation as a 'noble savage', in the terminology of that era, who had inherited some of the Vikings' legendary wanderlust. A Victorian audience may well have been attracted to the notion of reading what a modern Viking made of contemporary society in islands where Vikings had once settled, as suggested in some reviews of the book: 'our Norseman laughs […] with the lungs of Thor himself'.[54] Perhaps the title could also be read in Vinje's typically ironic style, as well as connecting with the titular dalesman figure of his newspaper.

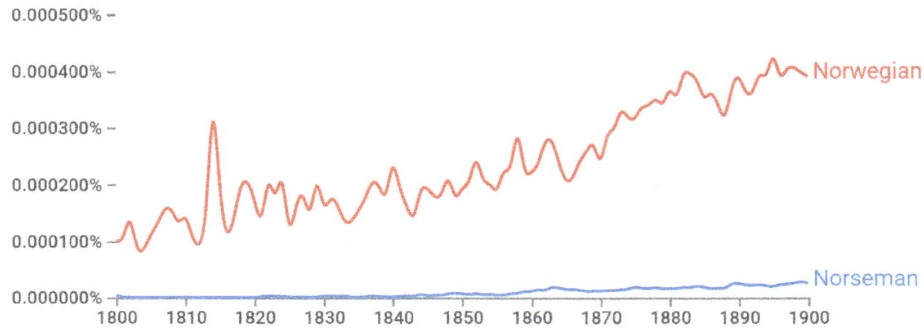

Figure 3: Comparative frequency of 'Norseman' and 'Norwegian' in 1800–1900, as seen in the Google Books 2019 corpus of books predominantly in English. *Google Books Ngram Viewer*, http://books.google.com/ngrams. Accessed 4 March 2022.

As for the Norwegian title, the name *Bretland* is also quite unusual, harking back to earlier times. Vinje has picked up an Old Norse term that *Store norske leksikon* claims was mainly used for Wales, Cornwall, and Brittany – in other words the main areas where the Brythonic languages Welsh, Cornish,

---

54. *The Athenæum* 1863: 268.

and Breton are still in use, albeit now as minority languages.[55] In that sense, *Bretland* denotes two parts of the island of Great Britain that Vinje did not seek to cover in any detail, and one part of present-day France, but it was still an apposite name to use. After all, the geographical nomenclature of this group of islands to the south-west of Norway is fraught with complexity. Hungarian-born writer George Mikes joked almost a century later that '[w]hen people say England, they sometimes mean Great Britain, sometimes the United Kingdom, sometimes the British Isles – but never England'.[56] The pattern can be even more pronounced in other languages, especially when colloquial terms have the upper hand over what might be geographically correct.

In a festschrift for Arne Kruse, a great scholar of place-names, some further toponomastic reflections seem appropriate. The most widespread term in English for the whole archipelago is still *the British Isles*, but this can be controversial, not least in Ireland, and especially in the Republic of Ireland. In fact, use of that term seems to have peaked in 1941 (see Figure 4). Wordier alternatives such as *the British and Irish Isles, the Anglo-Celtic Archipelago*, or *the Northwest European Archipelago* have found some limited acceptance but remain relatively rare. Many avoid names altogether by speaking of *these islands*, but if the author and translator of *Bretland og Britarne* were at home in Norway, would they refer to *those islands*, and if so, which islands are those? *The[se] islands* is also the term used by the British-Irish Council, the international body formed as a result of the Good Friday Agreement of 1998, and which brings together representatives of eight governments: those of Ireland, the United Kingdom, Guernsey, the Isle of Man, Jersey, Northern Ireland,

---

55. *Store norske leksikon* 2020.
56. Mikes 1946: 10.

Scotland, and Wales. More recently, the name-avoiding term has acquired a different currency as the name of a public affairs debate group that characterises itself as '[e]nthusiastic about the Union'.[57] These brief considerations of geographical naming still hardly scratch the surface of how the inhabitants define their national identity, but the terminological challenges do point to a political situation that has historically been in flux and is still subject to change.

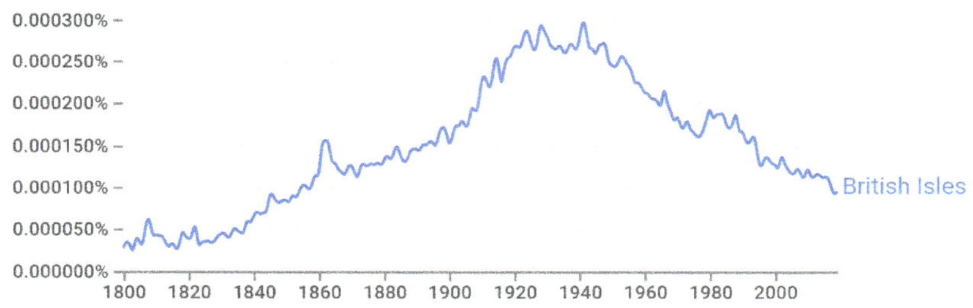

Figure 4: Occurrences of 'British Isles' (1800–2019) in the Google Books 2019 corpus of books predominantly in English. *Google Books Ngram Viewer*, http://books.google.com/ngrams. Accessed 4 March 2022.

Naming all the islands as a group was not a major concern for Vinje. He wrote some passages about Ireland, and very little about Wales except in articles for *Dølen*, but the elements of the book that could be considered travel literature mainly covered England and Scotland, which are predominantly situated on the same island. In Norwegian, although *Bretland* had previously mainly denoted other specific parts of the archipelago's largest island (plus a neighbouring territory on the European mainland), it was still a fitting name to adopt into *dølemål*, and *(Stóra(-))Bretland* has some wider use as the island's name in Faroese and Icelandic. That said, it is not certain without

---

57. These Islands [n.d.].

manuscript evidence whether *Bretland* was chosen by Vinje or, for instance, by Halfdan Halvorsen later in the translation process. There seems to be no occurrence of the word *Bretland* in Vinje's own writing beyond the Norwegian translation of the book, but instead *Britain*, whether when writing in Norwegian or in English.[58] In any case, Vinje clearly appreciated these nuances of naming, or perhaps John Caven made sure he did. In Vinje's book and in many of the letters he wrote, he was fairly careful to specify if he was referring to England, Scotland, or both. There were some exceptions, such as writing from Edinburgh 'I promised to write You a letter from England in English and I am now about to redeem my promise'.[59] Exceptions aside, such a generally meticulous approach cannot be taken for granted in travel writing in this part of the world, even among authors from the islands in question: 'As in many other fields, "British" is often used when "English" would be more accurate, and "English" sometimes silently includes texts that might be better described as Scottish, Welsh, or Irish'.[60]

Vinje begins his first letter in the book by stating his intentions:

> I came to Britain, as you are aware, with the fixed resolution of examining and studying the institutions of this great commercial land, and the manners, habits, and pursuits of its people. [...] I have wandered far, seen much, and learned something. [...] I have played the pedestrian for hundreds of miles, backwards and forwards, through the lonely glens and sheep-farms of the Scottish highlands. I have witnessed military displays on Wimbledon Common, and beneath the Crags

58. See e.g. [Vinje] 1863b; Vinje 1969: 147 (letter 77, 27 April 1863).
59. Ibid.: 137 (letter 73, 24 December 1862).
60. Pettinger 2016.

of Arthur's Seat. I have listened to the debates in the Houses of Parliament, and spent weeks in the Great Exhibition. I have even caught a distant glimpse of a fox-hunt.[61]

Although much of what Vinje described may have been based on fleeting glimpses, his biographer, Olav Midttun, described the book as one of the first Norwegian works of sociology, as Vinje was attempting to find the common characteristics of other societies.[62] While the book does have some characteristics of travel writing, Djupedal concurs that Vinje was not a tourist; he was carrying out fieldwork.[63]

Characteristically for the time, Vinje seemed to believe that there were organic patterns in society and history dependent on country, climate, and race. His views are sometimes quite crude in their espousal of what might be early social Darwinism, although Vinje often tempered such statements. Charles Darwin's *On the Origin of Species* (1859) had been published less than three years before Vinje arrived in Edinburgh, the same city where Darwin had earlier embarked upon his abortive medical training, studied marine life of the Forth, and learned taxidermy skills from John Edmonstone, a freed slave from what is now Guyana. Vinje was open to new ideas and impulses, but it seems he may have rejected evolutionary biology: 'I am seeking for reason and coherence, and, without going so far as some learned men in their disputes about the missing link between the gorilla and the man, I go pretty far'.[64] Vinje repeats somewhat crude ideas of ethnic superiority,

---

61. Vinje 1863a: 1. Unless it is relevant to include the Norwegian translation, quotations will be given from Vinje's original English text, as it is the primary source text.
62. Midttun 1960: 83.
63. Djupedal 1968: 32.
64. Vinje 1863a: 4.

attributing to contemporary ethnographers the idea that 'the superiority of the British people is due to the cross mixture of races from which it has sprung'.[65] He then retreats from that line of argumentation: 'My limited knowledge of the workings of nature in this way will not allow me to enter upon such a subject'.[66] Nevertheless, he continues with some racial judgments inferring that there are shared qualities with Scandinavians like himself:

> The British are really a good race. You cannot be long among them before you see that. In the south of England you can clearly trace the prevalent infusion of Roman blood, but as you go northwards you discover more and more of the Gothic, till you come to Yorkshire, and Scotland, where the relationship to the Scandinavian tribes is obvious.[67]

There is also some considerable tension between the romantic and the rational in Vinje's writing. For instance, another feature typical of the period is Vinje's attempt to explain certain cultural traits through reference to the landscape or climate. He believes that the maritime climate may have had a positive effect on his health, and thereby assumes it is likely that the inhabitants are also healthy. Even the industrial impact on the atmosphere is incorrectly ascribed health-enhancing qualities, although this may well be meant ironically, with Vinje's typical *tvisyn*: 'The climate is invigorating, and even the smoke and coal dust are healthy'.[68]

---

65. Ibid.: 14.
66. Ibid.: 15.
67. Ibid.
68. Ibid.

Vinje's observational methods, compared to Andersen's

While Vinje's project was not strictly scientific in nature, if Olav Midttun described it as one of the first Norwegian works of sociology, then it is worth considering Vinje's methods, which may make him partially a social anthropologist. Georg Sibbern, the aforementioned Norwegian Prime Minister in Stockholm, was one of those who had provided Vinje with letters of introduction, but Vinje writes that he barely used them:

> I have them still in goodly numbers occupying an honourable place in my writing-desk. And why? Because it is an opinion I hold, that the formal visits, invitations of ceremony, and parties of pleasure, which are the usual results of letters of introduction, teach a man nothing. They are in all nations the same, their character being generally 'much ado about nothing.' They contain, moreover, this element of evil, that they may very easily engender prejudices and prepossessions in the mind of the stranger. I therefore prefer to remain unknown, and from my obscurity study real life.[69]

Vinje had already more than hinted at this approach in his funding application:

> *Den, som vil og kan sætte sig ind i det meget, vi allerede vide om disse Lande, han vil altid finde en Ledetraad; men det tør dog forudsættes, at meget i denne Henseende endnu er at lære, især naar Tingen saa at sige sees nedenfra, og at der ikke som vanligt mest gaaes efter officielle Indberetninger. Og i denne Henseende*

---

69. Ibid.: 2.

tør jeg maaske uden at gaa Beskedenheden for nær sige, at jeg som opfødt blant vore med den skotske saa nær beslægtede Almue ikke vilde have liden Hjælp i denne Omstændighed [...].[70]

Whoever wishes to familiarise themselves with the great deal we already know about these countries, and who is able to do so, will always find some relevant clues, but it may nonetheless be assumed that there is still much to learn in that respect, especially when the object of interest is seen, so to speak, from below, and if official reports are not taken as the main sources, as is usually the case. And in this regard I dare say, without being too modest, that I would have no small advantage in such circumstances, having been brought up among our common people, so closely related to those of Scotland.

The idea of seeing society from the bottom up was not shared by all writers travelling at that time, as can be seen if we compare Vinje's approach to observing society with that of another contemporary Scandinavian writer, Hans Christian Andersen (1805–75), who visited England and Scotland, including Edinburgh, almost exactly fifteen years before Vinje, in the summer of 1847.

Andersen's visit was much shorter than Vinje's, at just over two months, and the celebrated Danish writer spent most of that time in or around London. It is no exaggeration to say that Vinje and Andersen were quite different personalities. While Vinje had to address an application to the king for his funding to visit Britain, Andersen's situation was the reverse, as he describes it in his autobiography, *Mit livs eventyr*:

---

70. Vinje 1969: 112 (letter 57, 16 June 1860).

En Dag spurgte Kongen mig, om jeg dog ikke ogsaa skulde see England. Jeg svarede: jo, og at jeg netop i den tilstundede Sommer tænkte paa at komme der. 'De kan jo faae Penge hos mig!' sagde hans Majestæt. [...] 'De repræsenterer nu i England den danske Literatur, og De maa derfor leve nogenlunde smukt og godt!'[71]

One day the King asked me if I ought not also to see England. I said, 'Yes,' and added that I was thinking of going there the following summer.

'Then you can have the money from me,' said His Majesty. [...] '[Y]ou represent Danish literature in England now, and so you must live well and in comfort.'[72]

Still, Andersen turned down the offer as he had sufficient funds of his own, and several other wealthy friends. As mentioned above, Vinje had been provided with letters of introduction but preferred not to use them. Andersen, meanwhile, did not need letters of introduction: his work was already well known in Britain, and he had contacts among the aristocracy and royalty.

Further contrasts are evident from their descriptions of the moment they stepped ashore. On 23 June 1847, Andersen wrote in his diary: [...] *Engelænderne ombord havde varet mig Ingen at troe, naar jeg steeg i Land, Ingen at indlade mig med* ('[...] the Englishmen on board had warned me not to trust anyone when I went ashore, not to take up with anyone').[73] Vinje claims to have been immediately much more trusting:

When I landed near London Bridge, I addressed a man who had come to meet some acquaintance that he expected to arrive by our steamer from the Continent. I asked him

---

71. Andersen 1855: 403.
72. Andersen 2013: 369.
73. Andersen 1974: 205; Andersen 1990: 165.

for some hints as to lodging and the like, and he acted as a most excellent friend. He took such a deal of trouble with me during the whole of my stay in London, that I really got ashamed of all the kindness he shewed me.[74]

Andersen did not delay in attending high-ranking appointments. The day after his arrival, he visited the Danish ambassador and then went to meet royalty: *Kjørt ud til Marlbor[o]ugh-House, blev indladt i et kongeligt Værelse; Arvestorhertug kom, faldt mig om Halsen, kyssede mig, vi sad sammen [...]* ('Drove out to Marlborough House; was admitted to a royal chamber. The hereditary grand duke [Charles Alexander of Saxe-Weimar-Eisenach] came, embraced me and kissed me. We sat together [...]').[75] Vinje, as already noted, preferred a different approach to expanding his social network, seeking to gain a more representative picture:

> Some of my countrymen, however, at the Great Exhibition [in London], were of a decidedly different frame of mind; and their perseverance in importuning our Secretary of Legation, our Consul, and Commissioner, for tickets of invitations to parties and festivals, made me oftentimes feel pity for these pestered officials, and ashamed for their persecutors.[76]

Andersen felt quite comfortable in the company of aristocrats, writing on 26 June 1847: *Man siger, at Aristocratiet i Engeland udelukker alle Kunstnere fra deres Kreds, jeg kan ikke sige det, jeg fandt de venligste Menneske[r,] den hjerteligste Modtagelse* ('People say that the aristocracy in England excludes all artists from their circle; I can't say that – I found the friendliest people,

---

74. Vinje 1863a: 8.
75. Bredsdorff 1954: 559; Andersen 1974: 205–206; Andersen 1990: 165.
76. Vinje 1863a: 2.

the heartiest reception').[77] For Vinje, meanwhile: 'The British are certainly good-looking, but I have been disappointed in not finding the aristocracy the best looking portion of the population, as I have often been led to believe'.[78]

The two travellers' accounts are full of many more contrasts, although the essential difference is that Vinje was so eager to see life from more marginalised viewpoints. Andersen was also interested in real life and social conditions, but the journalist Vinje was keen to explore this in a different way:

> One evening I followed a different method, and put myself under the guidance of a London detective, whose acquaintance I had purposely made. Among the indescribable haunts of misery and crime, I on that night learned more of modern civilization than was possible in the suffocating crowd of the Guildhall festival, though in neither society do I think that much is to be got worth the keeping.[79]

This method of embedding himself with a representative of local law enforcement shows some journalistic enterprise and a significant determination to see other viewpoints, in keeping with the *tvisyn* for which he is known. In the Norwegian translation, this passage also contributed to the expansion of the Norwegian lexicon by allowing Vinje to coin the word *Uppsnusare* (in some later editions *oppsnusar*) to describe a detective, although the term does not seem to have caught on. Vinje did not rely only on observation as a method, though; newspapers were another key source, albeit one that could be problematic.

---

77. Andersen 1974: 209; Andersen 1990: 169.
78. Vinje 1863a: 19.
79. Ibid.: 2–3.

Vinje's social criticism and the book's reception

Throughout the book, Vinje was quite scathing in his criticism of some aspects of British life, not least social inequality, the role of capital, elitism, and land ownership. This stood in contrast to the generally positive views of Britain held in Norway at the time, and his criticisms did not escape the attention of reviewers. For Vinje, industrialised Britain was not as progressive as he may have once thought, but conservative and reactionary.[80] The London *Standard* called Vinje 'a lunatic pure and simple', as did its sister papers the *Evening Standard* and *Morning Herald*.[81] A leading article in the *Glasgow Daily Herald* described him as 'like a special pleader retained by Louis Napoleon for the glorification of France and the disparagement of Great Britain', while a follow-up two days later claimed that 'there is little to be got from Mr. Vinje's letters'.[82] According to the magazine *John Bull*, the book was 'full, indeed, of valuable hints', but Vinje was plagued by 'very strong prejudices'.[83]

In his skilful overview of the book's initial reception, Sigmund Skard located twelve reviews in English from 1863 of Vinje's book (nine in the London press and three from Edinburgh).[84] Through extensive searches in digital repositories I have thus far found a further nine, spanning the years from 1863 to 1917 (three from Glasgow, and one each printed in Aberdeen, Dublin, Edinburgh, Liverpool, New Orleans, and New York). In addition, there are other newspapers that

80. Fjågesund 2021: 301.
81. *The Standard* 1863: 2.
82. *Glasgow Daily Herald* 1863a: 4; 1863b: 3.
83. *John Bull* 1863: 444.
84. Skard 1939a; 1939b.

printed extracts without a review (including publications in Brechin, Brighton, Dublin, Glasgow, Kirkwall, and Nairn), one reader's letter about the book (in Glasgow), and one of the reviews Skard had previously uncovered was reprinted in the *Bombay Gazette*.

When appraising the book's reception in his selection of reviews, Skard recognised that many critics showed clear satisfaction with the status quo, coupled with unconscious snobbery.[85] Paradoxically, this reaction may even have reinforced some of the points Vinje had sought to make, when publications such as the *London Review* claimed that: 'The author of the book before us tells us nothing new when he says that we have an extraordinary reverence for rank and money. [...] But we see what he does not, that to both there is a bright as well as a dark side'.[86] Such reviewers may not have picked up that he was reacting to the less critical Anglomania that he described as rampant in many countries and that only saw a bright side. As Vinje wrote: 'Shallow observers might even call the state of things here perfect'.[87]

Aside from ideological opposition to Vinje's criticisms, many reviewers pointed to possible exaggerations or inaccuracies. Vinje's usual audience in Norway knew to expect unusual leaps of thought and ironic *tvisyn*, while readers abroad were less sure what to make of this.[88] Arguably Vinje's *tvisyn* was an antidote to what otherwise would have been more shallow observation. Furthermore, Peter Fjågesund points out that the description of Vinje on the title page as 'Advocate before the High Courts of Justice' might have misled readers; Vinje did indeed have legal training, but his main occupation was

---

85. Skard 1939a: 333.
86. *London Review* 1863: 638.
87. Vinje 1863a: 90–91.
88. Skard 1939a: 332.

as a writer occupying a very particular position in Norwegian culture.[89] But there is an intriguing pattern in that the book's reception was occasionally more positive in reviews from beyond London, perhaps reflecting the more marginalised viewpoints Vinje supported.

The fact Vinje spent more time in Scotland was picked up by many reviewers in England too, remarking for instance that 'on the whole, his letters, written from Edinburgh as they are, seem written chiefly from Edinburgh information, and from an Edinburgh point of view'.[90] Already in the second 'letter' in his book, Vinje writes about coming to Scotland, where he felt more at home: 'I got tired of London, its bustle and din; and in order to make the change as complete as possible, I betook myself to the far-off valley of Glencoe. [...] It much resembles, on a small scale, the Vestfiordale, and many of our Norse dales'.[91] He felt similarly of urban Scotland: 'In Scottish cities, more particularly in Edinburgh, I can almost fancy that I am walking in our Norse towns'.[92] Vinje wrote at length comparing the landscape of Scotland and Norway, the people, and place-names. The aforementioned early social Darwinist ideas are evident in how Vinje compared the so-called 'races' he encountered. He often related these comments to more social concerns, such as the Highland clearances:

What a noble race these Caledonians are! It was regiments of them that stood like a wall against the Imperial Guard at Waterloo. It is all very well to have sheep instead of people in these Highland nurseries for soldiers, but sheep will not

89. Fjågesund 2021: 291.
90. *The Reader* 1863: 576.
91. Vinje 1863a: 11.
92. Ibid.: 15.

repel invasion, or fight England's battles. Perhaps the consumers of mutton in the large cities, tradesmen, operatives, and artists will fight well. This remains to be seen. [...] When men now-a-days are shooting and feeding sheep where the Caledonians lived in days of old, they no doubt think that great progress has been effected. *Nous verrons.*[93]

While many Victorian commentators on this side of the North Sea romanticised the wildness of the Highlands, Vinje saw it as a warning:

The Highlands is a graveyard, and the passing bell seemed ringing in my ears as I saw parish on parish laid out for sheep. How very picturesque! exclaimed some Londoners, as their carriage bowled along through the wilderness. Picturesque! certainly. Come hither, my artist friend, when you design a sketch from Faust, throw me in those Scottish Highlands as a scene for Mephistophiles [sic] to gloat over pleasantly. [... H]e would exult to see human beings making way for sheep, and grouse, and deer. Some day he may probably see the greater part of Europe in this condition. The Highlands are but the beginning of the end. It is the beginning of a higher civilisation, we are told; but independent people do not like this civilisation.[94]

Vinje's concerned reactions were not shared by all contemporary Scandinavian visitors. For instance, Reidar Djupedal contrasted Vinje's reactions to the Highlands with those of Norwegian poet Andreas Munch (1811–84). While Vinje perceived a human tragedy, Munch was swept away by the

---

93. Ibid.: 13–14.
94. Ibid.: 14.

beauty of the landscape.[95] In the most recent newspaper review of Vinje's book, an outlier from the midst of the First World War, David MacRitchie writes positively in an article for the Glasgow *Daily Record and Mail*, and seems appreciative of Vinje's 'lament over the depopulation of the Highlands'.[96]

Perhaps tellingly, several reviewers criticised Vinje for not using his letters of introduction to meet more highly ranking individuals on his travels, but Vinje had made a point of this, as discussed above. For the *Saturday Review*, this meant that Vinje 'disdained to set about the right way of obtaining reliable information' and 'deliberately refused to avail himself of the only method of effectually studying [British society]'.[97] This clearly shows that such reviewers saw access through more privileged channels as 'the right way' to study society. The *Aberdeen Journal* was more measured on this point:

> [...] the Norseman's criticisms are more cynical than they probably would have been if he had gone into circles to which his letters might have gained him access. At the same time his animadversions contain truth, – perhaps more truth, coming as they do from a perspicacious and candid stranger, than many of us may be willing to admit; and at all events, it may do us no harm to take a look at some of our national features as pourtrayed by such a one.[98]

Skard noted that some reviews, while still including criticisms of Vinje, appeared more receptive to hearing his ideas, and that *skotsk lokalpatriotisme* ('Scottish local patriotism') may have

---

95. Djupedal 1968: 27.
96. MacRitchie 1917: 2.
97. *Saturday Review* 1863: 802.
98. *Aberdeen Journal* 1863: 6.

been a factor.[99] One reason why some Scottish publications were more open to Vinje's ideas could be down to his portrayal of the Scots.

> We and the Swedes are much better friends than [the Scots and English] are. I have, therefore, independently endeavoured to form my opinion of the mutual relations between them, and have come to the conclusion that the Scots are the superior people. The more mountainous country is sufficient to account for this; besides, the popular education is much better in Scotland than in England [...]. My own experience, and that of other foreigners I have spoken with, certainly convinces me that the Scottish population, as a whole, stands intellectually higher than that of England.[100]

This may explain the apparently more extensive reprinting of such extracts in Scottish newspapers. It is also worthy of note that the mountainous landscape he credits with making a people 'superior' is the very aspect of the Scottish landscape he has already compared to Norway, and the mountains are where the dalesman lives: *Dølen* himself.

With higher praise reserved for Scotland, some reviews took aim at Vinje's tutor, John Caven – unnamed in the book – blaming him for the criticism of British society:

> M. Vinje, whose book is published at Edinburgh, is so convinced of the superior intellect and education of the Scotch to those of the English nation, that we should much regret if he had been induced by this consideration to make so unfortunate a choice of an interpreter. M. Vinje has

---

99. Skard 1939a: 334.
100. Vinje 1863a: 18–19.

discovered that the old hatred between the English and the Scotch still burns lustily; but it would be a pity if a member of the latter nation had given vent to his bitterness of feeling, not only by translating a virulent attack on the sister-country, but by perpetrating murder by his own hand on the language of its Sovereign.[101]

Other reviews were a little softer on this point. While still noting Vinje's preferences, they saw that Vinje had 'no hatred for the British. [... H]e testifies to their open kind-heartedness, and compliments their roast beef with having relieved him of some of his wrinkles. "The British," he says, "are really a good race." But his preference is for the North Britons [...]'.[102]

With Vinje's many criticisms, some reviewers believed Vinje was placing himself or Norway on a pedestal with a 'self-complacent assumption of superiority'.[103] However, with his questioning of power structures and of pre-conceived ideas of superiority among and about the inhabitants of an island at the centre of a global empire, was he instead trying to show that Britain – or specifically England and Scotland – were not so unlike Norway, or other countries?[104]

The most effusive praise of all seems to have come from newspapers outwith England or Scotland. The *New York Herald* writes that it 'is a very droll book, and pays off British writers for the absurd slanders and misrepresentations which they have published in reference to this country', although this may be a backhanded compliment.[105] In Dublin, *The Nation* wrote of Vinje as an 'honest thinker and manly writer' who 'has

---

101. *Saturday Review* 1863: 803.
102. *London Review* 1863: 639.
103. *Illustrated London News* 1863: 707.
104. Solberg 1992: 44–45.
105. *New York Herald* 1863: 7.

no sooner gained footing in Britain than he lays about him in the good old Scandinavian fashion, *i.e.*, right pluckily, with the battle-axe of the nineteenth century – "the pen"'.[106] While sharing in Vinje's 'measured' condemnation of the clearances, this review focuses especially on his treatment of Ireland. A review by the London-based *Athenæum* had earlier described Vinje's characterisation of the British state's response to the Great Famine in Ireland as 'the most unfounded of all lies', but for *The Nation* this shows that Vinje is 'possessed of a very accurate insight into the true state of things'.[107] Crucially, this Irish newspaper also remarked:

> Not one of your complaisant tourists is he – who so readily chime in with the tones of the dominant or ruling powers in whatever lands they may happen to visit, never daring to question wrong, but meekly accepting might as right. He is rather of that class of impartial philosophical observers and notetakers, becoming, we are happy to say, every day more enlarged […].[108]

Vinje's perspectives, coming from a political and geographical periphery of Europe himself, were not lost on all readers. Similarly, *tvisyn* could come into its own when focusing on stark social contrasts, bringing matters to the fore that might not otherwise be immediately apparent, especially to readers less familiar with the geographical context in question.

---

106. *The Nation* 1866: 554.
107. *The Athenæum* 1863: 268; *The Nation* 1866: 554.
108. Ibid.

Conclusion: An emerging Nynorsk world view

The appendix Vinje wrote about the Norwegian language struggle is an early statement of the Nynorsk movement's programme, and perhaps the first time that a Norwegian wrote about the language debate in English, as Ottar Grepstad has pointed out.[109] In examining Anglophone reviews of the book, none I have seen thus far make much mention of the appendix, except the following comment, which contains a fairly egregious error: 'Herr A.O. Vinje [...] is [...] favourably known in his own country as a zealous partisan of a movement for the revival and encouragement of the Norse tongue as the ancient language of Sweden [sic]'.[110] Nevertheless, the short appendix contains a great deal of interesting material on the language question, not least the way Vinje creates an almost mythological image of Ivar Aasen, as described in the introduction above.

It is, however, not only this appendix that makes the book Vinje wrote in Edinburgh an important chapter in the history of Nynorsk. Although the book was originally published in English, it is evidence of some significant traits in the emerging counter-hegemonic Nynorsk world view, which would come to be characterised by a radical and democratically inspired tendency for critical stances towards power structures.[111] A particular mix of National Romantic and Enlightenment ideas – themselves impulses from abroad – had shaped the Norwegian cultural climate at the time Aasen embarked on his linguistic project, and those ideas were still influential. A distinct Nynorsk culture was still in its early days, but *A Norseman's Views of Britain and the British* marks a key moment

---

109. Grepstad 2018.
110. *The Press* 1863: 765.
111. Puzey 2011.

when Nynorsk ideologies – as represented by Vinje, a pioneering user of the language – encountered contemporary impulses from the wider world that helped to crystallise that oppositional, power-critical stance in a wider context than the Scandinavian sociocultural and historical *milieux* in which the language originally known as Landsmål had been created.

Returning to Vinje's mission, this was, after all, a chance for *Dølen*, the Dalesman, to venture out even further than *By og Bygd* and into the wider world, engaging with social debate on many levels. To a greater degree than many travel writers of the time would have done, he attempts to portray this world from the bottom up, with his ironic tone and satirical content, showing many typical traits of his character and writing. Harald Beyer wrote of Vinje: *Han er omskiftelig som ingen annen, springende, impulsiv, lettrørt og kynisk, hjertevarm og taktløs, radikal og konservativ, upålitelig og trofast, halvt bondegutt, halvt europeer* ('He is unpredictable like no other, leaping, impulsive, emotional and cynical, warm-hearted and tactless, radical and conservative, unreliable and loyal, half farmer's boy, half European').[112] Beyer's description has been criticised as imprecise, with Digernes arguing that Vinje was in fact unusually consistent.[113] However, in this book, we see examples of all these attributes, and, not least, Vinje shows that it is possible to be both a farmer's boy and a European, demonstrating what that might mean in practice. He participates in international social debate with an independent mind. By venturing out into the world, and reflecting on his experiences and discoveries, he implicitly reflects back on Norwegian society too.

While there are many outdated elements in the book, there is also much that is still of relevance. On the bicentenary of Vinje's birth, philosopher Gunnar Skirbekk wrote that this particular

---

112. Beyer 1952: 242.
113. Digernes 1954.

book is *hyperaktuell* [...] *i den pågåande diskusjonen om forholdet mellom globalisert kapitalisme og statlege institusjonar* ('hypertopical [...] for the ongoing discussion about the relationship between globalised capitalism and state institutions').[114] Skirbekk feels the book is helpful as he wonders: *I vår tid, med spenningar mellom USA og Europa, og mellom Storbritannia og EU, kor står så vi, her i Skandinavia, her i Noreg?* ('In this age, with tensions between the USA and Europe, and between the UK and the EU, where do we stand, here in Scandinavia, here in Norway?')[115] In the appendix on the language question, Vinje writes in relation to Norway's close relationship with Denmark and Sweden: 'But that this holding together may not prove a failure like the Calmar union, no one of these nationalities must be absorbed by the others, but have its own autonomy in language, literature, legislation, and government'.[116] With such thoughts in mind, Vinje's book may indeed be equally topical on both sides of the North Sea to this day.

Bibliography

Aberdeen Journal. 'Literature'. 1 July 1863, 6.

Aftenbladet. 'Kristiania'. 11 October 1860, [2].

The Albion. 'New Publications'. 22 June 1863, 6.

Andersen, H.C. 1855. *Mit Livs Eventyr.* Copenhagen: C.A. Reitzel.

———. 1974. *H.C. Andersens dagbøger, 1845–1850.* Helga Vang Lauridsen and Tue Gad (eds). Copenhagen: Det Danske Sprog- og Litteraturselskab.

———. 1990. *The Diaries of Hans Christian Andersen.* Patricia L. Conroy and Sven H. Rossel (eds and trans.). Seattle: University of Washington Press.

———. 2013. *My Fairy-Tale Life.* W. Glyn Jones (trans.). Sawtry: Dedalus.

---

114. Skirbekk 2018: 17.
115. Ibid.
116. Vinje 1863a: 6 (appendix).

The Athenæum. '[Review of] *A Norseman's Views of Britain and the British*'. 29 August 1863, 267–268.

Barnes, Michael. 2010. 'The Study of Norn'. In Robert McColl Millar (ed.), *Northern Lights, Northern Words: Selected Papers from the FRLSU Conference, Kirkwall 2009*. Aberdeen: Forum for Research on the Languages of Scotland and Ireland, 26–47.

Beyer, Harald. 1952. *Norsk litteraturhistorie*. Oslo: Aschehoug.

Bredsdorff, Elias. 1954. *H.C. Andersen og England*. Copenhagen: Rosenkilde og Bagger.

Charlottetown Guardian. 'Dr Caven'. 27 August 1914, 3.

Dewar, Caitlyn. '"Emancipation Street" and "Teach Colonial History" Signs Appear around Edinburgh from BLM Activists'. *Edinburgh Evening News*, 26 June 2020. https://www.edinburghnews.scotsman. com/news/people/emancipation-street-and-teach-colonial-history- signs-appear-around-edinburgh-blm-activists-2896293. Accessed 4 March 2022.

Digernes, Ivar. 1954. 'Den konservative Vinje'. *Fossegrimen* 1:3, 102–108.

Djupedal, Reidar. 1968. 'Aasmund Vinje i Britland'. *Syn og Segn* 74, 22–33.

Draaisma, Muriel. 'Toronto City Council Votes to Rename Dundas Street'. *CBC News*, 14 July 2021. https://www.cbc.ca/news/canada/ toronto/toronto-renaming-dundas-street-1.6103260. Accessed 4 March 2022.

Fjågesund, Peter. 2021. 'Utsyn frå utkanten: Vinje, Hamsun og det anglo- amerikanske'. In Arnfinn Åslund et al. (eds), *Tvisyn, innsyn, utsyn: Nærblikk på A.O. Vinje*. Oslo: Scandinavian Academic Press, 287–321.

Glasgow Daily Herald. 1863a. [Leading article]. 22 June 1863, 4.

———. 1863b. 'Literature'. 24 June 1863, 3.

Grepstad, Ottar. 2018. 'Då Vinje såg Noreg utanfrå'. [Vinje]: Nynorsk kultursentrum/Vinje-senteret.

Halvorsen, J.B. 1885. *Bjørnstjerne Bjørnsons Liv og Forfattervirksomhed*. Kristiania: Det Mallingske Bogtrykkeri.

'Hugleik'. 'Klognæs Gaard og gamle Minder'. *Gudbrandsdølen*. 9 January 1912, 2.

Illustrated London News. 'Current Literature'. 27 June 1863, 707.

John Bull. '[Review of] *A Norseman's Views of Britain and the British*'. 11 July 1863, 444.

Knooihuizen, Remco. 2005. 'The Norn-to-Scots Language Shift: Another Look at Socio-Historical Evidence'. *Northern Studies* 39, 105–117.

London Review. 'A Norseman's Views of Britain'. 13 June 1863, 638–639.

MacRitchie, David. 'A Norse View of Scotland'. *Daily Record and Mail.* 2 July 1917, 2.

Midttun, Olav. 1960. *A.O. Vinje.* Oslo: Det Norske Samlaget.

Mikes, George. 1946. *How to be an Alien: A Handbook for Beginners and More Advanced Pupils.* London: Wingate.

Mo, Kristian. 1969. 'Historia åt Garden Klones'. In Sigurd Steen (ed.), *Klones jordbruks- og husmorskule: 50 års melding.* Otta: Engers Boktrykkeri, 7–14.

Montgomery MacDonald, L.M. 1927. 'The Day Before Yesterday'. *College Times* 3:3, 29–34.

Mullen, Stephen. 2021. 'Henry Dundas: A "Great Delayer" of the Abolition of the Transatlantic Slave Trade'. *Scottish Historical Review* 100:2, 218–248.

The Nation. 'Literature'. 21 April 1866, 554.

New York Herald. 'Literary Intelligence'. 17 September 1863, 7.

Pettinger, Alasdair. 2016. 'Travel Writing'. *Oxford Bibliographies: British and Irish Literature.* doi: 10.1093/obo/9780199846719-0119. Accessed 4 March 2022.

Post Office. 1862. *Edinburgh and Leith Directory 1862–63.* Edinburgh: Ballantyne.

The Press. 'Our Library Table'. 8 August 1863, 765.

Puzey, Guy. 2011. 'Wars of Position: Language Policy, Counter-Hegemonies and Cultural Cleavages in Italy and Norway'. PhD thesis. University of Edinburgh.

The Reader. 'Notices'. 13 June 1863, 575–576.

Saturday Review. '[Review of] *A Norseman's Views of Britain and the British*'. 20 June 1863, 802–803.

Schiötz, Eiler H. 1986. *Itineraria Norvegica: Utlendingers reiser i Norge inntil år 1900. En bibliografi*, vol. II. Oslo: Universitetsforlaget.

The Scotsman. 'Opening of Edinburgh University'. 4 Nov 1862, 4.

————. 'Publications'. 30 May 1863, 4.

Skard, Sigmund. 1939a. 'Den engelske domen over Vinjes Bretlandsbok'. *Edda* 26, 327–360.

————. 1939b. 'Kva tykte engelsmennene om Vinjes Englandsbok?'. *Syn og Segn* 45, 433–446.

Skirbekk, Gunnar. 2018. 'Vinje – hyperaktuell'. *Klassekampen*. 6 April, 16–17.

Solberg, Olav. 1992. 'Vinje på utanlandsferd: Bretland og Britarne'. In Eli Glomnes et al. (eds), *'At føle paa nationens puls': Åtte artiklar om Aasmund O. Vinje*. Oslo: Novus, 39–49.

The Standard. 'England through Foreign Spectacles'. 14 December 1863, 2.

Store norske leksikon. 2020. 'Bretland'. http://snl.no/Bretland. Accessed 4 March 2022.

These Islands. 'Our Driving Values'. http://www.these-islands.co.uk/values/d2. Accessed 4 March 2022.

Vesaas, Olav. 2001. *A.O. Vinje: Ein tankens hærmann*. Oslo: Cappelen.

[Vinje, A.O.]. 1851. 'Om Goldschmidt og hans Skribentvirksomhed (fremkaldt ved Iduns Kritik)'. *Andhrimner*, 2nd quarter, col. 55–62, 72–76.

[————]. ['Dølens fyrste Ord']. *Dølen.* 10 October 1858, 1–2.

————. 1861. *Ferdaminni fraa Sumaren 1860*, vol. II. Christiania: Bergh & Ellessen.

————. 1863a. *A Norseman's Views of Britain and the British*. Edinburgh: William P. Nimmo.

[————]. ['Mine Damer!']. *Dølen.* 12 April 1863, 1–4.

————. 1873. *Bretland og Britarne*. Kristiania: Det Norske Samlaget.

————. 1969. *Brev*. Olav Midttun (ed.). Oslo: Det Norske Samlaget.

————. 2018. 'Den norske språksituasjonen'. Ottar Grepstad (trans.). [Vinje]: Vinje-senteret.

Vislie, Vetle. 1890. *A.O. Vinje*. Bergen: Boklaget.

· VI ·

'Over hill, over dale':
Reviewing the Distribution and Significance
of Old Norse dalr in Scottish Place-Names

Alan Macniven

Over hill, over dale,
Thorough bush, thorough brier,
Over park, over pale,
Thorough flood, thorough fire,
I do wander everywhere,
Swifter than the moon's sphere;

Shakespeare, W. c. 1595.
A Midsummer Night's Dream, Act II, Scene I

Introduction

The names used to label and describe the natural features in any given landscape form part of a complex cultural narrative. As Shakespeare implied in his *Midsummer Night's Dream*, their generic elements alone equip users to anticipate and navigate topographies – both real and imagined – without ever having seen them. Beyond this basic cognitive function, however, the analysis of place-names and their linguistic building blocks has the potential to help settlement historians negotiate the changes in language, outlook, and cultural norms, which separate the modern users of those names from the communities that first coined them. Indeed, in areas and periods for which traditional historical sources are lacking, the contextualised review of place-name material can help add crucial nuance to narrative accounts of the past. This is particularly true in the study of the largely undocumented events and developments which together comprise Scotland's Viking Age.

There may have been a delay of a millennium or so before the dedicatee of this volume, Arne Kruse, undertook his own *landnám*. But when he arrived in Edinburgh in the late 1980s, Arne spared little time in developing the toolkit needed to assess the impact of his predecessors. Amongst his intellectual luggage was a wealth of experience in the theory and practice of place-name research, a keen familiarity with the typology and function of Scandinavian place-names, and an enduring interest in the Viking Expansion. As the underpinning for much of his teaching, research, conference papers, publications, and editorial work, this combination soon germinated into a notably multi-disciplinary *milieu* for investigating the Scandinavian dimension of Scotland's onomastic heritage. I myself have been a direct beneficiary of this environment, first as a student, then as a supervisee, and then as a colleague and friend. I offer the following in the spirit of celebration this festschrift represents.

Mapping and analysing the development of Norse settlement

In the 1960s, Bill Nicolaisen initiated the large-scale mapping of onomastic markers for Norse activity along the north and west coasts of Scotland, their hinterlands, and off-lying islands. The volume and density of this material inspired him to label the area *Scotia Scandinavica* (Figure 1). Nicolaisen's investigation of Old Norse settlement generics such as *staðir*, *bólstaðr*, and *setr* (Figure 2) fed into a series of influential assumptions on the evolution of Viking settlement, from its opening stages, through its expansion, to its internal consolidation.[1]

Taking his lead from Hugh Marwick's 'Farm Chronology',[2] and F.T. Wainwright's distillation of the same,[3] Nicolaisen argued that the widespread but diffuse distribution of *staðir*-names was indicative of an initial phase of land-taking, in which large, landed estates were demarcated[4] – the so-called 'primary settlements'. The clustering of *bólstaðr*-names, on the other hand, was thought to point to the subdivision of those parent estates at a later stage into 'secondary' units – indicating the maximum extent of Norse settlement.[5] By way of contrast, names of the *setr*-type were thought to reflect a stage in the consolidation of initial settlement, into what we might extrapolate as centres of specialised yet economically subordinate activity, whose more limited distribution is 'a pointer to the period of confrontation between Norse and Gaelic speakers'.[6]

While most scholars would still agree with the general tenor of these observations, the tendency nowadays is to view the relationship between the different naming elements in this

---

1. For a summary, see Nicolaisen 2001: 109–155, but also i.a. 1969; 1976; 1977–80; 1980; 1982; 1994.
2. Marwick 1952: 235–251.
3. Wainwright 1964: 139.
4. Nicolaisen 1969: 17; 2001: 113–116.
5. Nicolaisen 1969: 9–11, 14–16; 2001: 119–122. Of course, the interpretation of Scotland's Old Norse *bólstaðr*-names has since been substantially revised by Peder Gammeltoft (2001).
6. Nicolaisen 2001: 116–119; 1969: 11–14.

system as hierarchical rather than chronological.[7] Even with the first wave of Norse colonists there would have been a will, if not always a way, to establish the full range of agricultural and cultural facilities demanded by contemporary societal norms. The large agricultural landholdings of the leading settlers would have needed mills, smithies, summer pastures, and so on from the outset. This is what appears to have happened in fairly short order when the Norse first arrived in the untamed wilderness of Iceland.[8]

Considering that *Scotia Scandinavica* was no cultural *tabula rasa* when the Norse arrived but a fully developed settlement landscape, it is all but inevitable that planned differentiation would have been a feature of societal organisation from the very start. The relative economic viability of given sites within their localities will have determined their success or failure as settlement units, and the speed and stability with which the associated names became embedded in their local namescapes, or – alternatively – disappeared.

Of far greater controversy are Nicolaisen's observations on names containing the Old Norse nature generic *dalr* ('valley').[9] Whereas the bulk of his better-known surveys foreground cultural generics – all of which could reasonably be associated with agricultural settlements of one type or another – the interpretation of *dalr*-names presented a problem, in as much as it concerned a word whose most self-evident function was to designate topographical features. For that reason, Nicolaisen argued that there was 'no reason to think that [the element *dalr* in Scottish place-names] has ever meant anything but what it still means in Norwegian today, i.e. "a valley"'.[10] By extension, he

---

7. Crawford 1987: 105, 108; Thomson 1995, 42–62.
8. Vésteinsson 1998; Karlsson 2000.
9. Nicolaisen 2001: 112–113, 122–124.
10. Nicolaisen 1969: 16–17; 2001, 122–124.

reasoned that the widespread distribution of this name type was indicative of the 'sphere of Scandinavian influence', rather than 'a map of permanent Norse settlement', and most likely reflected patterns of seasonal exploitation, such as hunting, fishing, summer grazing, the odd military raid, or even friendly visits.[11]

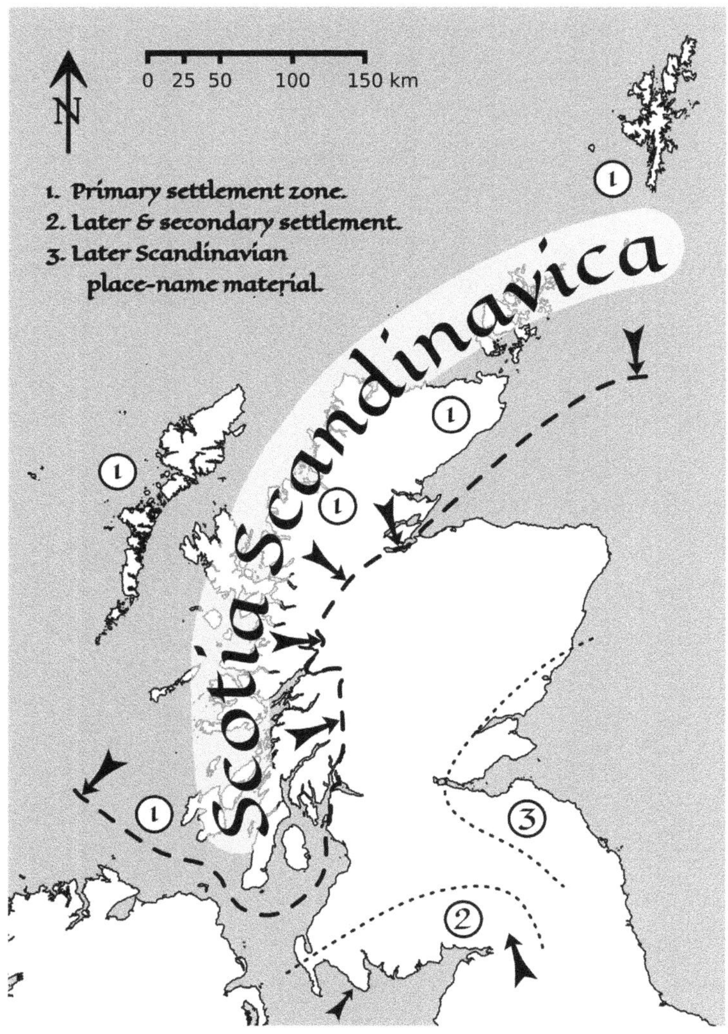

Figure 1: *Scotia Scandinavica*.[12]

11. Nicolaisen 2001: 122.
12. After Nicolaisen 1994: 31; 1980: 219–220. See also Crawford 1995: 5.

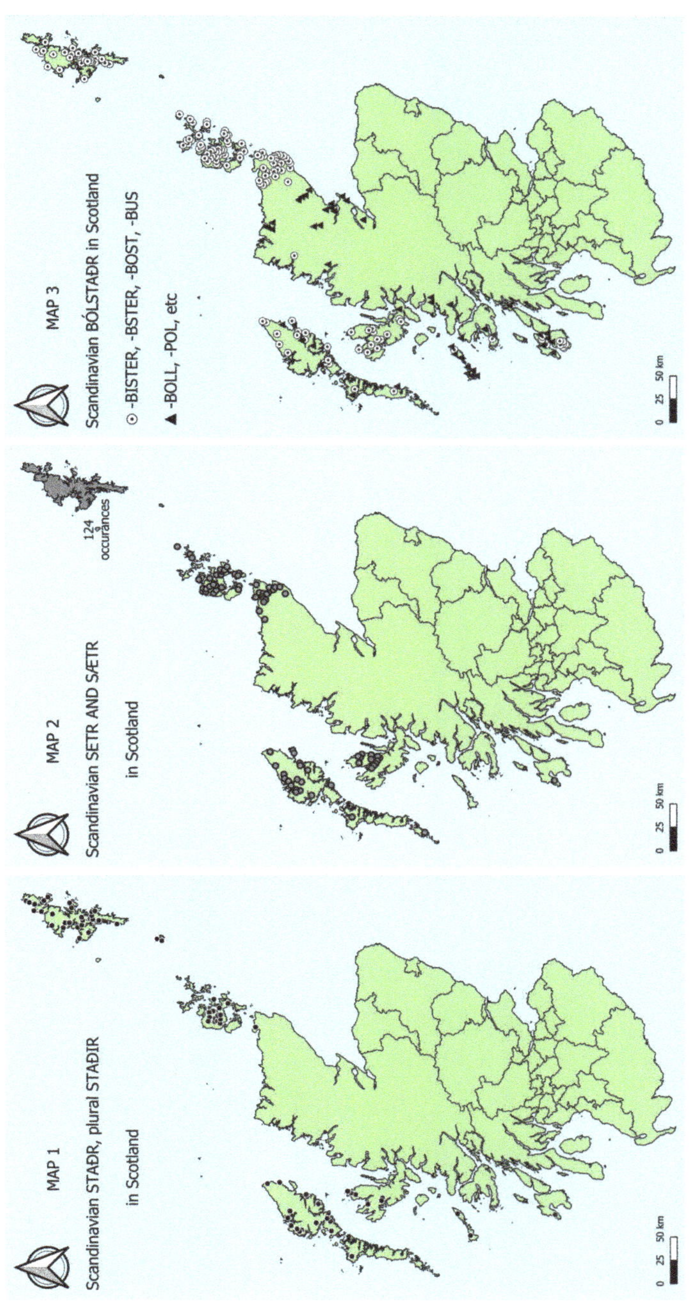

Figure 2: Distribution of Old Norse *staðir*, *setr*, and *bólstaðr* on OS one-inch-to-the-mile sheets.[13]

13. After Nicolaisen 1969: pull-out between pp. 8–9. These maps have been reprinted multiple times since, e.g. Nicolaisen 2001: 114, 115, 121.

It is perhaps not surprising that this straightforward and rhetorically compelling argument was quickly accepted as the settlement-historical orthodoxy. However, its simplicity has since been shown to belie a fundamental misunderstanding of ancient Scandinavian naming traditions,[14] and the transmission of place-name material in general.

Amongst the most neatly argued critiques of this position from an onomastic perspective are those of Scandinavian place-name scholar Arne Kruse. As Arne has pointed out over a series of articles, the namescapes of the Scandinavian homelands evolved over an extended period of time – as settlement expanded, retracted, or intensified, with new land being broken, old land abandoned, and cultural and economic emphases changing. The end result was the repository of name typologies, as well as cognitive toponymies exported by Viking Age colonists to Scotland.[15]

Logic dictates that at least some of the oldest surviving settlements in Scandinavia itself will have been named for the most prominent natural feature in their locality, whether that happened to be a bay (e.g. ON *vík*), a mountain (ON *fjall*) or a valley (ON *dalr*). With early settlement sites most likely chosen for their convergence of ecological, and therefore economic potential – as opposed to making-do-and-mending with whichever spare land was left – it follows that they enjoyed an elevated chance of success and, with it, survival – which also explains the relatively high values often associated with these sites in the earliest taxation lists.[16] When Scotland's first Norse *landsnámsmenn* set about naming their new environment, we might therefore expect them to begin with nature generics – either for practical, geographical reasons, to commemorate

---

14. Crawford 1987: 111 and 111n19; Crawford and Taylor 2003: 9.
15. See, for example, Kruse 2004; 2005; 2007; Jennings and Kruse 2009.
16. Kruse 2004: 105–106.

what they saw as important typological markers, or icons of nostalgia or success from back home. In so doing, they would have been unpacking and arranging their onomastic baggage.[17]

While Nicolaisen later turned away from the idea of rigid place-name chronologies,[18] and accepted that topographic generics like *dalr* could also be used for farms, he did so with the caveat that they must surely indicate 'less permanency in occupation, or at least a very different attitude towards the land'.[19] Yet for this material to have survived *in situ* from the Viking Age to its written crystallisation in later medieval charters, rentals, and – later still – maps, we can assume that it was maintained and preserved by permanently settled Norse-speaking communities until the names lost their appellative meaning, and passed into the sphere of lexically opaque address labels.[20] The alternative – of heritage communities of Gaelic speakers, eschewing their own naming traditions in favour of neologisms left behind like used chewing gum by transient Norse interlopers – is rather more difficult to accept.

To cut a long story short, and contrary to Nicolaisen's assessment, the distribution of Old Norse *dalr*-names has clear potential to serve as a starting point in the study of Scandinavian settlement in Scotland. Determining whether all of the names in the surviving corpus had dual referents – to both a settlement and a natural feature – would require the close and contextualised study of each name in turn. And to confirm whether they pointed collectively to concurrent usage and therefore the maximum extent of Norse settlement would

---

17. Kruse 2007. For a discussion of Old Norse *dalr* in the namescapes of Kintyre, see Jennings 2004.

18. Nicolaisen 2011: 213–214.

19. Ibid.: 214.

20. See Nicolaisen 2011: 308–309 for a brief overview of the factors which influence meaning and longevity in names.

depend on the relationship of *dalr*-names to the wider body of settlement-historical evidence, including other place-names, archaeological material, genetics, and even folk-traditions.[21]

Identifying Old Norse *dalr*

Before embarking on such a monumental task, it makes sense to review how we might go about identifying the surviving examples of these names, the areas and forms in which we expect to encounter them, which – if any – observations might help to narrow or expand the list, and which issues and problems might complicate the search. The most convenient starting point is the suite of modern maps produced by the Ordnance Survey, which provide both relative certainty of location and geographical accuracy. This was the approach taken by Nicolaisen himself, leading to the identification of several hundred *dalr*-names, comprising around 340 examples on the mainland and isles to the west, with the observation that it also 'occurs frequently' in the Northern Isles (Figure 3).

Before reviewing the situation, it is important to be clear about how a given name is assigned to this category. Ideally, the process would involve a thorough programme of scientific research for each and every name. The onomastic methodologies required to confirm etymological suspicions are well established. At a minimum, they comprise the collection and comparison of the earliest written forms of the names with long-standing local pronunciation, and a consideration of local topography, alongside other relevant aspects of the environmental, cultural, and economic context.[22] As a diagnostic

---

21. Cf. Nicolaisen 2011: 215.
22. See, for example, Christensen & Kousgarrd-Sørensen 1972; Waugh 1998.

precursor to this work, however, it is necessary to consider the possibilities suggested by the attested place-name typologies of the likely source language(s) – in this case Old Norse, and Scottish Gaelic, as well as Scots and standard English.

As there is no part of *Scotia Scandinavica* for which locally coined Norse name material did not survive as oral phenomena – in some cases for half a millennium or more – before being transcribed, a certain degree of transformation can be expected. As this process has taken place at different times and under different circumstances in different parts of the country, there is no clearly established framework of spelling to work with. The forms recorded in the Northern Isles and Caithness, for example, tend to be limited to *dale*, and occasionally *daal*.[23]

By way of contrast, in the West Highlands and Islands, the added complication of transmission through a Gaelic-language environment means that the variety of written forms encountered is, to say the least, diverse. With *dalr* and its reflexes occurring in simplex names, compounds, and in *ex-nomine* onomastic units used as the basis for later Gaelic-language constructs,[24] they can be difficult to unpack from their onomastic matrices. Fortunately, there are numerous guides to likely linguistic transformations, with some focusing on discrete phonemes and morphemes,[25] and others considering names as a whole.[26] From these, it is possible to lay out a range of orthographic variants, encompassing *dal(l)*, *dail(l)*, *dil(l)*, *dle*, *dul(l)*, *tal(l)*, *tale*, *tail*, *tel(l)*, *til(l)*, *tle*, *tul(l)*, and others.

---

23. See, for example, Stewart 1987: 71–78.
24. Cox 1988–9: 3; 2002: 36–39.
25. E.g. Henderson 1910: 342–357; MacBain 1911; Marstrander 1915; Oftedal 1961–2; Stewart 2004; Cox 2022 (vol. 1).
26. E.g. MacBain 1922; Marwick 1952; Oftedal 1954; Stewart 1987; Stahl 1999; Gammeltoft 2001; Cox 2001; 2022; Sandnes 2010; Márkus 2012; Macniven 2015.

Screening the data

Given the potential number of place-names involved, this kind of investigation presents a considerable challenge, which would almost certainly benefit from being broken down into a series of more manageable chunks. Ultimately, the need for an appropriate geopolitical context might warrant the use of administrative boundaries, such as those of the pre-1976 counties, pre-1891 parishes, or – more productively – the medieval landholdings and territories familiar from earlier sources. Before doing that, there are a few simple ways to pre-screen the data and filter out a significant number of 'false friends'.

It is worth remembering that Nicolaisen's survey was undertaken in the days before GIS or any other kind of easily accessible computer software. By current standards, his use of paper copies of maps is a process which is far more susceptible to error and omission than it needs to be. But thanks to the wonders of modern information technology, and the output of the GB1900 project, we have the ability to undertake computer-aided searches of a UK-wide place-name gazetteer, comprising over a million rows of data, transcribed and geocoded from the Ordnance Survey's second edition of County Series (six-inch-to-the-mile) sheets, originally produced between 1888 and 1914. Scotland alone is served by almost 260,000 rows of data – which translates into a daunting number of names.

Fortunately, not all of these need to be considered here. For the area outwith Nicolaisen's primary settlement zone, there is still very little historical, archaeological, or place-name evidence to support the prospect of Norse settlement on any discernible scale. For this reason, the search can be restricted to the modern local authority areas of Shetland, Orkney, Na h-Eileanan an

Iar, Argyll and Bute, Highland, and North Ayrshire. So doing reduces the number of rows to just over 110,000. Working with these, a standard search for place-names containing the most common reflex of Old Norse *dalr*, 'dale', returns 1,621 hits (Figure 3). Of these, only 1,227 are found within *Scotia Scandinavica*. For names encountered to the east and south, the *prima facie* assumption for most must be origins in English 'dale' or 'dell', which are not relevant to this study.[27]

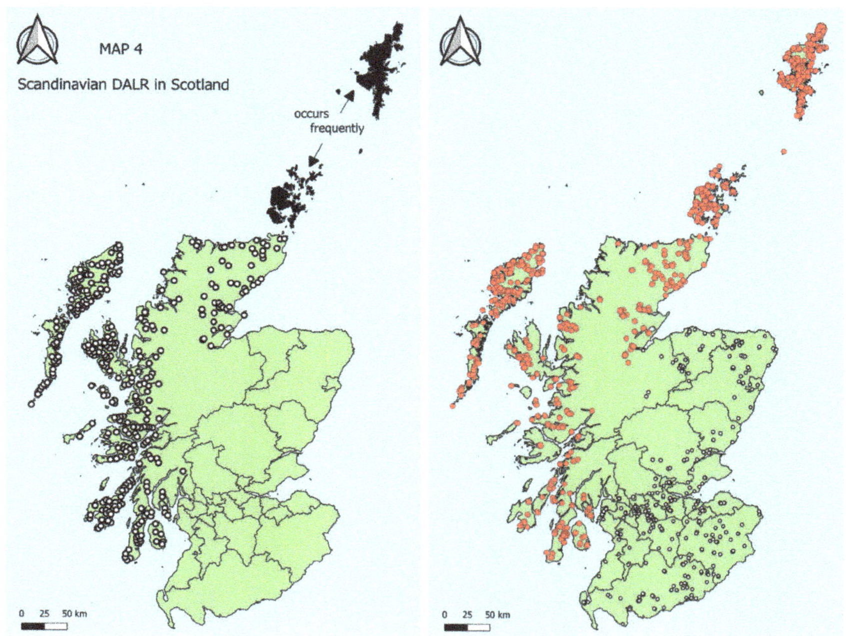

Figure 3: Distribution of Old Norse *dalr* on OS one-inch-to-the-mile sheets (left);[28] place-names containing 'dale' in the GB1900 database (right).

Given the chequered linguistic history of the main study area, however, and the distinctly non-standardised spelling of its

---

27. E.g. Nicolaisen 1969: 17n1; 2001: 124.
28. After Nicolaisen 1969: pull-out between pp. 8–9. As with the maps shown in Figure 2, this example was reproduced in numerous subsequent publications, e.g. Nicolaisen 2001: 123.

place-names, a search for 'dale' alone will not capture everything. Coding the search using the 'regular expressions' feature of a standard spreadsheet filtering tool gives a better impression of the maximum number of names derived from Old Norse *dalr*.[29] Combining '[dt][aeiu]l' with '[dt]ail' and 'daal', for example, covers all of the variant spellings listed above, returning almost 2,800 hits for the target area – substantially more than that indicated by Nicolaisen's survey (Figure 4).

Nevertheless, it is clear from even superficial analysis that not all of this material reflects Old Norse origins. There are a quite a few obvious cuckoos in the nest, where derivation is from a transparently English word, such as *ho**tel*** (126 hits), *dis**till**ery* (forty-two), *tel**egraph*** (thirty-seven), and *hosp**ital*** (thirty-five), among others. There are also forty-two examples where the name itself does not meet the search criteria, but the name field for that entry also contains a parish name which does, such as 'South Knapdale Ph.'.

In addition to this, the search inevitably returns a large number of names built from exclusively Gaelic material. Some, such as *tull*[*o/i*]*ch* (sixty-one: 'hillock'), *dalach* (twenty-two: potentially the genitive form of *dail*, 'meadow', or *dàil*, 'assembly'), *tailleir* (twelve: 'tailor'), and *talamh*(*anta*) (ten: 'earth') – with those forms – are readily apparent. But the proliferation of variant spellings resulting from the historical lack of standardisation, and even diacritics, in map-names means that others are potentially more difficult to spot.

---

29. In theory, the prospect of more sophisticated 'fuzzy matching' is offered by machine-learning programmes such as the KNIME analytics platform. There is certainly no shortage of 'skeleton material' with which to develop potential algorithms. Considering the flexible position of the generic in each string of onomastic data, and the potential linguistic variety in the rest of the matrix, however, the best results of this approach are likely to be limited to searches for names which were originally both typologically and etymologically identical or at least very similar.

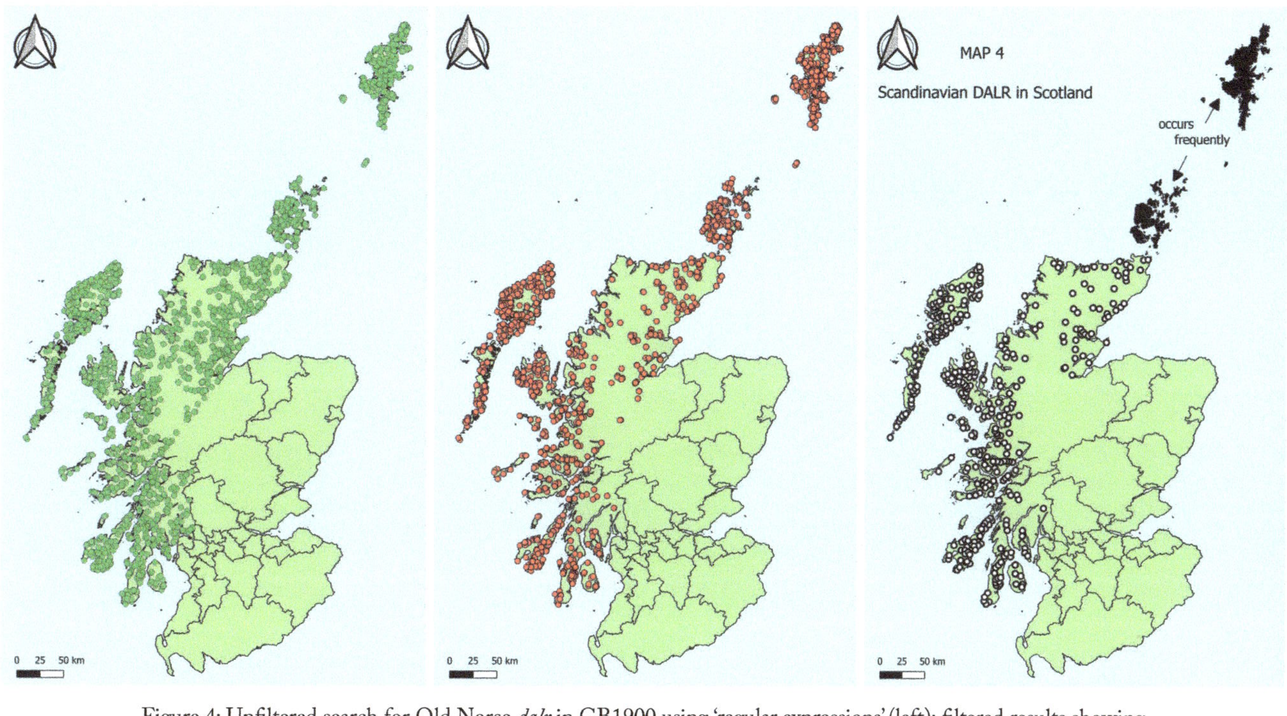

Figure 4: Unfiltered search for Old Norse *dalr* in GB1900 using 'regular expressions' (left); filtered results showing relatively certain *dalr* compounds only (middle); Nicolaisen's 1969 distribution map (right).

Features of name typology can serve as important diagnostic tools here. Names beginning with epexegetic onomastic units, for example, can help to identify Old Norse generics in the *ex-nomine* onomastic units which follow. Take the Islay names Glenastle, Glenegedale, Gleann Ghàiredail, and Gleann Chòireadail – all of which are associated with settlements and/or valleys, thus providing extra justification for the interpretation of the original *Ast<u>le</u>*, *Ege<u>dale</u>*, *Gàire<u>dail</u>*, and *Còirea<u>dail</u>* as Old Norse *dalr*-names.[30]

There are also bound to be cases, particularly with simplex names, where differentiation between originally Old Norse and Gaelic material will only be possible after detailed examination of the local topographical and cultural circumstances. Amongst the most ambiguous of these are potentially simplex examples of Old Norse *dalr* and stand-alone examples of the Gaelic generics *dail* ('meadow') and *dàil* ('assembly').

In Islay, the etymology of the traditional farm-name Daill (*Dal* in 1509) has been seen variously as Gaelic and Norse. While there are a number of factors which point more strongly towards the latter, including the linguistic origins of the other large land-holdings in the vicinity, the wider toponymic context is crucial here.[31] Daill is only a few kilometres from the head of the major waterway, Loch Indaal (likely from a preceding *Loch na Da/àl[ach]*). It also commands a fertile spot in the district of Islay known as The Glen in English, and *An Gleann* ('The Valley') in Gaelic. With such a close connection between these three names, it is not unreasonable to posit common origins in Old Norse *dalr*. But with the bulk of this subset of material likely to derive from Gaelic tradition, it makes sense to separate it – as a category – from the main group of *dalr*-candidates.

---

30. Macniven 2015: 152–154, 154–155, 175, 284.
31. Macniven 2015: 203–204.

Based on the crude analysis of spelling alone, there were twenty-three examples of 'Dal' / 'Dell' and 254 of 'An Dàil' / 'Dail' etc., which can be removed from the total (Figure 5).

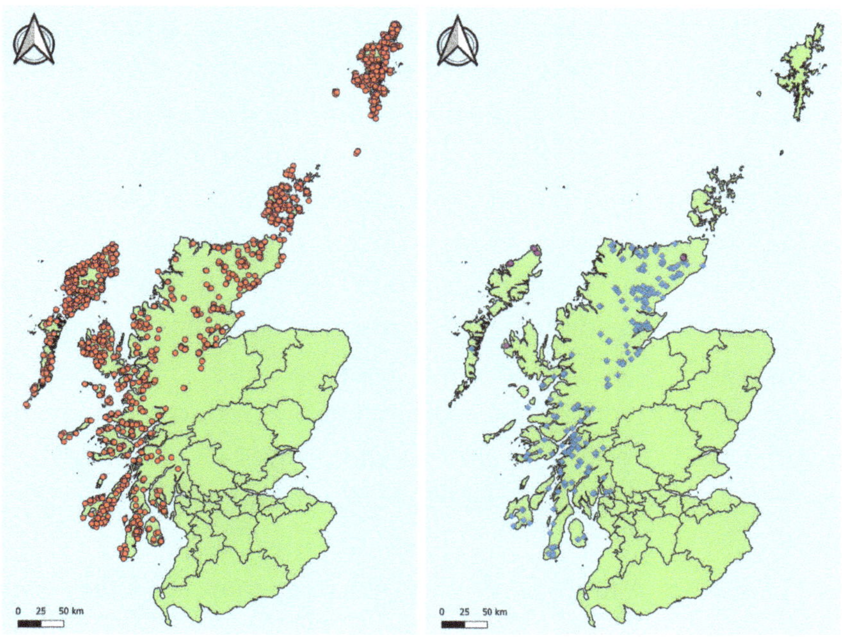

Figure 5: Likely compound *dalr*-names in GB1900 (left); originally simplex 'dal' and 'dale' names (red) and discrete 'dail' names (blue) (right).

Discussion

Following the methodology outlined above, it would seem that 1,750 or so *dalr*-names are preserved in the GB1900 entries for *Scotia Scandinavica* – a substantially higher volume of material than that identified by Nicolaisen. While closer scrutiny of individual names in the corpus could reduce the total, re-evaluation of certain erstwhile Gaelic *dàil* or *dail* names could increase it. Of course, it is possible that the strictly defined boundaries of the study area exclude some outliers. But it could also be the case that they include further examples, which await discovery in older, albeit less reliable maps, or non-cartographic sources, such as charters and rentals – as can be seen in the collation of the Islay *bólstaðr*-names.[32]

At the same time, it is important to stress that not all of the potential *dalr*-names in this list represent unique locations. In fact, a notable portion of the total can be attributed to clusters derived from a single original referent. These range from simple contrastive pairings, such as Doodilmore and Doodilbeg from Islay – from Old Norse *Dúfadalr* ('Dovedale')[33] – to more complex phrasal derivatives such as Loch Laingeadail Beag – from Old Norse *Langadalr* ('Longdale').[34] While pruning back names of this type to single, parent constructs will inevitably reduce the overall number of *dalr*-sites, the clusters themselves serve to highlight the cultural significance of those sites and the surrounding areas.

As seen in Figure 6, the revised base-map for Old Norse *dalr*-names in *Scotia Scandinavica* brings certain potential routes of communication into sharp relief, especially those linking the coasts of Caithness, Sutherland, and Ross to their hinterlands. This aligns with the observations by Barbara Crawford on the expansion of the jarldom of Orkney under Sigurðr *digri* Hlöðvisson (Sigurd 'the Stout', c. 991–1014), and his son Þorfinnr *inn ríki* (Thorfinn 'the Mighty', c. 1016–65).[35] Consolidation of Norse settlement during this period would have been necessary to safeguard Orcadian interests in the West.

---

32. Macniven 2015: 71–73 [Map 72].
33. Ibid.: 259–260.
34. Ibid.: 298.
35. See, for example, Crawford 1986, 1987, 1995b, 2003, and 2013.

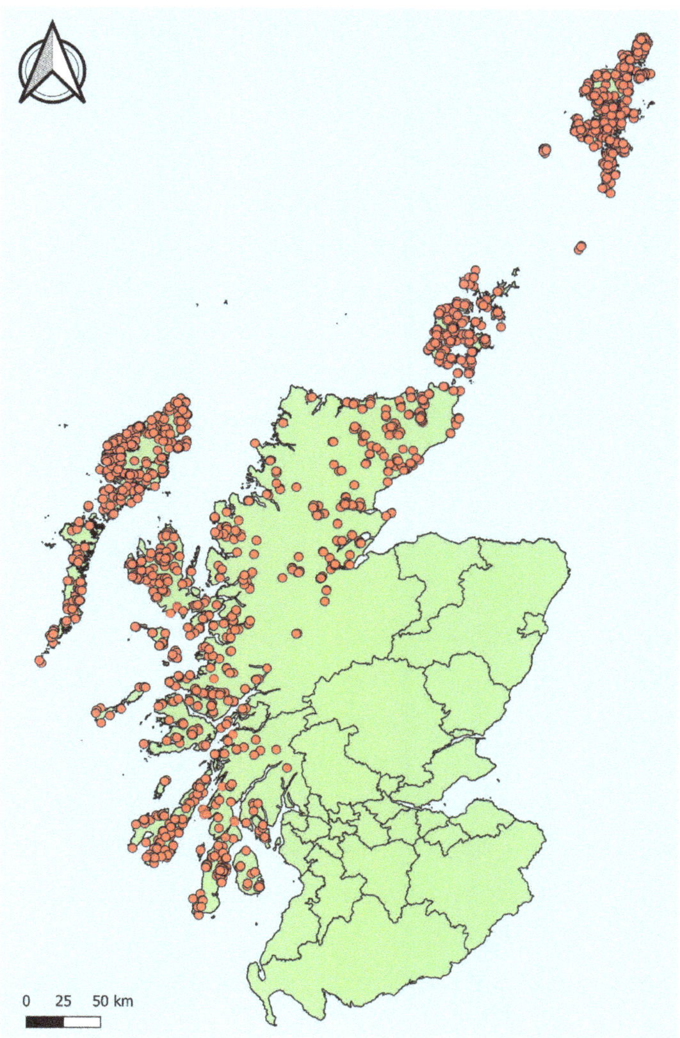

Figure 6: Base-map for Old Norse *dalr*-names in *Scotia Scandinavica*.

According to the thirteenth-century literary work *Brennu-Njáls saga*, for example, Sigurd is said to have had 'this dominion in Scotland: Ross and Moray, Sutherland and the Dales',[36] with the

36. *Jarl átti þessi ríki í Skotlandi: Ros ok Mýrhæfi, Syðri-lönd ok Dali.* Sveinsson 1954: 206–207; Crawford 1995b: 5.

dali or 'dales' in question likely to reflect both ancient Dàl Riata, or Argyll, and the coastal valleys linking the mainland part of that territory to Sutherland.[37] As Crawford has also stressed, however, jarldom aspirations are likely to have involved control of the overland transit routes from the Firthlands of Easter Ross and Sutherland to the Great Glen and beyond – as well as the inland timber resources crucial for maintaining both naval strength and (prestige) building programmes in relatively tree-less Orkney.[38]

Through close-reading of the semi-historical *Orkneyinga saga*,[39] Crawford builds a particularly strong case for the domination of the northeast coast under Thorfinn between about 1040 and 1065, when the attentions of the Scottish throne appear to have been turned elsewhere.[40] The apparent floruit of Dingwall – Old Norse *Þingvǫllr* ('Assembly Plain') – during this period as a Norse administrative and likely also market centre may only have been possible under the protection of the Orkney jarls.[41] It may also have led to the expansion and consolidation of Norse settlement in the surrounding area, resulting in the introduction (or revival?) of a layer of Old Norse place-names.[42] But it would be wrong to assume that the scope for Norse settlement in the preceding centuries would have been curtailed by the agendas of powerful neighbours to the south. These were clearly no impediment to the Norse *landnám* in Orkney itself, which was once controlled by a powerful hierarchy of Pictish kings,[43] presumably alongside large stretches of the adjacent mainland.

---

37. Sveinsson 1954: 207n1; Taylor 1938: 401.
38. Crawford 1986: 40-44; 1987: 25; 1995b: 11–17; 2003: 4–7.
39. See Taylor 1938; Guðmundsson 1965.
40. E.g. Crawford and Taylor 2003: 4–6.
41. Crawford 1995b: 17–21.
42. For a review of the historical namescapes to the south-west of Dingwall, see Crawford and Taylor 2003.
43. See, for example, Márkus 2017: 89, 96, 103, 160.

The early arrival of Norse settlers in the interior of Caithness, Sutherland, and Ross may have amounted to the opening phase in the long-term cycle of control between Norse and Celtic overlords. But it was no doubt predicated on the benefits offered by local resources and connections, just as it was elsewhere in *Scotia Scandinavica* – the same advantages which had previously been exploited by the displaced Celtic landowners, and would later be developed by their own descendants. The economic infrastructure reflected in the later medieval and early modern drove-roads, for example, may not have exact parallels in the Viking Age.[44] But what they might reveal are the main routes along which goods, people, and news are likely to have travelled. It seems little coincidence that one of the main thoroughfares between the east and west coasts today, the A835, links Ullapool in the west with Ulladale and nearby Dingwall in the east. Could it be that the common referent points to some aspect of shared community across the span of the route?

In terms of the overall distribution of *dalr*-names, the emphasis placed by Nicolaisen on their frequency in the Northern Isles – and effective downplaying of their density elsewhere – also needs to be reconsidered. Of the 1,754 examples tentatively identified here, only 212 are in Orkney, and 382 in Shetland. Far more are found in Highland, with 500 examples to the west and north of the Great Glen, another 400 in Na h-Eileanan an Iar, 247 in Argyll and a further thirteen on Arran in North Ayrshire.

As far back as 1978, Ian Fraser had argued that *dalr*-names should be considered as candidates for Norse control in areas lacking habitative names. But perhaps the scale of the dataset now coming to light points to an even bolder conclusion – that the scope and aspirations of Norse settlement in these areas was once as ambitious as it was in the far north? With further development

---

44. Baldwin 1986.

of the data, it seems likely that Scotland's Old Norse *dalr*-names could inform our understanding of not only the extent of Norse settlement but also the lines of communication and control which initially held it together but ultimately helped to hasten its demise.

Bibliography

Baldwin, J. 1986. 'The Long Trek: Agricultural Change and the Great Northern Drove'. In J. Baldwin (ed.), *Firthlands of Ross and Sutherland*. Edinburgh: Scottish Society for Northern Studies, 183–220.

Brennu-Njáls saga. E.Ó. Sveinsson (ed.). Reykjavík: Hið íslenzka fornritafélag, 1954.

Christensen, V. and Kousgård Sørensen, J. 1972. *Stednavneforskning I: Afgrænsning, terminologi, metode, datering*. Copenhagen: Universitetsforlaget i København i kommission hos Gyldendal.

Cox, R.A.V. 1988–9. 'Questioning the value and validity of the term "hybrid" in Hebridean place-name study'. *Nomina* 12, 1–9.

———. 2002. *The Gaelic Place-Names of Carloway, Lewis: Their Structure and Significance*. Dublin: Dublin Institute for Advanced Studies.

———. 2022a. *Ainmean Tuineachaidh Leòdhais / The Settlement Names of Lewis*. Vol. 1. Tigh a'Mhaide, Brig o'Turk: Clann Tuirc.

———. 2022b. *Ainmean Tuineachaidh Leòdhais / The Settlement Names of Lewis*. Vol. 2. Tigh a'Mhaide, Brig o'Turk: Clann Tuirc.

Crawford, B.E. 1986. 'The Making of a Frontier: The Firthlands from the Ninth to Twelfth Centuries'. In J. Baldwin (ed.), *Firthlands of Ross and Sutherland*. Edinburgh: Scottish Society for Northern Studies, 33–46.

———. 1987. *Scandinavian Scotland*. Leicester: Leicester University Press.

———. (ed.). 1995a. *Scandinavian Settlement in Northern Britain: Thirteen Studies of Place-Names in Their Historical Context (Studies in the Early History of Britain)*. Leicester: Leicester University Press.

———. 1995b. *Earl and Mormaer: Norse-Pictish Relationships in Northern Scotland*. Rosemarkie: Groam House Museum Trust.

———. 2013. *The Northern Earldoms: Orkney and Caithness from AD 870 to 1470*. Edinburgh: John Donald.

Crawford, B.E. and Taylor, S. 2003. 'The Southern Frontier of Norse Settlement in North Scotland: Place-Names and History'. *Northern Scotland* 23, 1–76.

Fraser, I.A. 1978. 'The Norse Element in Sutherland Place-Names'. *Scottish Literary Journal, Language Supplement* 9, 17–27.

GB1900 Gazetteer. https://www.visionofbritain.org.uk/data/#tabgb1900. Accessed 2 February 2022.

Guðmundsson, F. (ed.). 1965. *Orkneyinga saga: Legenda de Sancto Magno. Magnúss saga Skemmri. Magnúss saga Lengri. Helga þáttr ok Úlfs.* Reykjavík: Hið íslenzka fornritafélag.

Henderson, G. 1910. *The Norse Influence on Celtic Scotland.* Glasgow: J. Maclehose and Sons.

Jennings, A. 2004. 'The Norse Place-Names of Kintyre'. In J. Adams and K. Holman (eds), *Scandinavia and Europe 800–1350: Contact, Conflict, and Coexistence.* Turnhout: Brepols, 109–119.

Jennings, A. and Kruse, A. 2009. 'From Dál Riata to the Gall-Ghàidheil'. *Viking and Medieval Scandinavia* 5, 123–149.

Karlsson, G. 2000. *Iceland's 1100 Years: The History of a Marginal Society.* Iceland: *Mál og menning.*

KNIME. https://www.knime.com. Accessed 2 February 2022.

Kruse, A. 2004. 'Norse Topographical Settlement Names on the Western Littoral of Scotland'. In J. Adams and K. Holman (eds), *Scandinavia and Europe 800–1350: Contact, Conflict, and Coexistence.* Turnhout: Brepols, 97–107.

———. 2005. 'Explorers, Raiders and Settlers: The Norse impact upon Hebridean Place-Names'. In P. Gammeltoft, C. Hough, and D. Waugh (eds), *Cultural Contacts in the North Atlantic Region: The Evidence of the Names.* Lerwick: NORNA, Scottish Place-Name Society, 141–156.

———. 2007. 'Fashion, Limitation and Nostalgia: Scandinavian Place-Names Abroad'. In P. Graves and A. Kruse (eds), *Images and Imaginations: Perspectives on Britain and Scandinavia.* Edinburgh: Lockharton Press, 3–33.

MacBain, A. 1911, *An Etymological Dictionary of the Gaelic Language.* Stirling: Eneas MacKay.

———. 1922. *Place Names, Highlands & Islands of Scotland*. Stirling: Eneas Mackay.

Macniven, A. 2015. *The Vikings in Islay*. Edinburgh: John Donald.

Márkus, G. 2012. *The Place-Names of Bute*. Donington: Shaun Tyas.

———. 2017. *Conceiving a Nation: Scotland to AD 900*. Edinburgh: Edinburgh University Press.

Marstrander, C.J.S. 1915. *Bidrag til det norske sprogs historie i Irland*. Christiania: Det Kongelige Norske Videnskabernes Selskab.

Marwick, H. 1952. *Orkney Farm-Names*. Kirkwall: W.R. Mackintosh, 227–251.

Nicolaisen, W.F.H. 1969. 'Norse Settlement in the Northern and Western Isles: Some Place Name Evidence'. *Scottish Historical Review* 48, 6–17.

———. 1976. 'Scandinavian Place-Names in Scotland as a Source of Knowledge', *Northern Studies* 7/8, 14–24.

———. 1977–80. 'Early Scandinavian Naming in the Northern and Western Isles'. *Northern Scotland* 3:1, 105–121.

———. 1980. 'Place-names as evidence for linguistic stratification in Scotland'. In V. Dalberg et al. (eds), *NORNA-Rapporter 18. Sprogvidenskabelig udnyttelse av stednavnematerialet*. Uppsala, 211–231.

———. 1982. 'Scandinavian's and Celts in Caithness: The Place-Name Evidence. In J. Baldwin (ed.), *Caithness: A Cultural Crossroads*. Edinburgh, Scottish Society for Northern Studies, 75–85.

———. 1989. 'Place-Name Maps – How Reliable are They?' In L. Peterson (ed), *Studia Onomastica. Festskrift till Thorsten Andersson, 23 Feb 1989. Lund*. Stockholm : Almqvist & Wiksell, 261–278.

———. 1994. 'Viking place-names in Scotland'. *NORNA Rapporter* 54, 31–50.

———. 1995. 'Name and Appellative'. In E. Eichler et al. (eds), *Name Studies: An International Handbook of Onomastics*, vol. I. Berlin: Walter de Gruyter, 384–392.

———. 2001. *Scottish Place-Names: Their Study and Significance*. New Edition. Edinburgh: John Donald.

———. 2011. *In the Beginning was the Name. Selected Essays by W.F.H. Nicolaisen*. Lerwick: The Scottish Place-Name Society.

Oftedal, M. 1954. 'The Village Names of Lewis in the Outer Hebrides'. *Norsk tidsskrift for sprogvidenskap* 17, 363–409.

———. 1956. *The Gaelic of Leurbost. A Linguistic Survey of the Gaelic Dialects of Scotland*, vol. III. *Norsk tidsskrift for sprogvidenskap*, supplementary vol. IV. Oslo: Aschehoug.

———. 1961–62. 'On the frequency of Norse loan-words in Scottish Gaelic'. *Scottish Gaelic Studies* 9, 116–127.

———. 1962. 'Norse Place-names in Celtic Scotland'. In B. Ó Cuív (ed.), *The Impact of the Scandinavian Invasions on the Celtic-speaking Peoples c. 800–1100 AD: Introductory Papers read at Plenary Sessions of the International Congress of Celtic Studies, held in Dublin*. Dublin: Dublin Institute of Advanced Studies, 43–50.

Orkneyinga Saga. A.B. Taylor (trans.). Edinburgh: Taylor & Burt, 1938.

Sandnes, B. 2010. *From Starafjall to Starling Hill. An investigation of the formation and development of Old Norse place-names in Orkney*. The Scottish Place-Name Society. https://www.spns.org.uk/Starafjall.pdf. Accessed 16 May 2022.

Stahl, A.-B. 1999. 'Place-Names of Barra in the Outer Hebrides'. PhD thesis. University of Edinburgh.

Stewart, J. .1987. *Shetland Place-Names.* Lerwick: Shetland Library and Museum.

Stewart, T.W. 2004. 'Lexical imposition. Old Norse vocabulary in Scottish Gaelic'. *Diachronica* 21:2, 393–420.

Thomson, W.P.L. 1987. *History of Orkney.* Edinburgh: Mercat Press.

———. 1995. 'Orkney farm-names: a re-assessment of their chronology'. In B.E. Crawford (ed.), *Scandinavian Settlement in Northern Britain: Thirteen Studies of Place-Names in their Historical Context.* London: Leicester University Press, 42–62.

Vésteinsson, O. 1998. 'Patterns of Settlement in Iceland. A Study in Prehistory'. *Saga-Book* 25:1, 1–29.

Wainwright, F.T. (ed.). 1964. *The Northern Isles.* London: Nelson.

Waugh, D.J. 1998. ' "From the Inside": The Value of Local Knowledge in Onomastic Research'. In W.F.H. Nicolaisen (ed.), *Proceedings of the XIXth International Congress of Onomastic Sciences.* Aberdeen: University of Aberdeen, Department of English, 378–383.

· VII ·

Þursasker: A Note

Brian Smith

I am an admirer of Arne Kruse's essay on 'Laithlind'.[1] In this note I try to track down another mysterious geographical feature from the Viking Age, albeit a much smaller one.[2]

In the thirty-second chapter of *Orkneyinga saga*, the compiler, writing 150 years after the event, becomes lyrical about Earl Þorfinnr Sigurðarson. He says that Þorfinnr had been the most powerful of all the Orkney earls, and, ridiculously, that he 'owned nine earldoms in Scotland, and all the Hebrides, and a large realm in Ireland'.[3] He then quotes a verse by Arnórr Þórðarson, the so-called 'earls'-poet', which is likely to have been composed soon after Þorfinnr's death in the mid-eleventh century. Folk from *Þursasker* to Dublin, according to Arnórr, were forced to heed the earl:

Hringstríði varð hlýða
herr frá Þursaskerjum
— rétt segik þjóð, hvé þótti
Þórfinnr – til Dyflinnar.[4]

---

1. Kruse 2017.
2. I am very grateful to Diana Whaley for advice.
3. *Orkneyinga Saga* (trans. Taylor): 189.
4. *Poetry of Arnórr jarlaskáld* (trans. Whaley): 128.

I tell the people truth, everyone was thought to be
Thorfinn's subject from *Þursasker* to Dublin.

There is no debate about the meaning of the name. *Þursaskerjum* – in later texts *Þussaskerjum* – derives from Old Norse *þurs* ('giant'), and thus translates to 'skerries of the giants'. But where were they? There have been several suggestions. The least unconvincing, in my opinion, is the one given in 1873 by Gilbert Goudie and Jón A. Hjaltalín, the Shetlander and Icelander who were the first translators of the saga into English. They assumed, given what the saga-compiler said, and what Arnórr said, that *Þursasker* was in Ireland. Arnórr's verse, they said, 'seems to have reference only to Þorfinnr's conquests in Ireland. Doubtless the extent of these is considerably exaggerated'. I could not agree more. They suggested that the *Þursasker* was the same as the Tuskar Rock, near Rosslare Harbour, a notorious site for shipwrecks.[5]

It is not a bad idea. George W. Dasent, who translated the saga in 1894, and A. B. Taylor, translating it in 1938, reached the same conclusion.[6] Dasent adds a question mark; Taylor renders the name 'Tuscar Skerries' in both text and index. Arnórr seems to be writing about Þorfinnr's alleged realm in Ireland. He therefore gave what he thought were the Irish boundaries of it. Others, however, want *Þursasker* to be the northerly extreme of Þorfinnr's supposedly vast dominions.

The Orcadian Samuel Laing, translating *St Olaf's Saga* in the 1840s, where there is a similar version of Arnórr's verse, said that it might have been at Thurso in Caithness.[7] Carl Richard

---

5. *Orkneyinga Saga* (ed. Anderson): 44 and note. Irish toponymists have not considered the etymology of the name, but a derivation from *sker* is very likely. I am grateful to Conchubhar Ó Crualaoich for discussion.
6. *Orkneyingers' Saga* (trans. Dasent): 468; *Orkneyinga Saga* (trans. Taylor): 437.
7. *Heimskringla* (trans. Laing): 145.

Unger, the great Norwegian philologist and historian, thought the same.[8] Guðbrandur Vigfússon was the first, as far as I can see, to propose that *Þursasker* was in Shetland. He suggested that it might have been the Out Skerries, east of the Shetland mainland.[9] In 1905, Eiríkr Magnússon came up with a variety of possibilities. He said that *Þursasker* might be in Shetland or off Thurso – 'but perhaps the Giants' Causeway in Ireland is meant'.[10]

In the past sixty years, the suggestions have become wilder. Nowadays almost all commentators want *Þursasker* to be in Shetland. If you believe that Þorfinnr Sigurðarson had a vast realm, you want it to stretch from Dublin to Unst.

In the early 1960s, Finnbogi Guðmundsson, an Icelander who was editing a new edition of *Orkneyinga Saga*, came to Shetland to look for saga-places. His proposal about *Þursasker* was startling. He made the mysterious claim that it was very likely north of Unst, because there are high skerries there, or east of Whalsay, because there are smaller ones there with access to good harbours. Finnbogi said that he had followed A.B. Taylor in that idea, which (as we have seen) was not the case.[11]

Eventually Barbara Crawford took up the subject. She is convinced that Arnórr's verse is 'a succinct assessment of the [Orkney] earldom thalassocracy at its widest'.[12] So *Þursasker* must be in Shetland. Browsing in Jakob Jakobsen's work on Shetland place-names, Crawford came upon a fishing-ground called *Da Tussek*. Jakobsen said that it was in North Unst, but he gave no information about its meaning, or its exact locality.[13]

---

8. *Heimskringla* (ed. Unger): 858.
9. *Orkneyinga Saga and Magnus Saga* (ed. Gudbrand Vigfússon): 409.
10. *Stories of the Kings of Norway* (trans. Eiríkr Magnússon): 251.
11. *Orkneyinga saga* (ed. Finnbogi Guðmundsson): 81–82.
12. Crawford 2013: 162.
13. Jakobsen 1936: 168.

Crawford thought that it was 'a possible pointer to the former existence of a very similar name for skerries in that locality'. It was 'exactly the place', she thought, 'where outlying rocks (such as the Muckle Flugga group) would be well-known to Norse mariners as the first indication of the islands in the western sea'.[14]

Crawford's navigational suggestion is wrong. No one sailing from Norway to Shetland can see Muckle Flugga en route. But it is worth looking as closely as we can at *Da Tussek*.[15] The termination *-ek* suggests strongly that it is a diminutive. Peder Gammeltoft suggested to me that *Tussek* might be a name related to the Shetland dialect word *tusk*, meaning tangled hair, perhaps referring to seaweed.[16] I then noticed the word *truss-ibelt* ('a kind of long-stalked seaweed') in Jakobsen's Shetland dictionary. Noting similar seaweed words in Iceland and the Faroes – *þussaskegg* and *tussingur* – Jakobsen derived the first part of the Shetland word from Old Norse *þurs* ('giant' or 'ogre'), the same word that gave rise to *Þursasker*.[17]

We shall never know much about *Da Tussek*. We do not even know where it was in the north of Unst. The name is obsolete. But we can guess that it was a little stretch of seaweed, somewhere offshore; not a spectacle for Arnórr or Þorfinnr to get excited about. In any case – this is a complex point – the 'giant' content of each of the names (*Þursasker* and *Da Tussek*) must involve skerries or seaweed – not both!

Meanwhile, there is a complication. In *Hákonar saga Hákonarsonar*, the king of Scotland is said to have announced in 1248 that he did not mean to pause

---

14. Crawford 1987: 75.
15. I am grateful to Peder Gammeltoft for discussion about the name.
16. Jakobsen 1932: 950.
17. Jakobsen 1932: 973.

[...] *fyrr en hann hefði merki sitt sett austr em Þursasker ok undir sik unnit allt Nóregs konungs ríki, þat er hann átti fyrir vestan Sólundarhaf.* [18]

[...] before he had set his standard east in Þursasker, and brought under himself all the Norwegian king's dominion that he owned to the west of the Solund Sea.[19]

P.A. Munch, perhaps with Arnórr's verse in mind, thought that King Alexander's *Þursasker* 'must have been a rock or skerry eastward either of Orkney or Shetland, the place of which we have not been able to find'.[20] But the saga says that 'Alexander was very greedy for the [Norwegian] realm in the Southern Isles' (*Suðreyjar*) – that is, the Hebrides. As a result, the most recent editors of the saga say that this *Þursasker* was west of the Hebrides, and not in the north at all.[21]

Summing up: it seems to me likely that (a) the name *Þursasker*, in *Orkneyinga saga* and *Hákonar saga Hákonarsonar*, refers to different places; (b) both places were in the west, in Ireland and the Hebrides, rather than the north; or even that (c) the term refers to far-flung imaginary places. My last option is perhaps least likely; if it is right, I suspect that the name would appear more frequently in literary sources. I propose that there is more than one *Þursasker*, both in the west.

Bibliography

Crawford, B.E. 1987. *Scandinavian Scotland.* Leicester: Leicester
   University Press.

---

18. *Hákonar saga Hákonarsonar* (ed. Sverrir Jakobsson et al.): 146.
19. The Solund Sea is between Norway and Scotland.
20. *Chronicle of Man* (ed. Munch): 106n.
21. *Hákonar saga Hákonarsonar* (ed. Sverrir Jakobsson et al.): 337.

———. 2013. *The Northern Earldoms, Orkney and Caithness from A.D. 870 to 1470*. Edinburgh: John Donald.

Hákonar saga Hákonarsonar, vol. II. 2013. Sverrir Jakobsson, Þorleifur Hauksson, and Tor Ulset (eds.). Reykjavík: Hið Íslenzka Fornritafélag.

Heimskringla eller Norges kongesagaer af Snorre Sturlasson. 1868. C.R. Unger (ed.). Christiania: Brøgger and Christie.

Heimskringla, or chronicle of the kings of Norway, vol. II. 1844. Samuel Laing (trans.). London: Longman, Brown, Green and Longmans. 1844

Jakobsen, J. 1932. *An Etymological Dictionary of the Norn Language in Shetland*, vol. II. London and Copenhagen: David Nutt and Vilhelm Prior.

———. 1936. *The Place-Names of Shetland*. London and Copenhagen: David Nutt and Vilhelm Prior.

Kruse, Arne. 2017. 'The Norway to be: Laithlind and Avaldsnes'. In Christian Cooijmans (ed.), *Traversing the Inner Seas: Contacts and Continuity in and around Scotland, the Hebrides, and the North of Ireland*. Edinburgh: Scottish Society for Northern Studies, 198–231.

Orkneyinga Saga. 1938. A.B. Taylor (trans.). Edinburgh and London: Oliver and Boyd.

Orkneyinga Saga. 1965. Finnbogi Guðmundsson (ed.). Reykjavík: Hið Íslenzka Fornritafélag.

Orkneyinga Saga and Magnus Saga. 1887. Gudbrand Vigfusson (ed.). London: H.M.S.O.

The Chronicle of Man and the Sudreys. 1860. P.A. Munch (ed.). Christiania: Brøgger and Christie.

The Orkneyinga Saga. 1873. J. Anderson (ed.). Edinburgh: Edmonston and Douglas.

The Orkneyingers' Saga. 1894. Sir G.W. Dasent (trans.). London: H.M.S.O.

The Poetry of Arnórr jarlaskáld. 1998. Diana Whaley (trans.). London: Brepols.

The Stories of the Kings of Norway called the Round of the World (Heimskringla), vol. IV. 1905. Eiríkr Magnússon (trans.). London: Bernard Quaritch.

· VIII ·

Norse Shielings in Caithness:
'A Perverse Distribution'

Ryan Foster

I initially contacted Arne about a potential part-time PhD project in Edinburgh. He suggested that I apply for the recently advertised Northern Scholars Scholarship, which I duly did and was exceptionally lucky to be awarded. Arne then took on the role of one of my supervisors, and it is that project that this chapter is based on. Arne was brilliant as a supervisor; he is a superb scholar, highly organised, thorough, methodical, and logical in his approach. The stress of supervising me – a dyslexic geographer with a grasshopper brain – should not be underestimated, but he took it all with his usual good humour and calm demeanour. It was a pleasure and a privilege to have spent four happy years under his guidance, and I feel deeply honoured to have been asked to contribute to this volume.

Introduction

The use of shielings as part of an infield-outfield system has been characteristic of Scandinavian farming from the Iron Age and into the modern period. The infield around the home farm was used to grow cereal crops and hay, and was surrounded by the *garðr* ('fence') separating it from the outfield.[1] Shielings were secondary farming units found in the outfield and inhabited by people with livestock during the summer months. This removed livestock from the farm, protecting the hay and crops,[2] and also provided areas of fresh grazing for livestock, the opportunity to collect winter fodder, and complete ancillary tasks, such as hunting, iron working, textile manufacturing, and some dairying.[3] The export of this type of farming system has been suggested through onomastic evidence in Britain,[4] as well as archaeological evidence in the Faroes,[5] Iceland,[6] and Greenland.[7]

In Norway, shielings are most commonly referred to as *sætr*,[8] though there are regional variations.[9] *Sætr* was also the most commonly used generic to denote shielings in Scandinavian settlements around the North Atlantic, with two exceptions, *sel* (n.) in Iceland[10] and *ærgi* in Britain[11] and the Faroes.[12] Whereas *sel* was an Old Norse (ON) element and used as a shieling name – albeit with a limited distribution in Norway[13] – *ærgi* was a loanword from Gaelic.[14] In the Hebrides, Northern Isles, and Cumbria, *ærgi* would seem to have been used as a shieling name in more fertile locations than *sætr*-names.[15] I have

---

1. Øye 2005: 360.
2. Zimmermann 1999: 315.
3. Øye 2004: 91; Bjørgo 2005: 219, 225.
4. Pearsall 1961; Whyte 1985; Fellows-Jensen 1980.
5. Dahl 1970; Mahler 1991; 1993; 2007.
6. Hitzler 1979; Guðrún Sveinbjarnardóttir 1991.
7. Albrethsen and Keller 1986.
8. Beito 1949: 274–275.
9. Beito 1949.
10. Guðrún Sveinbjarnardóttir 1991: 91.
11. Pearsall 1961; Fellows-Jensen 1985; Whyte 1985; Higham 1996; Foster 2018.
12. Dahl 1970; Mahler 1991; 1993; 2007.
13. Beito 1949: 118–122.
14. Fellows-Jensen 1980: 67.
15. Pearsall 1961: 84; Fellows-Jensen 1985: 74; Whyte 1985: 105; Higham

argued elsewhere that the link between *ærgi*-names and more fertile locations is due to the need for richer grazing to fulfil the nutritional demands of lactating cattle.[16] The one exception is Caithness, where *sætr*-names would seem to be located on more favourable sites when compared to *ærgi*-names.[17] The aim of this chapter is to examine why the distribution of *sætr*- and *ærgi*-names in Caithness seems so atypical or perverse.

Definitions

The most common place-name element for an ON shieling in Scotland is derived from either *setr* (n.) or *sætr* (n.),[18] which under the influence of Gaelic often take the form of *siadar/ seadar*.[19] *Setr* had the meaning of (1) 'seat, residence', or (2) 'a mountain pasture or dairy lands'; while *sætr* was a specific term for a mountain pasture.[20] It is now impossible to distinguish between the two elements in Scottish place-names,[21] even if both elements were present in Scotland,[22] and for simplicity they will be referred to as *sætr* hereafter.

Ærgi (n.) has the same definition as *sætr*,[23] and has traditionally been taken as adopted from the Scottish Gaelic *àirigh* (f.), meaning either 'hill pasture' or 'shieling'.[24] However, several scholars have suggested that the original meaning of *ærgi* may

---

1996: 56; Foster 2017: 124–125; 2018: 496.

16. Foster 2017: 128; 2018: 504.

17. Foster 2018: 381–397, 465–488.

18. Beito 1949: 11–84.

19. Nicolaisen 1969, 13; Cox 1990, 95–98.

20. Cleasby and Vigfússon 1874: 525, 619; Haegstad and Torp 1909: 370, 451.

21. Crawford 1987: 102–103.

22. Cox 1990: 111.

23. Cleasby and Vigfússon 1874: 133, 619; Haegstad and Torp 1909: 546.

24. MacBain 1911: 10.

have been closer to the Old Irish *áirge* (f.),[25] being a 'herd of cattle', a 'pasture', a 'herdsman's hut', or a 'milk herd'.[26] However, the difference in meaning between the Old Irish and Scottish Gaelic terms may have developed from agricultural changes that occurred in the post-Norse period.[27]

Ærgi is one of only a handful of Gaelic words adopted into ON.[28] By comparison, Peder Gammeltoft found around 200 ON words adopted into Scottish Gaelic.[29] Contact linguistic theory suggests that language borrowing usually occurs in one direction when two languages meet, with the less prestigious language borrowing from the more prestigious one.[30] The difference in the number of words adopted by the respective languages would suggest that ON had been the more prestigious during the Viking Age. The adoption of *ærgi* is therefore unusual, and all the more so when considering that ON already had its own term for a shieling.[31]

The reasons behind why ON speakers adopted *ærgi* led to a long-running debate between Mary Higham[32] and Gillian Fellows-Jensen.[33] One solution to this problem can be found in Uriel Weinreich's 'concrete loanwords'[34] and Carol Myers-Scotton's theory of cultural borrowing.[35] The two theories involve the adoption of words that cover new ideas, concepts, or objects.

---

25. Cox 1992: 139; 2002: 220; Macniven 2015: 69; Foster 2018: 463; Edmonds 2019: 166.
26. Dineen 1904: 24.
27. Cox 2002: 122–123; Raven 2005: 384, 463; James 2009: 54.
28. Cox 1991: 486.
29. Gammeltoft 2004: 63–64.
30. Weinreich 1968: 3; Myers-Scotton 2002: 41.
31. Weinreich 1968: 1–3.
32. Higham 1977–78; 1996.
33. Fellows-Jensen 1977–78; 1980; 2002.
34. Weinreich 1968: 56–58.
35. Myers-Scotton 2002: 41.

Weinreich suggests that there are three possibilities when there are two competing words for the same object or idea: (1) confusion in usage, leading to the abandonment of one of the terms; (2) the replacement of the old word with the foreign term; or (3) the specialisation over time of the old and new term.[36]

The continued use of *sætr* alongside *ærgi* in Cumbria[37] and Sutherland[38] would seem to rule out options one and two, leaving only option three, a specialisation in usage.[39] I have suggested that ON *sætr* encompassed a more general meaning of summer grazing and winter fodder collection, possibly with some dairying.[40] Scandinavian settlers to Gaelic-speaking areas of the Irish Sea encountered the intensive dairy shieling, a new concept to them.[41] The adoption of *ærgi* most likely fulfilled a 'need-filling motive' in ON as their own term did not sufficiently cover this new concept.[42]

Location and physical geography

Caithness occupies the far north-eastern part of mainland Scotland, separated from the rest of the mainland by Sutherland and from Orkney by the Pentland Firth. The area forms a rough triangle, running around 49 km from the northern tip at Duncansby Head to Reay in the west, then south-east from Reay, 49 km south to the Ord of Caithness. Sutherland – ON *suðrland* ('southern land') – lies to the west and south, isolating Caithness from the rest

---

36. Weinreich 1968: 54–56.
37. Oram 2000: 248.
38. Fraser 1979: 19–20; 1986: 29.
39. Foster 2018: 504–505.
40. Bjørgo 2005: 225.
41. Foster 2018: 506.
42. Anttila 1989: 155.

of Mainland Scotland. Doreen Waugh has made a compelling argument that the whole northern coastline of Scotland could be considered as part of Caithness in the Viking Age.[43]

Figure 1: Map of Northern Scotland.

The landscape of Caithness is formed from Middle Old Red Sandstone, which was created in a lacustrine environment

---

43. Waugh 2000: 22–23.

and has produced a low-lying, gently sloping landscape. There is a change in geology along the south-western border with Sutherland, where the land becomes more mountainous, as the bedrock changes to metamorphosed fine-grained semipelite and igneous intrusions of felsic Strath Halladale granites.[44]

Figure 2: Photograph of Assary, Caithness, possible site of *Ásgrimsærgin* ('Ásgrim's-*ærgi*') in *Orkneyinga saga* (author's photo).

Overlaying this geology are wide expanses of blanket peat, peaty gleys, and peaty podzols, which cover around 65% of Caithness.[45] Blanket peat forms an acidic, nutrient-deficient soil that is used for rough grazing.[46] It covers much of the west and the south-west of Caithness, and includes a band

44. 'Onshore GeoIndex', *British Geological Survey*, https://mapapps2.bgs. ac.uk/geoindex/home.html. Accessed 30 July 2021.
45. Board of Agriculture for Scotland 1912: 52–57.
46. *Scotland's Soils*, https://map.environment.gov.scot/Soil_maps/?layer=5#. Accessed 30 July 2021.

running up to the far north-east. There are scattered pockets of more fertile alluvial and brown forest soils, the latter forming a discontinuous band along the north-west and with pockets along the south-east coast. There are two small areas of humus iron podzols, one around Reay in the north-west and a second smaller one just north of the Ord of Caithness. Though these soils are naturally acidic and nutrient deficient, they are improvable and are often converted to growing arable crops.[47]

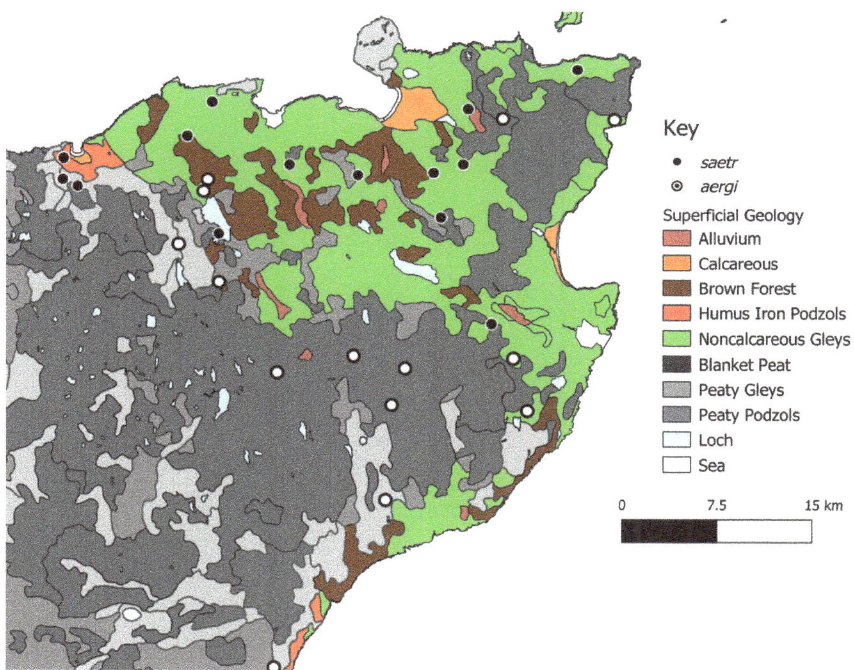

Figure 3: Map of superficial geology in Caithness (Soils 250K shapefile copyright and database right: The James Hutton Institute, used with permission. All rights reserved).[48]

47. 'Humus-Iron Podzols', *The James Hutton Institute*, https://www.hutton.ac.uk/learning/exploringscotland/soils/humusironpodzols. Accessed 30 July 2021.
48. *The James Hutton Institute*, https://www.hutton.ac.uk. Accessed 7 August 2018.

Noncalcareous gleys are the second most common soil in Caithness, being found along much of the coastline and also forming a wide band between Reay and Wick. Being naturally poorly drained, they are usually exploited as grazing land.[49] However, in Caithness, they are often used for arable farming, but this requires artificial drainage, and it is likely that their use in arable production was less widespread in prehistory.

Climate

Rainfall is relatively low across Caithness and varies between 800 mm in the north-east to 1100 mm a year in the south-west. Temperatures are generally lower at more northern latitudes, but there is also a split between coastal and inland locations. In winter, coastal areas are warmer, but in summer the opposite is true, inland sites reaching a maximum temperature of 18.1°C inland, while along the coast this is between 16.2–16.6°C.[50] At Wick John O'Groats Airport and Strathy East along the coast (both 36 m asl), minimum air temperature rises above the growing degree-day[51] from May until October, which gives a six-month growing season.[52] The growing degree-day is the average daily air temperature needed for plant growth to start, and for grass this is around 5°C. At Kinbrace (103 m asl), situated 23 km inland, the growing season drops to only four

---

49. 'Noncalcareous Gleys', *The James Hutton Institute*, https://www.hutton.ac.uk/learning/exploringscotland/soils/noncalcareousgleys. Accessed 30 July 2021.
50. 'UK climate averages (Kinbrace, Sutherland, Strathy East, Sutherland Wick John O'Groats Airport)', *Met Office*, https://www.metoffice.gov.uk/research/climate/maps-and-data/uk-climate-averages. Accessed 30 July 2021.
51. Skaugen and Tveito 2004: 221.
52. 'UK climate averages', *Met Office*, https://www.metoffice.gov.uk/research/climate/maps-and-data/uk-climate-averages. Accessed 30 July 2021.

months (June–September), which also experiences eighty-six days of air frost, compared to forty-three to forty-five days at coastal sites.

A cool climate in Caithness leads to low levels of evapo-transpiration, which means some soils can still be considered as wet, despite low levels of precipitation.[53] The available water capacity of soils is the volume of water a soil can provide for plant growth and is heavily linked to soil type. The calcareous soils found around Sinclair's Bay and the eastern part of Dunnet Bay have an available water capacity of only 47.63 mm. This increases to between 138.95 mm to 161.15 mm for the brown forest soils and noncalcareous gleys, while blanket bog has an available water capacity of 504.59 mm.[54]

Distribution

In Caithness, ON shieling names exhibit a complementary distribution, with distinct and separate concentrations of each place-name element. *Sætr*-names are found in an arc parallel to the northern coastline, stretching from Braxside in Reay Parish in the west to Seater in Canisbay Parish (Figure 4). There are small concentrations of *sætr*-names in Reay, Thurso, and Bower Parishes. The most southern example in Caithness is Thuster in Wick Parish, though it should be noted that there are some examples further south in Sutherland (see Figure 5).[55]

---

53. Futty and Towers 1982: 9.
54. *Scotland's Soils*, https://map.environment.gov.scot/Soil_maps/?layer=5#. Accessed 30 July 2021.
55. Fraser 1979: 19–20; 1986: 29.

Table 1: Old Norse shieling names in Caithness.

Sætr	Specific element	*Ærgi*	Specific element
Braxside, NC951634	ON *brekka* ('slope') or ScG *breac* ('variegated in colour')[56]	Assary, ND062624	ON *Ásgrimr* (m., personal name)[57]
Brimside, ND049669	ON *brim* (n., 'surf')[58]	Badrinsary,[59] ND118240	
Carriside, ND074590	ON *Kári* (m., personal name)[60]	Blingery, ND306489	ON *Blæingr* (m., personal name)[61]
Fryster, ND184638	ON *Friði* (m., personal name) or ON *Frey* or *Freyja*[62]	Dorrery,[63] ND074550	
Helshetter, NC963628	ON *hella* (f., 'a flat stretch of rock')[64]	Golsary, ND206375	
Hunster, ND243640	ON *Húni* (m., personal name)	Halsary, ND180491	*Hall* or ON *Hallvard* (m., personal name)[65]
Reaster, ND257654	ON *hreysi* (n., 'heap of stones')[66]	Kensary, ND221481	
Sandside, NC952652	ON *sandr* (m., 'sand, shore')[67]	Leurary, ND065634	
Seater, ND357725	simplex[68]	Munsary,[69] ND211452	
Seater, ND249603	simplex	Raggra, ND317446	ON *Ragi* (m., personal name)[70]
Shalmstry, ND130647	ON *Hiálmr* (m., personal name)[71]	Scoolary, ND298684	ON *Skúli* (m., personal name)[72]
Syster, ND270691	ON *sjár* (m., 'the sea')[73]	Shurrery, ND042581	ON *Sióvarr/ Sævarr* (m., a personal name)[74]
Thuster, ND289517	ON *þuríðr* (m., personal name[75]	Skirza, ND387682	ON *Skerrir* (m., personal name[76]
Thuster, ND068698	ON *þuríðr* (m., personal name), possibly ON *Fjós-* from ON *fé-hús* ('cow house')[77]	Smerary, ND120478	ON *smjör* ('butter')[78]

56. Waugh 1985: 65.
57. Waugh 1993: 123–124.
58. Waugh 1985: 147.
59. Waugh 1993: 124.
60. Waugh 1995: 75.
61. MacBain 1922: 290; Waugh 1993: 123–124.

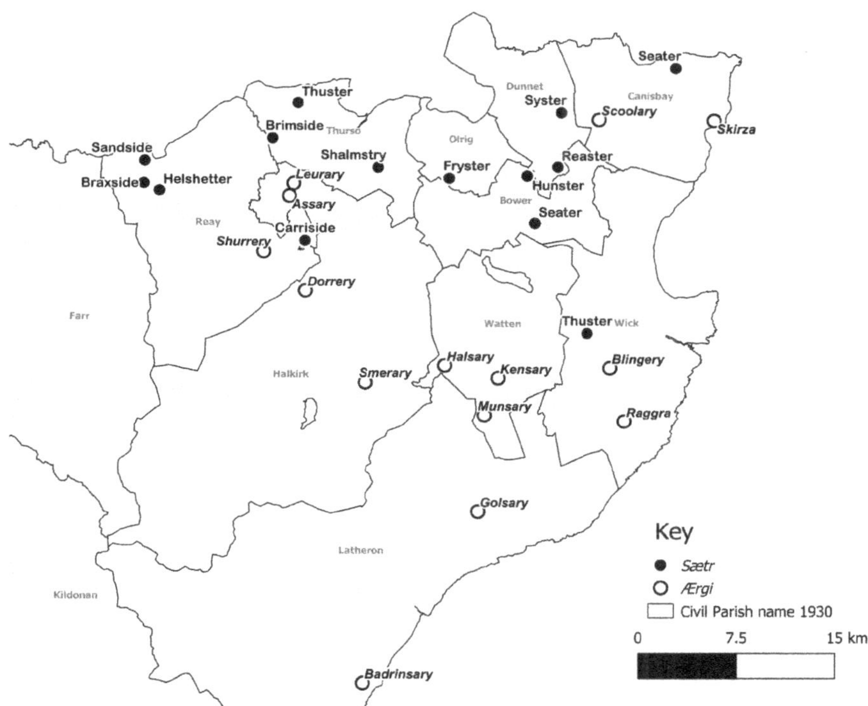

Figure 4: Map of *sætr*- and *ærgi*-names in Caithness.

62. Waugh 1985: 216.
63. MacBain 1922: 173, 290.
64. Waugh 1985: 74.
65. MacBain 1922: 173, 290.
66. Waugh 1985: 258
67. Waugh 1995: 80.
68. Waugh 1985: 306–307.
69. Waugh 1993: 123–124.
70. Ibid.
71. Waugh 1985: 169.
72. Ibid.: 306.
73. Ibid.: 16.
74. Ibid.: 81; Waugh 1993: 123–124.
75. Gammeltoft 2001: 313.
76. Waugh 1985: 308; 1987: 103.
77. Waugh 1985: 175.
78. For similar derivation, see Fellows-Jensen 1980: 70.

Ærgi-names in comparison are found inland and further to the south than *sætr*-names, with a distribution pattern concentrated in Halkirk, Wick, Watten and Latheron Parish. Two outliers, Scoolary and Skirza,[79] are found in the most north-eastern parish of Canisbay. In Halkirk Parish, Assary has been suggested as the *Ásgrimsærgin* ('Ásgrim's-*ærgi*') from *Orkneyinga saga*,[80] the only known reference in ON literature to an *ærgi*-name.

Comparison of location factors

There is little difference in the altitude of shieling names in the Northern Isles, Hebrides, or Cumbria, with an average difference of only around 5–9 m. However, in Caithness, ærgi-names are found at almost twice the altitude of *sætr*-names; even so, the difference is only around 40 m, with 71% still below 100 m asl and all below 150 m asl.

Sætr-names have a more coastal distribution than *ærgi*-names (except in Cumbria), with *ærgi*-names some 300 m further inland in the Hebrides and Northern Isles. Caithness is somewhat of an anomaly in this respect, as *ærgi*-names are on average 2,500 m further inland than *sætr*-names. Proximity to the coast is normally indicative of an agriculturally more favourable position, with flatter land, deeper and more fertile soil, and the ameliorating effect of the sea in winter. However, in the Western and Northern Isles, high winds increase the risk of damage from salt spray to coastal vegetation.[81] Although inland locations are less likely to suffer from salt spray, there is a trade-off with a cooler climate, which could delay the start

---

79. Waugh 1985: 103.
80. Fellows-Jensen 1980: 67; 2002: 91.
81. Hudson et al. 1982: 15; Jóhansen 1985: 63.

of the growing season.[82] This would suggest the *sætr*-names in Caithness were located in far more favourable locations than *ærgi*-names.

Table 2: Location factors of shielings from selected Scandinavian settlement areas (the number of sites is given in brackets).

		Hebrides		Northern Isles		Cumbria		Caithness	
		sætr- (59)	*ærgi-* (44)	*sætr-* (196)	*ærgi-* (10)	*sætr-* (24)	*ærgi-* (26)	*sætr-* (14)	*ærgi-* (14)
Altitude (m asl)	Mean	53	44	33	38	141	135	46	90
	Median	40	45	30	30	151	125	45	90
Distance from sea (m)	Mean	885	1246	724	1056	21136	16930	4789	7415
	Median	543	1030	489	500	24330	16210	4445	6585
Soil (%)	Fertile	23	37	16	21	0	15	14	14
	Moderately fertile	22	21	40	21	17	19	64	29
	Infertile	55	42	44	58	83	66	22	57
Modern Vegetation (%)	Arable	17	18	20	21	37	38	26	24
	Grassland	22	21	30	24.5	12	38	28	24
	Damp grassland	17	22	15	27.5	33	17	26	18
	Rough grazing	44	38	35	27	18	7	20	34

Ærgi-names are more likely located on fertile soils than *sætr*-names in all areas except Caithness, where 14% of both

---

82. Anslow and Green 1967: 118.

sætr- and *ærgi*-names are located on these soils. In the Hebrides and Cumbria, around 20% of both *sætr*- and *ærgi*-names are located on moderately fertile soils. In the Northern Isles, 40% of *sætr*-names are on moderately fertile soils, while in Caithness this rises to 64%, compared to only 29% of *ærgi*-names. Around 35% more *sætr*-names than *ærgi*-names are located on moderately fertile soils in Caithness, while *ærgi*-names are 35% more likely to be located on infertile soils. When considering soil fertility, ON shieling names in Caithness would seem to be an anomaly.

Discussion

Overall, when comparing soil fertility and height above sea level, Caithness does not conform to the perceived view that *ærgi*-names were located in more favourable locations than *sætr*-names. However, the idea that *ærgi*-names in Caithness are atypical is not as clear-cut as at first glance. The difference in altitude between *ærgi*- and *sætr*-names is at best marginal and is likely to have had a minimal effect on the growing season. The more inland location of *ærgi*-names in Caithness have colder and longer winters,[83] giving a shorter growing season.[84] Shielings in the *Gulathing* law code were only occupied from around 14 June,[85] which would coincide with the start of the

---

83. July temperature inland at Kinbrace (103m asl) 18.1°C and 16.2°C at the coastal site of Wick John O'Groats Airport (36m asl). 'UK climate averages', *Met Office*, https://www.metoffice.gov.uk/research/climate/maps-and-data/uk-climate-averages. Accessed 30 July 2021.
84. Minimum air temperature of 5°C: June–September at Kinbrace (103m asl) and May–October at Wick John O'Groats Airport (36m asl). 'UK climate averages', *Met Office*, https://www.metoffice.gov.uk/research/climate/maps-and-data/uk-climate-averages. Accessed 30 July 2021.
85. Earliest Norwegian Laws: 94 (G81).

growing season at inland locations in Caithness. This would mean that there would be fresh grass for the livestock as they arrived at the shieling.

What is atypical is that *ærgi*-names in Caithness, when compared to *sætr*-names, are more likely to be located on soils classed as infertile and with vegetation classed as rough grazing. Around 71% of *sætr*-names are located on soils with less than 200 mm available water capacity, compared to only 43% of *ærgi*-names. *Ærgi*-names are twice as likely to be located on soils with an available water capacity exceeding 350 mm.[86] This would suggest *ærgi*-names were preferentially located on damper soils, reducing the risk of water stress. One factor which may help explain this is the geology of Caithness – sandstone is permeable, allowing water to more freely percolate down through the soil. Alongside low precipitation levels, this increases the possibility of water stress for plants during dry periods. Water stress occurs when water extraction from the soil by roots is lower than that lost through respiration, leading to wilting and reduced photosynthesis.

The higher soil moisture capacity of peat-based soils may have been attractive in regions at risk of summer drought. These damper soils could help promote plant growth over a longer period, especially if grazed or used for hay. A key component of damp grassland are sedges (*Carex spp.*) and rushes (*Juncus spp.*). Torstein Garmo found these to be higher in crude protein and lower in crude fibre than grass species between July to August.[87] Dairy cows have been shown to select a diet with a higher protein content to produce milk.[88] This would suggest that the 'perverse' distribution of

---

86. *Scotland's Soils*, https://map.environment.gov.scot/Soil_maps/?layer=5#. Accessed 30 July 2021.
87. Garmo 1986: 17.
88. Tolkamp et al. 1998: 2669; Sæther et al. 2006: 385.

ærgi-names in Caithness is more illusionary than real when seen from the perspective of dairying. Interestingly, despite over half of *ærgi*-names being located on what are considered infertile soils, only a third are classed as rough grazing, while half are utilised as arable. Similarly, in South Uist, *ærgi*-names were preferentially situated on the Blacklands,[89] formed from a mix of peaty soils and windblown calcareous sand,[90] which has formed the basis of settlement since the Middle Ages.[91]

The lack of *sætr*-names in Southern Caithness may suggest that *sætr* had been abandoned in favour of *ærgi* by these Norse settlers.[92] However, there are a small number of *sætr*-names scattered throughout Sutherland (Figure 5). While many of those found along the northern coastline may be considered as part of the original settlement of Caithness,[93] three *sætr*-names are located in southern portion of Sutherland: Linsidemore (NH541991– ScG *Lionsaid*, ON *línsætr*, 'flax shieling'); Hòrasaid (NC886189 – ON *Þoris/Þorirs-sætr*, '*Thori*- or *Thorir's* shieling');[94] and Bosset (NC449058 – ON *búsætr*, 'cattle shieling').[95] The location of these three *sætr*-names and the fact that both generics were still active place-name elements during the later settlement of North-West England would strongly suggest *sætr* had not been replaced by *ærgi*.[96]

---

89. Foster 2017: 128.
90. Owen et al. 1996: 128.
91. Parker Pearson 2012: 14–15.
92. Kruse 2007: 7–8.
93. Waugh 2000: 22–23.
94. Watson 1905–6: 366.
95. Fraser 1979: 19–20; 1986: 29.
96. Wainwright 1948: 147–169; Foster 2021: 1–10.

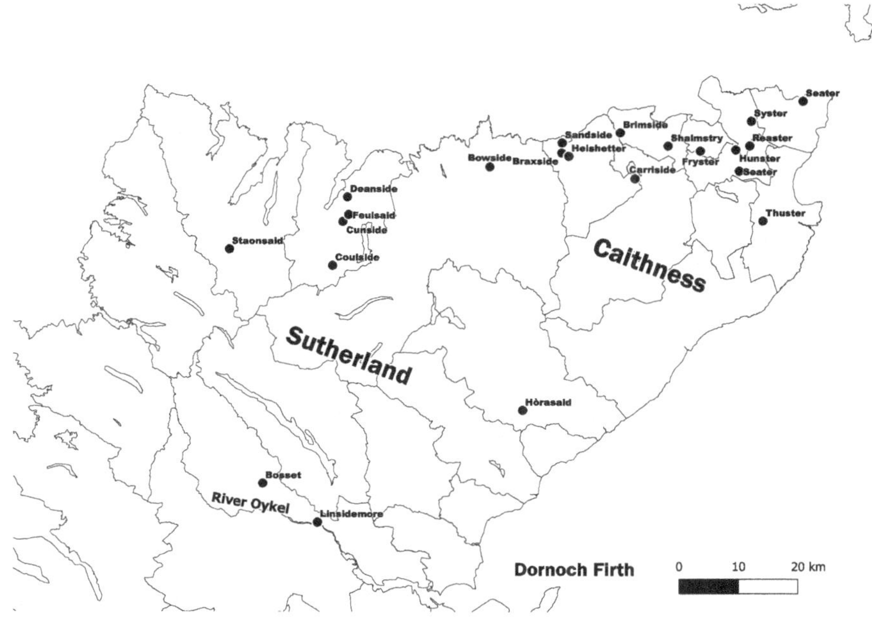

Figure 5: Map of *sætr*-names in Caithness and Sutherland (Soils 250K shapefile copyright and database right The James Hutton Institute, used with permission. All rights reserved).[97]

This distribution pattern of *sætr*-names could be explained by the scarcity of fertile land, which limited settlement. In Figure 6, areas of fertile soils are relatively small and scattered, both west and south of Caithness. South of Caithness, there are no large areas of fertile soil until the Dornoch Firth. The best soils for agriculture in this area are the small pockets of brown forest soil or humus iron podzols along some of the larger river valleys. Each fertile pocket which could be utilised for arable is separated by wide expanses of infertile peat, limiting settlement density. The function of a shieling in Norse agriculture was to provide summer grazing for cattle, which were needed to provide manure to fertilise the arable crops in the infield.

---

97. *The James Hutton Institute*, https://www.hutton.ac.uk. Accessed 7 August 2018.

When this aspect of Norse farming is considered, the scarcity of shieling names can be explained by the lack of arable land. What can be seen in Figure 6 is that where pockets of fertile soil do occur, an ON shieling name is also found close by.

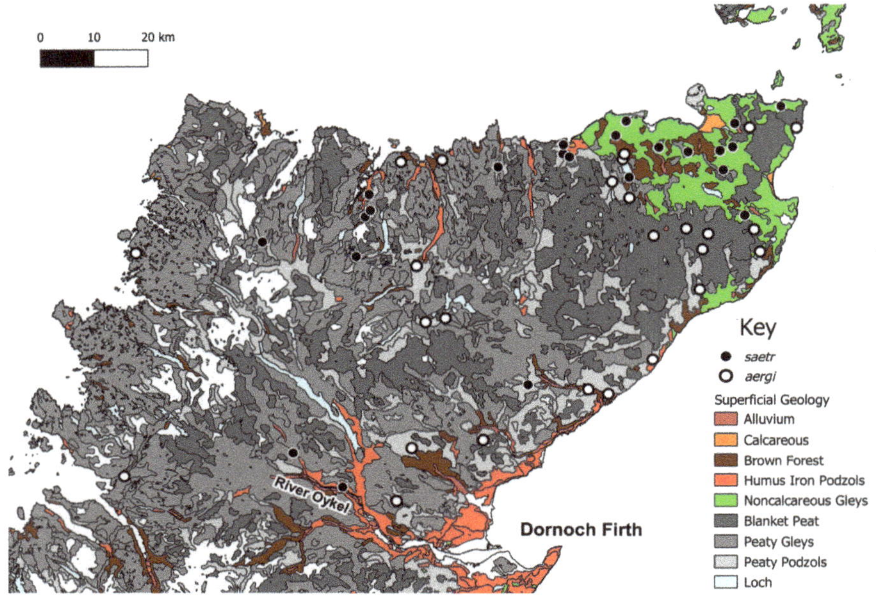

Figure 6: Map of superficial geology and Old Norse shieling names in Northern Scotland.

However, it is highly likely that the present distribution pattern has also been influenced by later language change. In the post-Norse period, eastern Caithness experienced a language shift from ON to Scots, and in western Caithness from ON to Gaelic and then to Scots.[98] The area with the greatest concentration of ON names in northern Caithness is also the most fertile. This would translate to a large ON-speaking population, which would not only increase the likelihood of ON

---

98. Bangor-Jones 1995: 82–83; Waugh 1995: 66.

place-names becoming cemented into the landscape,[99] but also act as a barrier to the introduction of Gaelic. It is in this region, where ON survived longest, that *sætr* is most commonly found, while *ærgi* in comparison predominates in areas that were more extensively Gaelic-speaking in the post-Norse period, such as Sutherland.[100] *Ærgi*, being a cognate of Gaelic *àirigh*, may have been more easily recognised and accepted by Gaelic speakers, making it more likely to survive.[101] *Sætr*, having no cognate in Gaelic, would be unintelligible to Gaelic speakers and consequently more likely to be replaced by a Gaelic term in areas where Gaelic came to predominate.[102]

The impact of language change on place-name survival[103] could arguably be best seen around the Dornoch Firth. This represents the first large area of fertile soil travelling south from Caithness. The area has some surviving Norse habitational names in the area,[104] and further south, there is possible evidence for it acting as a political centre with the names Dingwall – ON *þing-vǫllr* ('assembly field') – and Scatwell – ON *skattr-vǫllr* ('tax-field').[105] However, despite these names suggesting an established Norse presence, there are relatively few other ON names.[106]

The Dornoch Firth lies close to the old Pictish heartland of Moray,[107] which was also an area where Gaelic power and

---

99. Thomason 2001: 69–70; Gammeltoft 2006: 53; Caldwell 2008: 29.

100. Small 1986: 209; McNeill and MacQueen 2000: 426; Kruse 2005: 162; Gammeltoft 2006: 65; Jennings and Kruse 2009b: 95; Foster 2018: 346.

101. For similar conclusions on Islay, see Macniven 2015: 64.

102. Caldwell 2008: 29; Macniven 2015: 64.

103. Jennings and Kruse 2009a: 141, 138–143; Oram and Adderley 2011: 131–132; Macniven: 2013: 7.

104. Fraser 1986: 29–31; Jennings and Kruse 2009a: 143.

105. Crawford 1986: 34; Small 1986: 205.

106. Fraser 1986: 29; Small 1986: 206–209.

107. Nicolaisen 1982: 76.

language had become increasingly important.[108] The distance from other centres of Norse influence, combined with the proximity to the centre of Pictish and later Gaelic power, may have led to language shift away from Norse at a relatively early date. The pressure to adopt Gaelic is likely to have been even greater on any small populations of ON speakers found on the isolated pockets of fertile land to the north of Dornoch.[109]

This, however, does not fully explain why there is a complementary distribution of shieling names in Caithness itself. A similar distribution pattern of *sætr*- and *ærgi*-names can be seen between the Isle of Lewis and the Uists in the Western Isles,[110] but this is less evident in Cumbria.[111] I would argue that this may indicate a difference in chronology in the Scandinavian settlement of the Western Isles and north-eastern Caithness when compared to Cumbria. Caithness is believed to have been settled relatively early in the Viking Age, c. AD 800.[112] The Pentland Firth (ON *Pettlandsfjörðr*) separates Orkney from Caithness. The name would suggest that Norse settlers in Orkney knew that the land opposite was inhabited by Picts[113] and would also suggest that Caithness was settled after Orkney.[114]

A lack of characteristically Pictish names in Caithness[115] led Doreen Waugh to suggest that Scandinavian settlers imposed a new settlement pattern and land-use system, which replaced the original names.[116] Caithness and Lewis have both been

---

108. Nicolaisen 1993: 257; Shepherd 1993: 85–86; Crawford and Taylor 2003: 9.
109. Small 1986: 208; Jennings and Kruse 2009a: 141.
110. Foster 2017: 113.
111. Foster 2018: 35; 2021: 6.
112. Nicolaisen 1982: 75; Waugh 1987: 99.
113. Nicolaisen 1982: 76.
114. Waugh 1985: 2–3: Crawford and Taylor 2003: 2.
115. Nicolaisen 1982: 76.
116. Waugh 1985: 2–3; 1993: 124.

suggested as Pictish-speaking, a Brittonic-related language,[117] in the pre-Viking Age.[118] In Lewis[119] and Caithness, there are a few exceptions to what would seem a Norse onomastic whitewash. There is, however, no way of identifying whether many of these non-Norse names are pre-Norse, post-Norse, or formed during the Viking Age.[120]

Caithness – ON *Katanes* ('headland of the cats') – is one example of an ON name that incorporates a pre-Norse specific element,[121] which Nicolaisen suggests is probably the Gaelic term *cat* (m., 'cat').[122] There is little evidence to suggest that Caithness was Gaelic-speaking in the pre-Norse period.[123] However, Gaelic may have started to make inroads into Sutherland from around AD 800[124] and in western Caithness from the mid-ninth century.[125] Nicolaisen has suggested that the name *cat* was bestowed on the people by their Gaelic neighbours to the south,[126] though the element may well be a Pictish rather than a Gaelic term.

Doreen Waugh,[127] following Nicolaisen, proposed that ON-speaking settlers to Caithness encountered Gaelic speakers as they expanded their settlement to the south.[128] Waugh proposed that the complementary distribution of shielings in Caithness represented a contact zone between ON and

117. Jackson 1955: 129–166; Wainwright 1962: 91–112.
118. Bannerman 1974: 28; Taylor 2016: 4.
119. Fraser 1974: 19; Fellows-Jensen 1984: 152–153; Kruse 2004: 104;
2005: 158; Jennings and Kruse 2005: 251; Gammeltoft 2006: 65.
120. Waugh 1993: 120–121.
121. Nicolaisen 1982: 77.
122. Ibid.
123. Ibid.
124. Bangor-Jones 1995: 82–83.
125. Nicolaisen 1982: 80.
126. Ibid.: 76.
127. Doreen Waugh 1993: 123–124.
128. Nicolaisen 1982: 80.

Gaelic.[129] She suggested that it was along the edge of this onomastic contact zone where a higher number of Gaelic speakers led to the adoption and use of *ærgi* for a shieling.

However, the parish of Reay has evidence for the earliest and most intense Gaelic influence, containing twenty-two out of twenty-four Gaelic *achadh*-names ('field' and later 'farm') in Caithness.[130] Surprisingly, considering the density of Gaelic names, it is *sætr* that outnumbers *ærgi* by four to one. Whereas in Canisbay, in the extreme north-east, the ratio is two to one for *ærgi* to *sætr*, despite a complete lack of evidence for Gaelic ever being spoken there.[131] Jake King has suggested that some, at least, of the *achadh*-names in Caithness and Sutherland are very late formations. King proposes that Norse settlers to Caithness ignored the existing place-names, coining purely ON names, but later Gaelic speakers moved into the area, adapting existing ON names as well as coining new Gaelic ones.[132]

The lack of Gaelic place-names in Caithness and Orkney may point to both areas being settled before contact with Gaelic speakers.[133] David Dumville suggests that during the early part of the Viking Age, interactions between Scandinavians and Gaelic speakers was sporadic and violent.[134] It is only after AD 820 that encounters evolved from robbery and killing to taking prisoners and making alliances,[135] and it is only after AD 850 that groups of Vikings began to be identified in Irish sources, suggesting some form of communication.[136] It is likely that it was during this period that language contact developed to allow

---

129. Waugh 1993: 123–124.
130. Waugh 1985: 20.
131. Nicolaisen 1982: 77.
132. King forthcoming.
133. Nicolaisen 1979–80: 110; Smith 2001: 20.
134. Dumville 2008: 357.
135. *Annals of Ulster*: 363; Downham 2007: 238–239.
136. Dumville 2008: 358.

for the exchange of ideas. If the Northern Isles and northern Caithness were settled c. AD 800, then this would have been before language contact with Gaelic speakers had developed and the settlement would exhibit an insular Norse nomenclature.[137]

The idea that there was a difference in the timing of Scandinavian settlement of Caithness and Sutherland would seem to be corroborated by some Icelandic sagas. Icelandic sources sometimes refer to Scandinavian settlers and settlement in Scotland. A major issue with sagas is that they were written down some 300–400 years after the events they describe, and the accuracy of the material is open to question.[138] However, sagas are one of the earliest ON sources that refer to the Viking Age and are, in fact, the only source to discuss Caithness in this period.[139] It is therefore worth examining what evidence they may contain.[140]

Ketill flatnefr (Ketill 'Flatnose') was a well-known settler from Icelandic sources who had a close connection to the Gaelic west.[141] In *Laxdæla saga*, Ketill's daughter, *Auðr djúpaúðga* (Aud 'the Deep-Minded'), also referred to as *Unnr*, is reputed to have married *Áleifr hinn hvíti* (Óláf 'the White').[142] Óláf the White is believed to be *Amlaíb*, the Norse King of Dublin mentioned in Irish sources from c. AD 851–853.[143] Óláf the White had been, at various times, allied to a variety of petty Irish kings and even previously married to the daughter of one.[144]

Þórunn hyrna, another of Ketill's daughters in *Laxdæla saga*, married *Helgi inn magri* (Helgi 'the Lean'), son of *Eyvindr*

---

137. Foster 2018: 313.
138. Woolf 2007: 296; Jennings and Kruse 2009a: 127–129.
139. Dumville 2008, 351.
140. Jennings and Kruse 2009a: 127–129.
141. *Eyrbyggja saga*: 25; *Landnámabók*: chap. 11; *Laxdæla saga*: chap. 4; Jennings and Kruse 2009a: 127.
142. *Laxdæla saga*: 47.
143. Ó Corráin 1998: 298; Downham 2007: 15–23, 238.
144. Downham 2007: 238–239.

Bjarnarson (nicknamed 'the Easterner') and *Rafertach* (Rafarta), daughter of *Kjarval Írakonung* (Cerball of Osraige).[145] The sagas suggest Ketill was heavily connected to Ireland, including alliances with Norse rulers, who themselves were also strongly associated with Gaelic rulers. Andrew Jennings and Arne Kruse have argued that the Icelandic tradition concerning Ketill and Aud may have some validity, as the likely source was Ari Þorgilsson, one of their descendants.[146]

A common theme in many sagas connect this group of Norse settlers in the Irish Sea to later events in Caithness.[147] Ketill's grandson by Óláf the White and Aud was called *Þorsteinn rauði* (Thorstein 'the Red'). Thorstein was married to *Þuríður Eyvindardóttur* (Thurid, the daughter of Eyvind and Rafarta), further connecting the dynasty to the Gaelic west.

Laxdæla saga states that Thorstein raided widely in what later became Scotland, gaining half of it through treaty, but was later killed while in Caithness.[148] Some Icelandic sagas report that Thorstein the Red made an alliance with *Sigurðr inn riki* (Sigurd 'the Mighty'), the Earl of Orkney,[149] Sigurd and Thorstein reputedly conquering Caithness and Sutherland as far as *Ekkjalsbakki*.[150] Sigurd was killed shortly afterwards and buried at said place,[151] whose name may refer to the River Oykel in Sutherland.[152] The burial site has been suggested as referring to a mound, Cnoc Skardie, at Cyderhall.[153] The use of grave mounds as symbols of power and of land ownership in

---

145. *Laxdæla saga*: 47; Jennings and Kruse 2009a: 129.
146. Jennings and Kruse 2009a: 127.
147. Crawford 1986: 37.
148. *Laxdæla saga*: 51.
149. *Haraldr saga hins hárfagra*: 369; *Orkneyinga saga*: 27; *Eiríks saga rauða*: 126.
150. *Orkneyinga saga*: 27.
151. Ibid.
152. Crawford 1986: 38; Crawford 1987: 58–59; Crawford and Taylor 2003: 1.
153. Crawford 1987: 58–59; Crawford and Taylor 2003: 3.

Norway[154] is well known and would suggest that Scandinavian settlers felt confident enough in their control of the area to bury their leader here. There are a number of recorded furnished graves in Northern Scotland, especially in north-eastern Caithness. There are also two furnished graves located in the south-east of Sutherland,[155] which adds weight to the idea that this area was under Norse control at one time.[156]

The campaign of Sigurd and Thorstein likely expanded Norse control south from the coastal strip of Caithness into what is now Sutherland. Thorstein's powerbase was in the west, and his followers are likely to have been predominantly drawn from this area. These forces, having already been in contact with Gaelic speakers, would have had the opportunity to adopt *ærgi* into their farming system and lexicon. This concept may then have been introduced to Caithness by this group, who settled in the newly won areas of southern Caithness and Sutherland.

Thorstein's mother, Aud, had also travelled to Caithness, and according to *Laxdæla saga*, it was from there she secretly fled to Iceland on his death.[157] Though circumstantial, it is arguable that the story of Aud fleeing in secret might suggest that any surviving members of Thorstein's force are likely to have stayed behind.

Conclusion

ON shieling names in Caithness, at first glance, do have an atypical distribution pattern when compared to other areas of Scandinavian settlement. However, the difference in altitude

---

154. Skre 2001: 10.
155. Harrison 2008: 291.
156. Crawford and Taylor 2003: 3.
157. *Laxdæla saga*: 51–52.

between the two groups of shieling names is negligible, while either group's distance from the coast makes little impact concerning the use as a shieling in Scandinavian farming. The only aspect that can be considered odd concerning the location of shieling elements in Caithness is that *sætr*-names are located on more fertile soils compared to *ærgi*-names. However, even this may not be as unusual as it first seems when considering the available water capacity of soils. Despite peaty soils being considered infertile, their increased water capacity could arguably have been a benefit for livestock grazing in areas of relatively low rainfall. The fact that over half of *ærgi*-sites today are used for arable farming would suggest that the sites, though superficially infertile, were not as marginal as they first appear.

This difference in location of the two shieling elements, rather than being an indicator of marginality, may be the result of a combination of factors. The timing of each area's settlement is likely to have affected the choice of shieling name, with the northern coast being settled before language contact with Gaelic speakers had occurred. The insularity of Norse settlement is highlighted by the intensity of ON place-names and occurrence of furnished graves.[158] The density of settlement is no doubt a result of the general fertility of soil, which supported a large population of ON speakers. This would, in turn, have helped to retain distinctly Norse characteristics long enough for names to become mono-referential,[159] and in north-east Caithness stopped Gaelic from encroaching completely.[160]

When place-names are coined, they have appellative meanings in their respective language, such as 'hill' or 'field'. However, when they become established names for a location, they lose the appellative element and act purely as names, thus becoming

---

158. Waugh 1985: 2–3; 1993: 124.
159. Gammeltoft 2006: 53; Caldwell 2008: 29.
160. Nicolaisen 1982: 77.

mono-referential. As a place-name's main function is to single it out from other localities, it can then be easily transferred from one language to another, or as Peder Gammeltoft puts it, a name 'stops connoting and starts denoting'.[161]

The argument that the complementary distribution pattern of shieling names in Caithness is a result of a contact linguistic zone is difficult to prove. The evidence for large numbers of Gaelic speakers in Caithness in the pre-Norse period is weak. I would argue that the story found in Icelandic sources of a secondary later migration of Scandinavians who had spent time in the Gaelic west is supported circumstantially by the place-name evidence. Once the southern part of Caithness and Sutherland was subdued, Scandinavian settlers were able to set up their farming enterprises. These new settlers may have brought with them from the west a new concept and loanword *ærgi*, which they had incorporated into their farming economy.[162]

The distribution pattern of ON shieling names in Caithness is not perverse or atypical as it first seems, but fits into the general pattern of Scandinavian settlement in the Viking Age. The distribution pattern of shieling names in Caithness, rather than being the result of a single factor, is likely to be the result of a complex interaction of geography, settlement chronology, and later language shift.

Bibliography

Primary sources

Annals of Ulster, vol 1. 1887. W. Hennessy (trans. and ed.). Dublin: Kessinger.

---

161. Gammeltoft 2006: 55.
162. Foster 2018: 508.

Board of Agriculture for Scotland. Agricultural statistics, vol. I, part I. *Acreage and livestock returns of Scotland with a summary for the United Kingdom.* 1912. 52–57.

Eirik the Red and Other Icelandic Sagas. 1961. G. Jones (trans). Oxford: Oxford University Press.

Eyrbyggja saga. 1976. H. Pálsson and P. Edwards (trans.). London: Penguin.

The Earliest Norwegian Laws, being the Gulathing Law and the Frostathing Law. 1935. L.M. Larson (trans.). Menasha: Columbia University Press.

Futty, D.W. and Towers, W. (eds.). 1982. *Northern Scotland: Soil Survey of Scotland: Soil and Land Capability for Agriculture.* Aberdeen: The Macaulay Institute for Soil Research.

The James Hutton Institute. https://www.hutton.ac.uk. Accessed 30 July 2021.

Landnámabók: The Book of Settlements. 2006. H. Pálsson and P. Edwards (trans.).. Winnipeg: University of Manitoba Press.

Laxdæla saga. 1969. Magnus Magnusson and H. Pálsson (trans.). London: Penguin.

'Onshore GeoIndex', *British Geological Survey.* https://mapapps2.bgs. ac.uk/geoindex/home.html. Accessed 30 July 2021.

Orkneyinga Saga: The History of the Earls of Orkney. 1978. H. Pálsson and P. Edwards (trans.). London: Penguin.

Scotland's Soils. https://map.environment.gov.scot/Soil_maps/?layer=5#. Accessed on 30 July 2021.

Haraldr saga hins hárfagra. In *The Heimskringla.* 1884. S. Laing (trans.). London: Longman, Brown, Green and Longmans.

'UK climate averages (Kinbrace, Sutherland, Strathy East, Sutherland Wick John O'Groats Airport)', *Met Office.* https://www.metoffice.gov. uk/research/climate/maps-and-data/uk-climate-averages. Accessed 30 July 2021.

Secondary sources

Albrethsen, S.E. and Keller, C. 1986. 'The use of Sæter in Norse Medieval Greenland'. *Arctic Anthropology* 23:1–2, 91–107.

Anslow, R.C. and Green, J.O. 1967. 'The seasonal growth of pasture grasses'. *Journal of Agricultural Science* 68, 109–122.

Anttila, R. 1989. *Historical and Comparative Linguistics*, 2nd edition. New York: John Benjamins.

Bangor-Jones, M. 1995. 'Norse settlement in south-east Sutherland'. In B.E. Crawford (ed.), *Scandinavian Settlement in Northern Britain: Thirteen Studies of Place-Names in Their Historical Context*. London: Leicester University Press, 80–91.

Bannerman, J.W.M. 1974. *Studies in the History of Dalriada*. Edinburgh: Scottish Academic Press.

Beito, O. 1949. *Norske Sæternamn*. Oslo: Aschehoug.

Bjørgo, T. 2005. 'Iron Age House remains from mountain areas in Inner Sogn, Western Norway'. In K.A Bergsvik and A. Engevik. *UBAS Nordisk 1*. Bergen: Universitetet i Bergen, 209–228.

Caldwell, D. 2008. *Islay the Land of the Lordship*. Edinburgh: Birlinn.

Cleasby, R. and Vigfússon, G. 1874. *An Icelandic–English Dictionary*. Oxford: Clarendon Press.

Cox, R.A.V. 1990. 'The origin and relative chronology of shader-names in the Hebrides'. *Scottish Gaelic Studies* 16, 95–113.

———. 1991. 'Norse-Gaelic Contact in the West of Lewis: The Place-Name Evidence'. In P.S. Ureland and G. Broderick (eds). *Language Contact in the British Isle. Eighth International Symposium on Language Contact in Europe, Douglas, Isle of Man, 1988*. Tübingen: Max Niemeyer Verlag, 479–493.

———. 1992. 'The Norse element in Scottish Gaelic'. Proceedings of the 9th International Congress of Celtic Studies, Paris 1991. In Études Celtiques 29, 137–145.

———. 2002. *The Gaelic Place-names of Carloway, Isle of Lewis: their structure and significance*. Dublin: Dublin Institute for Advanced Studies.

Crawford, B.E. 1986. 'The Making of a Frontier: The Firthlands from the Ninth to Twelfth Centuries'. In J.R. Baldwin (ed.), *Firthlands of Ross and Cromerty*. Edinburgh: Scottish Society for Northern Studies, 33–46.

———. 1987. *Scandinavian Scotland: Scotland in the Early Middle Age*, vol. II. Leicester: Leicester University Press.

Crawford, B.E. and Taylor, S. 2003. 'The Southern Frontier of Norse Settlement in North Scotland: Place-Names and History'. *Northern Scotland* 23, 1–76.

Dahl, S. 1970. 'Um ærgistaðir og ærgitoftir'. *Fróðskaparrit* 18: 361–368.

Downham, C. 2007. *Viking Kings of Britain and Ireland: The Dynasty of Ívarr to A.D. 1014*. Edinburgh: Dunedin Academic Press.

Dineen, P. 1904. *Irish English Dictionary*. Dublin: Irish Text Society.

Edmonds, F. 2019. *Gaelic Influence in the Northumbrian Kingdom: The Golden Age and the Viking Age*. Studies in Celtic History 40. Woodbridge: Boydell Press.

Fellows-Jensen, G. 1977–78. 'A Gaelic-Scandinavian Loan-Word in English Place-Names'. *JEPNS* 10, 18–25.

———. 1980. 'Common Gaelic *Áirge*, Old Scandinavian *Ærgi* or *Erg*?' *Nomina* 4, 67–74.

———. 1984. 'Viking Settlement in the Northern and Western Isles'. In A. Fenton and H. Pálsson (eds), *The Northern and Western Isles in the Viking World*. Edinburgh: John Donald, 148–168.

———. 1985. 'Scandinavian Settlement in Cumbria and Dumfrieshire: The Place-Name Evidence'. In J.R. Baldwin and I.D. Whyte (eds), *The Scandinavians in Cumbria*. Edinburgh: Scottish Society for Northern Studies, 65–82.

———. 2002. 'Old Faroese *ærgi* yet again'. In A. Johansen (ed.), *Eivindarmál. Heiðursrit til Eivind Weyhe á seksti ára hansara 25. apríl 2002*. Torshavn: Annales Societatis Scientiarum Færoensis Supplementum 32, 89–96.

Foster, R. 2017. 'The use of the Scandinavian Place-Name Elements *-sætr* and *-ærgi* in Skye and the Outer Hebrides: a site and situation study'. In C. Cooijmans (ed.), *Traversing the Inner Seas: Contacts and Continuity around Western Scotland, the Hebrides and Northern Ireland*. Edinburgh: Scottish Society for Northern Studies, 107–139.

———. 2018. 'Norse shielings in Scotland: An interdisciplinary study of *setr/sætr* and *ærgi*-names'. PhD thesis. University of Edinburgh.

————. 2021. 'Reconstructing early shieling landscapes and land-use in Cumbria during the Viking Age'. *Folk Life*, 1–17.

Fraser, I.A. 1974. 'The Place Names of Lewis: The Norse Evidence'. *Northern Studies* 4, 11–21.

————. 1979. 'The Norse element in Sutherland Place Name'. *Scottish Literary Journal*. Supplement No. 9.

————. 1986. 'Norse and Celtic Place-Names around the Dornoch Firth'. In J.R. Baldwin (ed.), *Firthlands of Ross and Cromerty*. Edinburgh: Scottish Society for Northern Studies, 23–32.

Gammeltoft, P. 2001. *The Place-name Element Bólstaðr in the North Atlantic Area*. Copenhagen: Reitzels Forlag.

————. 2004. 'Scandinavian-Gaelic Contacts. Can Place-Names and Place-Name Elements be used as a Source for Contact-Linguistic Research?'. *NOWLE* 44, 51–90.

————. 2006. 'Scandinavian influence on Hebridean island names'. In P. Gammeltoft and B. Jørgensen (eds), *Names Through the Looking-Glass*. Festschrift in Honour of Gillian Fellows-Jensen. Copenhagen: C.A. Reitzel, 53–84.

Garmo, T. 1986. 'Chemical composition and in vitro digestibility of indigenous pasture plants in different plant groups (preliminary report)'. *Rangifer* 6, 14–22.

Harrison, S.H. 2008. 'Furnished insular Scandinavian burial artefacts and landscape in the early Viking Age'. PhD thesis. Trinity College Dublin.

Heggstad, L. and Torp A. 1930. *Gamelnorsk Ordbok, med Nynorsk tyding*. Kristiania: Norske Samlaget.

Higham, M.C. 1977–78. 'The "erg" place-names of Northern England'. *JEPNS* 10, 7–17.

————. 1996. '-ærgi names as indicators of transhumance: problems of the evidence'. In H.S.A. Fox (ed.), *Seasonal Settlement*. Vaughan Paper 39. Leicester: University of Leicester, 55–60.

Hitzler, E. 1979. *Sel, Untersuchungen zur Geschichte des isländischen Sennwesens seit der Landnahmzeit*. Oslo: Universitetsforlaget.

Hudson, G. et al. 1982. *Soil and Land Capability for Agriculture: Outer Hebrides*. Aberdeen: Macaulay Land Use Research Institute.

Jackson, K. 1955. 'The Pictish Language'. In F.T. Wainwright (ed.), *The Problem of the Picts*. Edinburgh: Thomas Nelson, 129–166.

James, H.F. 2009. 'Medieval rural settlement: a study of Mid-Argyll, Scotland'. PhD thesis. Department of Archaeology, University of Glasgow.

Jennings, A and Kruse A. 2005. 'An Ethnic Enigma – Norse, Pict and Gael in the Western Isles'. In A. Mortensen and S.V. Arge (eds), *Viking and Norse in the North Atlantic: Selected Papers from the Proceedings of the Fourteenth Viking Congress, Tórshavn, 19–30 July 2001*. Tórshavn: Føroya Fróðskaparfelag, 284–296.

————. 2009a. 'From Dál Riata to the Gall-Ghàidheil'. *Medieval Scandinavia* 5, 123–149.

————. 2009b. 'One coast – three peoples: names and ethnicity in the Scottish west during the early Viking period'. In A. Woolf (ed.), *Scandinavian Scotland – 20 Years on*. St Andrews: St John's House Papers 12, 75–103.

Jóhansen, J. 1985. *Studies in the Vegetational History of the Faroe and Shetland Islands*. Tórshavn: Annales Societatis Scientiarum Faeroensis Supplementum 11.

King, J. (forthcoming). 'Another Look at the Onomastic Frontier Zone in Caithness'. In R. Foster and C. Cooijmans (eds), *A'm grippit dis land: History, Language and Landscape in Caithness and the Northern Isles. Essays in Honour of Doreen Waugh*. Turnhout: Brepols.

Kruse, A. 2004. 'Norse Topographical Settlement Names on the Western Littoral of Scotland'. In J. Adams and K. Holman (eds), *Scandinavia and Europe 800–1350: Contact, Conflict and Coexistence*. Turnhout: Brepols, 97–107.

————. 2005. 'Explorers, Raiders, and Settlers. The Norse Impact upon Hebridean Place-Names'. In P. Gammeltoft et al. (eds), *Cultural Contacts in the North Atlantic Region: The Evidence of Names*. Shetland: NORNA, Scottish Place-Name Society and Society for Name Studies in Britain and Ireland, 141–156.

————. 2007. 'Fashion, Limitation and Nostalgia: Scandinavian Place-Names Abroad'. In A. Kruse and P. Graves (eds), *Images and Imaginations: Perspectives on Britain and Scandinavia*. Edinburgh: Lockharton Press, 3–33.

MacBain, A. 1911. *An etymological dictionary of the Gaelic Language.* Stirling: Eneas Mackay.

———. 1922. *Place-Names of the Highlands and Islands of Scotland.* Stirling: Eneas Mackay.

Macniven, A. 2013. 'Modelling Viking Migration to the Inner Hebrides'. Across the Sólundarhaf: Connections between Scotland and the Nordic World Selected Papers from the Inaugural St. Magnus Conference 2011. *Journal of the North Atlantic* Special Volume 4: 3–18.

———. 2015. *The Vikings in Islay: The place of names in Hebridean settlement history.* Edinburgh: John Donald.

Mahler, D.L.D. 1991. 'Argisbrekka: New Evidence of Shielings in the Faroe Islands'. *Acta Archaeologica* 61: 60–72.

———. 1993. 'Shielings and their role in the Viking-Age Economy'. In C.E. Batey et al. (eds), *The Viking Age in Caithness, Orkney and the North Atlantic.* Edinburgh: Edinburgh University Press, 487–505.

———. 2007. *Seteren ved Argisbrekka: økonomiske forandringer på Færøerne I vikingetid og tidlig middelalder:* economic development during the Viking Age and Early Middle Ages on the Faroe Islands. Annales Societatis Scientiarum Færoensis Supplementum 47. Tórshavn: Faroe University Press.

McNeill, P.G.B. and MacQueen, H.L. 2000. *An Atlas of Scottish History to 1707.* Glasgow: Scottish Society of Medievalists.

Myers-Scotton, C. 2002. *Contact Linguistics: Bilingual Encounters and Grammatical Outcomes.* Oxford: Oxford University Press.

Nicolaisen, W.F.H. 1969. 'Norse Settlement in the Northern and Western Isles: Some Place-Name Evidence'. *Scottish Historical Review* 48, 6–17.

———. 1979–80. 'Early Scandinavian Naming in the Western and Northern Isles'. *Northern Studies* 3:2, 105–122.

———. 1982. 'Scandinavians and Celts in Caithness: the place-name evidence'. In J.R. Baldwin (ed.), *Caithness: A Cultural Crossroads.* Edinburgh: Scottish Society for Northern Studies, 75–85.

———. 1993. 'Names in the Landscape of the Moray Firth'. In D. Sellar (ed.), *Moray: Province and People.* Edinburgh: Scottish Society for Northern Studies, 253–262.

Ó Corráin, D. 1998. 'The Vikings in Scotland and Ireland in the ninth century'. *Peritia* 12, 296–339.

Oram, R.D. 2000. *The Lordship of Galloway*. Edinburgh: John Donald.

Oram, R. and Adderley, W.P. 2011. 'Innse Gall: Culture and Environment on a Norse Frontier in the Scottish Western Isles'. In Imsen Steinar (ed.). *The Norwegian Domination and the Norse World c.1100–c.1400*. Norgesveldet, occasional papers 1. Trondheim: Tapir Academic Press, 125–148.

Owen, N. et al. 1996. 'The machair vegetation of the Outer Hebrides: A review'. In D. Gilbertson et al.(eds), *The Outer Hebrides: The Last 14,000 Years*. Sheffield Environmental and Archaeological Research Campaign in the Hebrides 2. Sheffield: Sheffield Academic Press, 123–131.

Øye I. 2004. 'Agricultural conditions and rural societies c. 800–1350'. In R. Almås (ed.), *Norwegian Agricultural History*. Trondheim: Tapir Academic Press, 79–140.

———. 2005. 'Farming and farming systems in Norse societies of the North Atlantic'. In A. Mortensen and S. Arge (eds), *Viking and Norse in the North Atlantic*. Select Papers from Proceedings of the Fourteenth Viking Congress, Tórshavn, 19–30 July 2001, Annales Societascientiarium Færoensis Supplementum 44. Tórshavn: The Faroese Academy of Sciences, 359–370.

Parker Pearson, M. (ed.). 2012. *From Machair to Mountains: Archaeological Survey and Excavation in South Uist*. Sheffield Environmental and Archaeological Research Campaign in the Hebrides 4. Oxford: Oxbow Books.

Pearsall, W.H. 1961. 'Place-names as clues to the pursuit of ecological history'. *Namn och Bygd* 49, 72–89.

Raven, J.A. 2005. 'Medieval Landscapes and Lordship in South Uist'. PhD thesis. Department of Archaeology, University of Glasgow.

Sæther, N.H. et al. 2006. 'Plant and vegetation preferences for a high and moderate yielding Norwegian dairy cattle breed grazing seminatural mountain pastures'. *Animal Research* 55, 367–387.

Shepherd, I.A.G. 1993. 'The Picts in Moray'. In D. Sellar (ed.), *Moray: Province and People*. Edinburgh: Scottish Society for Northern Studies, 75–90.

Skaugen, T.E. and Tveito, O.E. 2004. 'Growing-season and degree-day scenario in Norway for 2021–2050'. *Climate Research* 26, 221–232.

Skre, D. 2001. 'The Social Context of Settlement in Norway in the First Millennium AD'. *Norwegian Archaeological Review* 34:1, 1–12.

Small, A. 1986. 'Norse Settlement in Easter Ross'. In William Ritchie et al. (eds), *Essays for Professor R.E.H. Meller*. Aberdeen: University of Aberdeen Press, 205–209.

Smith, B. 2001. 'The Picts and the Martyrs'. *Northern Studies*, 7–32.

Sveinbjarnardóttir, Guðrún. 1991. 'Shielings in Iceland, an archaeological and historical survey'. *Acta Archaelogica* 61:1, 73–96.

Taylor, S. 2016. 'Charting a Course Through the Scottish Namescape'. In C. Hough and D. Izdebska (eds), *Names and Their Environment*, Proceedings of the 25th International Congress of Onomastic Sciences, Glasgow, 25–29 August 2014. Glasgow: University of Glasgow, 2–24.

Thomason, S.G. 2001. *Language Contact: An introduction*. Edinburgh: Edinburgh University Press.

Tolkamp, B.J. et al. 1998. 'Diet choice by dairy cows. 1. Selection of feed protein content during the first half of lactation'. *Journal of Dairy Science* 81, 2657–2669.

Wainwright, F.T. 1948. 'Ingimund's Invasion'. *English Historical Review* 247, 145–169.

———. 1962. *The Northern Isles*. Edinburgh: Nelson.

Watson, W.J. 1905. 'Some Sutherland Names of Places'. *Celtic Review* 2, 360.

Waugh, D. 1985. 'The place-names of six parishes in Caithness, Scotland'. PhD thesis. University of Edinburgh.

———. 1987. 'The Scandinavian Element *Staðir* in Caithness, Orkney and Shetland'. *Nomina* 11, 61–74.

———. 1993. 'Caithness and Onomastic Frontier Zone'. In C. Batey et al. (eds), *The Viking Age in Caithness, Orkney and the North Atlantic*. Edinburgh: Edinburgh University Press, 120–128.

———. 1995. 'Settlement names in Caithness with particular reference to Reay parish'. In B.E. Crawford (ed.), *Scandinavian Settlement in Northern Britain*. Leicester: Leicester University Press, 64–79.

———. 2000. 'A scatter of Norse names in Strathnaver'. In J.R. Baldwin (ed.), *The Province of Strathnaver.* Edinburgh: Scottish Society for Northern Studies, 13–23.

Weinreich, U. 1968. *Languages in Contact. Findings and Problems.* London: Mouton.

Whyte, I.D. 1985. 'Shielings and the Upland Pastoral Economy of the Lake District in Medieval and Early Modern Times'. In J.R. Baldwin and I.D. Whyte (eds), *The Scandinavians in Cumbria.* Edinburgh: Scottish Society for Northern Studies, 103–118.

Woolf, A. 2007. *From Pictland to Alba, 789–1070.* Edinburgh: University of Edinburgh Press.

Zimmermann, W.H. 1999. 'Why was cattle-stalling introduced in prehistory? The significance of byre and stable and of outwintering'. In C. Fabech and J. Ringtved (eds), *Settlement and Landscape: Proceedings of a conference in Århus, Denmark, May 4–7 1998.* Aarhus: Aarhus University Press, 301–318.

Place-Names of Mingulay

Anke-Beate Stahl

Arne served as one of the supervisors to my PhD thesis. In many ways, he and I are exact opposites. He was punctual, organised, and very serious, and in this way, I always thought he was much more German than me.

This chapter aims to provide an overview of the mapping and recording of place-names on Mingulay, located in the Outer Hebrides of Scotland. It will do so by employing evidence collected from maps, charts, gazetteers, letters, and from interviews with descendants of former inhabitants, local fishermen, and crofters.

Once considered to be more difficult to reach than North America, Mingulay (NL560830) is one of the remotest islands of the Hebrides. It lies 19 km south of Barra and 90 km west of Ardnamurchan Lighthouse, the nearest point on the Scottish mainland. Of the group of islands south of Barra, known as the Bishop's Isles,[1] Mingulay is the second largest in terms of area, measuring 4 km in length, just over 3 km in width, and covering 6.4 km². However, it is larger than its closest neighbours, Berneray (Ceann Bharraigh, Barra Head) to the

---

1. As such they appear in the rental of the bishopric of 1561. *Collectanea de Rebus Albanicis* 1839: 4. For further discussion of this term, see Buxton 1995: 50.

south and Pabbay to the north, and features the highest hills in the island group. Its size is likely to have inspired its descriptive name which is derived from Old Norse (ON) *mikil* ('big') and ON *ey* ('island').[2] In Gaelic, the island is known as Miùghlaigh [mju:əLaj].

Earlier versions of the name include:

1546 *Megaly*	George Lily
1654 *Megala*	Robert Gordon: Joan Blaeu's *Atlas novus* ('Vistus insula')
1703 *Micklay*	Martin Martin
1714 *Megala I.*	Herman Moll
1776 *Mingaly I.*	Murdoch Mackenzie
1794 *Mingalla I.*	Captain J. Huddart
1804 *Mingalay I.*	William Heather
1807 *I. Mingalay*	Aaron Arrowsmith
1827 *Minguly*	John Lothian, 'Western Isles'
1832 *Mingulay*	John Thomson
c. 1850 *Mingalay*	A. and C. Black
1880 *Mingulay*	OS six-inch map, first edition

The vertical cliffs of Mingulay, the tallest in Britain after St Kilda, run along the rugged northern and western shores and incorporate deep chasms, high sea stacks, and natural arches. They are home to colonies of guillemots, razorbills, puffins, and kittiwakes. From its highest cliff Biulacraig (NL549831) at 213 m, in the west, the land drops off gradually to the east where the ruins of the village (NL565834) sit by a sandy beach. Four hills, running in a semi-circle from north-east to south-west, break up the slope, with Carnan (NL553828) at 273 m serving as a triangulation point. The island is treeless

---

2. Borgström 1936: 287.

and appears barren with only a thin layer of acidic soil. The bedrock is mainly Lewisian gneiss with veins of basalt, which, being subject to erosion, contribute to the serrated look of the coast.

Figure 1: Biulacraig. Photo: Anke-Beate Stahl.

Settlement history

It is estimated that Mingulay has been permanently settled for at least 2,000 years. Although there are no obvious Iron Age buildings, such as brochs and duns, the more than 400 recorded archaeological sites on the island have left archaeologists confident that further fieldwork would most likely produce evidence of pre-Iron Age settlements.[3] Dùn Mingulay (NL545822, OS 1880) is a large peninsula with sheer cliffs and a narrow isthmus as access. It may have been a livestock enclosure rather than a defensive structure.[4] The OS also lists a *dùn* ('fort') on Geirum Mòr (NL548813, 1931), an islet with 15 m steep cliffs just 180 m south-west of Mingulay. Here appear to be the ruins of a chapel,[5] but no obvious signs of a fort.

The Viking raids on Iona and Skye in the period between AD 795 and 825, as described by the *Annals of Ulster* and *Annals of Innisfallen*, are most likely the cornerstones of the initial Norse settlement in the Hebrides.[6] Norse influence dominated for five centuries until 1266, when the Hebrides were sold to the Scottish Crown as a result of the Treaty of Perth.

Despite its remote location, Mingulay had around 150 inhabitants in 1881. Locals made a living from fowling, collecting eggs, selling feathers to mainland markets, crofting, and fishing. Peat provided a source of energy, but life was hard. The village, located in the east of the island, was relatively sheltered,

---

3. Branigan and Foster 2000: 128.
4. 'Mingulay, Dun Mingulay', *Canmore: National Record of the Historic Environment*, https://canmore.org.uk/site/272187/mingulay-dun-mingulay. Accessed 19 May 2022.
5. 'Geirum Mór, Mingulay', *Canmore: National Record of the Historic Environment*, https://canmore.org.uk/site/21381/geirum-mr-mingulay. Accessed 19 May 2022.
6. Jennings 1996: 61.

but houses were basic and some were overcrowded. Landing on the sandy beach was difficult, and taking cargo ashore or loading boats was dangerous.

Even the derrick, finally completed in 1901, proved not as practical as hoped for. Visitors could be marooned on the island for many weeks, unable to leave due to bad weather. Likewise, islanders who had travelled to Barra or beyond were prevented from returning. There was a limited amount of fertile land suitable for growing food and grazing cattle, the quality of the soil was poor, and seaweed was scarce so there was not much to be used as fertilizer. Unrest started, followed by emigration, encouraged by the prospect of some land on Vatersay, and by 1912, Mingulay was deserted.[7] Today, we can refer to audio recordings of former inhabitants, written accounts by locals and visitors, and maps and charts to get a glimpse of what life on the island was like.

Mingulay on maps and charts

The mapping of Mingulay evolved alongside the mapping of the Outer Hebrides as a whole. In early maps, the Hebrides appeared much further north than their actual location, but as surveying techniques progressed, the shapes of individual islands became more defined, and their positioning within the Minch – the strait to the west of the Scottish mainland – became more accurate. Abraham Ortelius' map 'Scotiae Tabula' of 1573 is significant, as it is the first to show the Inner and Outer Hebrides as clearly separated sets of islands. On it, the smaller islands south of Barra may be identified by location, although not yet by shape.

---

7. Buxton 1995: 123.

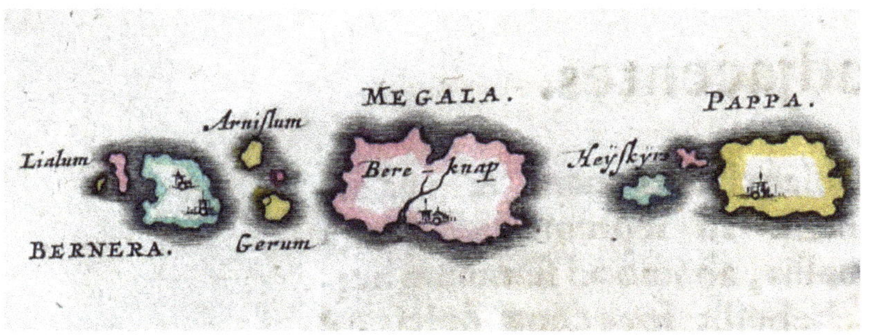

Figure 2: Joan Blaeu's *Atlas novus*. 1654. Reproduced with
permission of the National Library of Scotland.

Joan Blaeu's 'Vistus Insula' was published as part of his *Atlas
novus* in 1654. It was based on Robert Gordon's survey, which
in turn had been informed by the work of Timothy Pont.
On 'Vistus Insula', Mingulay appears as *Megala* and can be
clearly distinguished from its neighbouring islands. This map
shows one name in the interior of Mingulay, *Bere-knap*. Both
elements of this name are likely to be of ON origin, from *bere*
('naked', 'bare') and *knappr* ('top of a hill', 'knob'). *Bere-knap*
appears to be an older name for what is now known as Carnan
(NL553828), the most distinguishable hill on Mingulay. In
Atlas Novus, the sea stack *Arnislum* and the islet *Gerum* are
located to the south of Mingulay. These names − in contrast
to *Bere-knap* − are still in current use and appear as Arnamul
(NL545825), Geirum Mòr (NL547813), and Geirum Beag
(NL551814) on contemporary maps.

At 150 m, Arnamul is impressively high. The first element
of this name may be derived from ON *arnar*, genitive case of
örn, (m., 'eagle')[8] or from a personal name of the same form.[9]
The generic derives from ON *múli* ('sea rock'). Geirum may be
based on ON *geirr* ('spear') or possibly the ON personal name

---

8. There are sea eagles in this area.
9. A. Kruse, pers. comm. The personal name Qrn is popular in ON anthro-
toponyms. See Evemalm 2018: 197.

Geirr. The generic of this name, *-um*, is derived from ON *holmr* ('islet') and it is followed by Gaelic *mòr* ('large') and Gaelic *beag* ('small'), which were added at a later stage. Alternative spellings are *Gierum* (1892), *Gìrum* (1903) and *Gìrum Mhòr* (1931), with a number of variations also seen for the smaller of the two islands.

Figure 3: Caolas Àirneamuil (Caolas Arnamul). Photo: Anke-Beate Stahl.

In the aftermath of Culloden in 1746, the lack of detailed maps led to the Hanoverian army failing to capture Charles Edward Stuart. As a result, William Roy was commissioned to produce the *Military Survey of Scotland* between 1747 and 1755. Maps from this survey were considered so strategically important that public access was denied, leaving many eighteenth-century cartographers to draw information from earlier publications. However, Roy did not cover the Outer Hebrides at all, and only a small part of the Inner Hebrides.

John Thomson's *Atlas of Scotland* of 1832 proved to be a significant milestone in mapping the Hebrides as it showed the 'Southern Part of the Western Isles' in great detail. In addition to a more accurately depicted coastline, headlands and hills are shown with contour lines. For the first time, streams are shown – although not named – on Mingulay. The atlas contains more hill names than any previous map and also includes names for coastal features such as sea stacks, islets, promontories, and landing places. Considering the size of Mingulay, the number of names shown on the map is unusually large and suggests that the surveyor, MacLean, may have had a particular interest in recording this much detail. In contrast to previous publications, Thomson's map is rotated by ninety degrees, with the chain of the Outer Hebrides running from west to east, rather than the familiar south to north. In some places, names are difficult to read, as Thomson's ornamental horizontal lines separating the land mass from coastal waters interfere with the typescript.

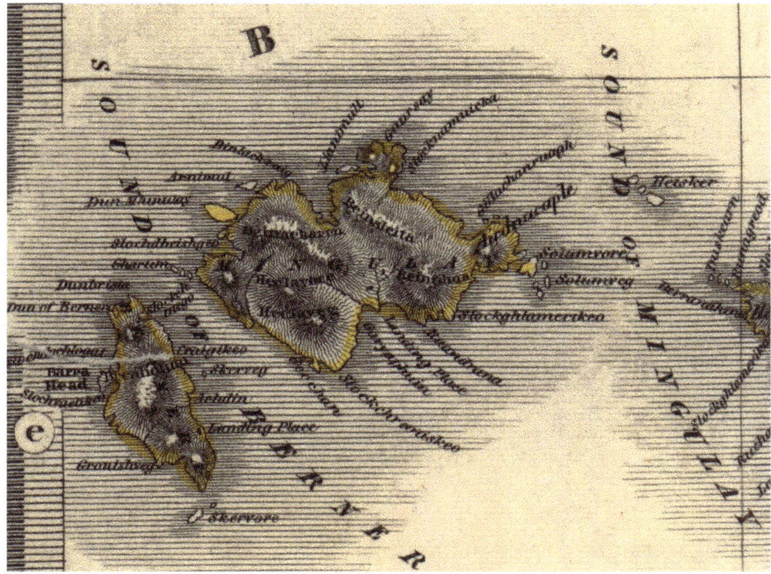

Figure 4: John Thomson, 'Southern Part of the Western Isles', Map of Barra, 1832.
Reproduced with permission of the National Library of Scotland.

Captain Otter's survey of Scotland's West Coast, 'Hebrides or Western Isles from Barra Head to Scarpa' (Sheet V, Chart 2474), published in 1865, added another dimension to mapping the Hebrides. His charts show the depths of the seabed in great detail and also record the heights of hills on Mingulay. For the first time, names appear in English translations, examples being *Ram Head* (Tom a' Reithean, NL568848), and *Green Island* (Greanamul). Some names receive English generics such as *Gnuarsay* [sic] *Point* (Guarsay Mòr, NL548844) or *Bay of Sonodal* (Bay Hunadu, NL572845), while others are given entirely new names in English such as in *Horse Island* (Geirum Mòr, see above), *Dun Bluff*[10] (Dùn Mingulay, see above), *Twin Rocks* (Bogha Dubh an Dùin, NL542819), and *Night Bay* (Bàgh na h-Aonaig, NL552833).

The six-inch OS maps published in 1880 show considerably more place-names on Mingulay than any previous map. They were preceded by the Ordnance Survey object name books, which listed all features considered for entry in the OS six-inch maps.

The object name books for Barra and its southern islands were compiled between 1876 and 1878, possibly by Captain J.C. MacPherson, whose name is noted on the last page.[11] The printed layout of these books provided space for each place-name, alternative spellings, authorities (i.e. contributors), and historical maps and charts from which information was obtained. Depending on the collector, detailed information about antiquities, natural history, and sometimes even social conditions were given. The

---

10. This name appears on only one historical record and is unknown amongst locals. In this case, the element *bluff* may be a topographic term for 'headland', mostly used in North America for prominent (inland) cliff-faces. The Admiralty use probably stemmed from the use of *bluff* during Canadian coastal surveys. Ian A. Fraser, pers. comm.

11. Ordnance Survey Name Books 1878. Inverness-shire, Outer Hebrides, II: 139.

OS provided clear guidelines that informants be recruited first from key professions in the local community, examples being landowners, tacksmen, clergymen, schoolmasters, and inn-keepers. In many areas, however, crofters and fishermen, who had an in-depth knowledge of the land and sea, were also consulted.

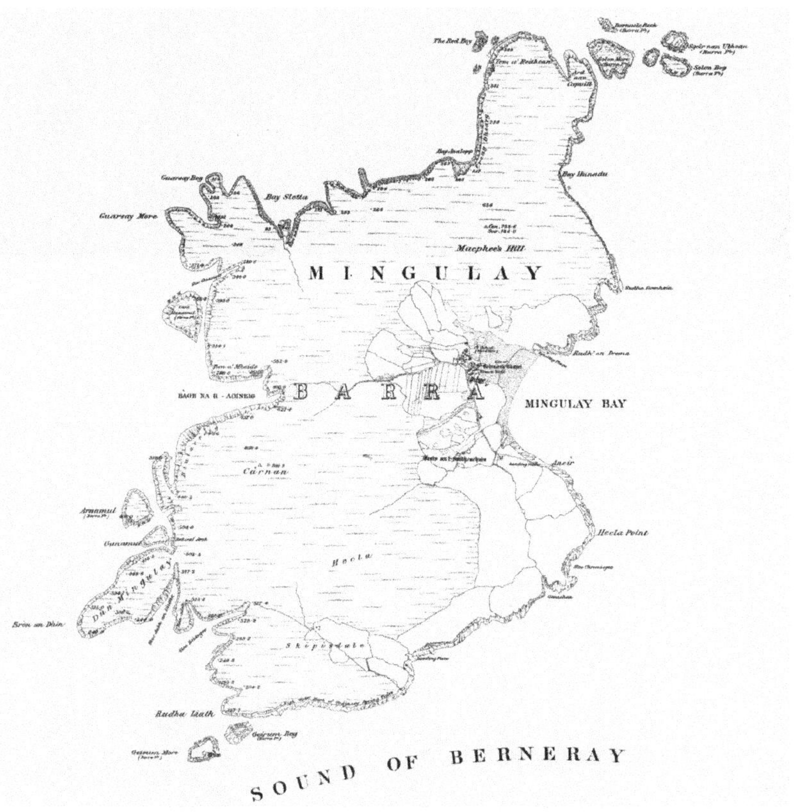

Figure 5: OS six-inch map, Mingulay, 1880. Reproduced with permission of the National Library of Scotland.

In Mingulay, all entries from the OS object name books appeared on the OS six-inch maps (1880). The contributors for Mingulay were listed as Mr John Sinclair (Iain Dhunnchaidh) from Mingulay, Mr Allan McNeil, assistant lighthouse keeper who would have lived on Berneray, and Mr Sinclair from

Barra Head.[12] A few names were verified by Mr McAulay from Castlebay, who was a boatman for the mail boat for the southern islands, and one by Rev. A. McDonald. All entries were confirmed by A.A. Carmichael, who acted as an authority on the correct spelling of the place-names. This Alexander Archibald Carmichael, a native of Lismore who had lived in South Uist for many years, was an exciseman, collector of folklore, antiquarian, and author of the *Carmina Gadelica*.[13] In a private letter, Carmichael expressed his concerns regarding the inclusion and exclusion of place-names on the final maps.

> I think Gaelic place-names are very descriptive and self-evident and intelligible to most intelligent Highlanders. There are not a few however which for various and obvious reasons are open to doubt. And let me here give my opinion of the O.S.D. [Ordnance Survey Department] which I am not sure is wholly blameless in this matter. When the work of the Barra SU B & U and Harris [i.e. Barra, South Uist, Benbecula, North Uist, and Harris – the Hebridean islands whose names Carmichael was asked to authorise] came out, I found that many of [the] place-names which I was at so much pains and expense in collecting were entire [sic] left out that some names on the old maps were left unaltered and that some were altered in form thus lending the meaning different. I took the liberty of drawing the attention of the Dir G of the OS to these alterations and the reply was that names were omitted to save expense that old names were left out as they were obviously incorrect & [so] as to avoid confusion and that the final mode of spelling rested with the Inspector General. Sir C. Wilson repeats that the final mode of spelling rests with the In.G.[14]

---

12. He is likely to be the brother of John Sinclair (Iain Dhunnchaidh).
13. Carmichael 1900.
14. Withers 2000: 547.

Individual place-names collectors

Interest in the island, its flora and fauna, and its inhabitants and their traditions increased in the second half of the nineteenth century, and Mingulay received visits from ornithologists, folklorists, and people who tried, unsuccessfully, to convert the local Catholic population to Protestantism. John Finlayson (1830–1904) was born in Lochcarron, Ross-shire, and came to Mingulay in 1859 to work as schoolmaster. He married Jane Campbell, a local woman, and remained on the island for the rest of his life. His letter to the botanist and naturalist John Alexander Harvie-Brown, who had visited Mingulay in 1870 and 1887,[15] was written on 9 March 1892 and contains a list of fifty place-names of the island. An invaluable source, each of Finlayson's place-names follows a brief description of each feature, which in some cases helps to distinguish the type of feature, particularly in cases where the origin of the name is opaque. He starts with *Soalum* (Solon Mòr, NL574849), an islet in the north-east, and works his way clockwise round the island, in some cases enabling at least an approximate location of now-lost place-names.

Eleven years after John Finlayson's compilation of Mingulay place-names, Fr Allan McDonald (1859–1905) conducted his own collection of place-names of the island. Also known as Maighstir Ailean or Fr Allan, he worked as a Roman Catholic priest on South Uist and Eriskay. He was also a poet, collected Hebridean folklore, was interested in philology, and worked as a political activist, fighting for crofters' rights. Both John Finlayson and Fr Allan were Gaelic speakers, and confident in writing in Gaelic too. In 1903, Fr Allan's 'List of non-Gaelic

---

15. See Buxton 1995: 21.

place-names in the island of Mingulay, near Barra-Head' was published.[16]

In his list of non-Gaelic place-names, Fr Allan attempts a phonetic spelling, placing accents on vowels and hyphenating names to facilitate pronunciation. For *Háwshŭm*, Fr Allan provides the alternatives *Sáwshŭm* and *Táwshŭm*, acknowledging that a name used by native Gaelic speakers may, under certain grammatical circumstances, have been lenited.

The first entry on Fr Allan's list is *Hiarigeo*, most likely located at the northern end of the sandy beach on Mingulay Bay (approx. NL568834). The list is ordered to follow the shoreline anti-clockwise around the island. The final entry is *Gūnarsay* (approx. NL567831), a rocky area south of the village just by the old school. The locations of the following names on the list are now unknown:

- *Căhăsdal*
- *Rōw-rye,* or *Trow-rye, Srow-rye*
- *Clet Annsa*
- *Alāvi*
- *Sheōw-a-dal*
- *Sūinsibost*
- *Orācri*
- *Háwshŭm,* or *Sáwshŭm, Táwshŭm*
- *Ugráiny*
- *Lianacui*

The coastline of Mingulay, as shown on a hand-drawn map titled 'Mingulay Place-Names as located by Donald MacPhee,

16. It appeared as an appendix to the article 'The Norsemen in Uist Folklore', which Fr Allan wrote for the *Saga-Book of the Viking Club* (McDonald 1901–1903: 413-433), and as such is not connected to the main text of his essay.

1931',[17] appears to have been traced from a six-inch OS map. Donald MacPhee (Dòmhnall Bàn) grew up on Mingulay and was considered to be exceptionally scholarly.[18] In general, this map has a flat appearance, as the contour lines of elevations were not recorded. It contains around eighty handwritten place-names. Each entry is numbered,[19] starting with *Na Gilleachan Ruadh* ('the red boys', NL566852)[20] in the north and continues clockwise round the island, concluding with a few interior features. Aside from well-documented names of major hills, main gullies, and prominent sea stacks, this map lists names of a number of smaller features, some of which initially appeared on John Finlayson's and Fr Allan's lists of place-names. Dòmhnall Bàn's map includes the names of most small streams on the island, none of which appeared on previous maps or previous place-name gazetteers.

- *Abhainn Lianagaidh* (NL557832) starts around the top of Biulacraig and cuts through the central valley towards Mingulay Bay (NL569831). An alternative name for this stream, *Abhainn a' Ghlinne*, is not listed on this map.

- *Abhainn a' Chàrnain* (NL559825) starts on the eastern slope of Carnan and flows into the sea at the village around *Soilis Bheag* (NL567828).

- *Abhainn Sumhsabaist* (NL555818) starts east of Sloc Heisegeo (NL549818) and flows in a south-easterly direction through Skipisdale (NL556817) into the sea.

---

17. I am indebted to Ben Buxton for sharing information about this map.
18. See Buxton 1995: 38.
19. Mairi Ceit MacKinnon, a Castlebay resident, numbered each entry at a later date.
20. This feature appears in its singular version, The Red Boy, on OS maps.

- *Abhainn Léite* (NL555837) runs in a north-westerly direction from the north-eastern slope of Tom a' Mhaide (NL554834) into Bay Sletta (NL555844).

- *Abhainn na h-Àirde* (NL569845) runs in an easterly direction along *Gàradh na h-Àirde* (NL568846) into Bàgh Hunadu (see above).

Figure 6: Abhainn a' Ghlinne (Abhainn Lianagaidh). Photo: Anke-Beate Stahl.

Both the date on the map and the confident use of Gaelic suggest that John Lorne Campbell may have advised on the spelling and possibly noted down the names supplied by Dòmhnall Bàn. John Lorne Campbell (1906–96), a Celtic scholar who extensively collected Hebridean folklore, lived on Barra in the 1930s.

Another map, a photocopied part of a six-inch second-edition OS map,[21] shows a number of handwritten place-names along the west coast of Mingulay, from Sloc Heisegeo (NL548819) in the south-west to Sloc na Muice ('gully of the pig', NL556843) in the north. This map mirrors all the names on Dòmhnall Bàn's map, except for one difference: the spelling of the river running through Skipisdale, which appears as *Abhainn Sûsabast*[22] rather than *Abhainn Sumhsabaist*, as on Dòmhnall Bàn's map.

During the author's research of place-names of Barra and its surrounding islands,[23] carried out between 1994 and 2000, a total of seven residents from Barra and Vatersay contributed place-names for Mingulay: Donald MacNeil (Dogain), Joseph Sinclair (Jaw), Roderick MacLeod (Roddy Dhòmhnall Uilleim), John MacLeod (Iagan an Dot), Domhnall Dhunnchaidh Campbell (DD), Peigi Anna Campbell, and Malcolm MacNeil (Calum a Chal) were all native Gaelic speakers. For years, the men of this group had fished and set creels around Mingulay and knew the area extremely well. Two of them had regularly taken visitors and research teams to the island. One of them had even belonged to a local syndicate of crofters, the Barra Head Isles Sheepstock Company, which owned the island until it was sold to the

---

21. Hugh Cheape sent a copy of this map to Ben Buxton in 1999. An annotation on the map states that it was from 'Canna House Library. J.L. Campbell's additions from Barra informants. This is the only section of the map'.
22. The quality of the reproduction of this document casts doubt over the last vowel of the specific, which could alternatively read as 'e', as in *Sûsabest*, or 'o', as in *Sûsabost*.
23. Stahl 2000.

National Trust of Scotland in 2000. Some of the above crofters had ancestors who originated from Mingulay, and all of them had a special interest in the local history of the island.

Unsurprisingly, eighty-five years since the last permanent inhabitants left Mingulay, the majority of place-names remembered lay in coastal locations. Most place-names collected during this survey were of Gaelic origin. Some place-names describing small features contained Norse place-name elements as specifics, helping to pinpoint the original Norse name on the map. In addition, the above contributors were instrumental in tracing the locations and supplying the pronunciation for a number of place-names previously listed by John Finlayson in 1892 and by Fr Allan in 1903.

The interaction of languages in the place-names of Mingulay

Norse place-names form the earliest linguistic evidence of settlement on Mingulay. Whereas a number of place-names are purely Gaelic, most place-names on the island contain elements from two languages, such as a Gaelic or English generic combined with an opaque Norse name. In such cases, the meaning of the ON element may no longer be transparent but it still works as a place-name as long as it is combined with a functioning generic.[24] Admiralty charts introduced English names − some of them translations of existing names, others entirely new creations such as Twin Rocks (NL542819) for *Bogha Dubh an Dùin* ('black reef of the fort'). In structure, Norse names are closer to English than Gaelic and would in most cases have been left unaltered by English-speaking topographers.

---

24. See Cox 1987: 91.

Figure 7: View from Druim na h-Aoineig (NL550828) with Dùn Mingulay to the
left, Arnamul to the right, and *Bogha Dubh an Dùin* (Twin Rocks) in the centre.
Photo: Anke-Beate Stahl.

Sea stacks and islets

Apart from the name Mingulay itself, most names of prominent
sea stacks and islets are of ON origin. South of Arnamul (see
above) is picturesque Gunamul (NL547825), a rock connected
to mainland Mingulay by a natural arch. The first element of
Gunamul (*Gonamul* 1892, *Gonnamul* 1903; 1931) may derive
from the ON personal name *Gunnarr*. Lianamul (NL549837),
a substantial sea rock to the north of Arnamul, is possibly a
combination of ON *lína* ('rope') and ON *múli* ('sea rock').[25]

The ON element *holmr* can be found in two prominent
islets to the north-east of Mingulay, Solon Mòr (NL574850)

---

25. In the past, ropes were used to gain access to the stack. See Buxton
1995: 15.

and Solon Beag (NL578849). Finlayson's spelling of this island, *Soalum* (1892), and Fr Allan's *Sòălum* (1903) suggest a derivation of the specific from ON *sauðr* ('sheep'), which is fitting, as sheep would have been kept there until the National Trust of Scotland purchased the island. As with Geirum, the Gaelic adjectives *mòr* ('big') and *beag* ('small') have been added at a later stage to differentiate between the two islands.

Figure 8: Caolas Lianamul (NL550836). Photo: Anke-Beate Stahl.

Another islet in this location is Sgeir nan Uighean (NL577850), which is derived from Gaelic *sgeir* ('skerry', a loanword from ON *sker*) and Gaelic *uighean* ('eggs'), suggesting that this place would have been an important source of food for the islanders. Other islets in this area are *Sgeir nam Bàirneach* (NL574852), the Gaelic name for the OS entry Barnacle Rock, and *An Adhrac* (NL576849 – *An Adhraic,* 1931) derived from Gaelic *adhrac* (f., 'horn').

The Red Boy (NL566852) is a distinctive red sea rock on the north-western side of Tom a' Reithean. On Johnson's map (1832), the name appears as *Gillachanruagh.* As previously mentioned, Dòmhnall Bàn refers to this place as *Na Gilleachan Ruadh* ('the red boys', 1931). The colour of this rock is reflected in *Creag Ruadh* or *A' Chreag Dhearg* ('red rock'), which is the name for the most north-westerly stretch of coastline on Mingulay itself, just opposite The Red Boy.

Mountains

The hills of Mingulay contain elements of all three languages: Norse, Gaelic, and English. An early version of the name for the highest point of Mingulay, *Beinacharrn* (1832), indicates that the modern name Carnan (NL553827) has been short-ened, that the original Gaelic generic *beinn* ('mountain') was lost, and that the previously specific Carnan was transformed into a generic. The area between Carnan and Biulacraig is called *Aonaig* (NL553830, 1931), with *Aonig* (1892) and *Aoinig* (1903) as variations. This element possibly derives from Gaelic *aoineadh* ('steep coastal cliff', 'very steep hillside').[26]

The name of the second highest hill, Hecla, probably derives from the ON adjective *hár* ('high') and ON *klettr* ('rock, cliff'), and is a place-name frequently used in Iceland, Norway, and other parts of Scotland.[27] In 1931, Dòmhnall Bàn dis-

---

26. For further discussion of this term, see Whyte 2017: 252; Fraser 1985.
27. Hecla is likely to be a transferred name. Transfer of name types can take place when a place-name from the homeland is semantically correctly applied to a similar looking feature in the new territory. For further

tinguished between *Hecla Bheag* and *Hecla Mhòr*, adding the Gaelic specifics 'small' and 'large', but is the only contributor to do so.

MacPhee's Hill, or *Beinn 'ic a' Phì* (NL566843), in the north, is the best-known mountain on Mingulay, despite being, at 224 m, only the third-highest on the island. Legend has it that the hill was named after the oldest son of Kenneth MacPhee, who originated from Eigg. The son travelled to Mingulay onboard a boat sent by the MacNeil of Barra to investigate why people from Mingulay had not visited Barra for a while. When the crew noticed that there was no human activity in the village, young MacPhee was sent over to find out what had happened. As soon as he realised that all the people on Mingulay had died, he reported it back to the boat. On hearing this, the crew feared it was the plague and decided it would not be safe to let MacPhee back onboard, so they left without him. Every day, the boy would climb the hill to see if anybody was coming to fetch him. After six weeks, the chief revealed to Kenneth MacPhee the reason for his son's disappearance, allowing Kenneth to crew a boat to travel to Mingulay. The son was alive, and in acknowledgment of the boy's courage, the MacPhees were given permission to settle on Mingulay rent-free.[28]

A smaller hill is Tom a' Reithean ('round knoll of the young ram', NL568847), with the alternative Gaelic version of *An Àird* ('promontory') and anglicised form *The Ard*.

---

discussion, cf. Stahl 2000: 38.
28. Bruford 1983.

Figure 9: Mingulay Bay overlooking MacPhee's Hill. Photo: Anke-Beate Stahl.

Promontories

Finlayson, Fr Allan, and Dòmhnall Bàn identify the south-westerly headland of Mingulay as *Ginish* (NL550815, 1892), *Gí-i-nish* (1903), and *Gi'inis* (1931). The ON place-name element *nes* (n., 'headland') also occurs in Bannish (NL547819) and *Meinish* (NL574830, 1892). Smaller headlands on Mingulay are Sròn an Dùin ('point of the fort', NL543819) and *Sròn Guarsay* ('point of Guarsay', NL549844) in the north-west. Ard nan Capuill (NL572851) or *Ard nan Capall* ('headland of the ponies', 1931) on the north-east side of Tom a' Reithean refers to the time when ponies would have transported the peat from this part of the island back to the village. Smaller promontories such as points are almost always Gaelic, as in Rubha Liath ('grey point', NL550814) and Rubh 'an Droma ('point of the ridge', NL571833).

The serrated west coast of the island is home to deep ravines. Many of them carry Norse names, but in most cases only the meaning of the generic, *geo*, from ON *gjá*, can be identified, as in *Heisegeo* (NL549818), with alternative spellings in *Hesigu* (1892), *Háishigeo* (1903), *Sloc Heisigeo* (1931), and the OS version Sloc Heisegeo.

The latter two versions of this name reveal a common feature in Hebridean place-names: the addition of a generic to an existing place-name. This process can result in names containing two elements that mean the same thing. In Sloc Heisegeo, the ON *gjá* and Gaelic *sloc* both mean 'chasm' or 'gully'. The creators of this name would have been unaware of the lexical meaning the original name once had. To them, *Heisegeo* was what Cox calls an *ex-nomine* unit,[29] to which they added a functioning generic, *sloc*, ensuring continuation of the name. On Mingulay, this can also be observed in names such as Sloc Ghremisgeo (approx. NL570821)[30] and *Sloc Lamarigeo* (NL573836, 1832).

The majority of smaller gullies on this island carry purely Gaelic names such as *Na Sluic* ('the gullies', NL551846), *Sloc a' Bhòcain* ('gully of the ghost', NL573846), *Sloc an Uisge* ('water gully', NL571844), or *Sloc na h-Àirde* ('gully of the headland', NL571850).

Streams and wells

There are no freshwater features beyond the streams mentioned above. Nor are there ponds or lakes except for a few peat bogs.

---

29. Cox 1987: 91.

30. Finlayson (*Tremisgu*, 1892), McDonald (*Tremmis-geo*, 1903), and MacPhee (*Sloc Hreimisgeo*, 1931) appear to position this place-name at NL568820.

There do not appear to be any sizeable wells.[31] A hollow in a rock near the school was used to obtain water for religious purposes. This place was called *St Columba's Well*. The islanders would have taken their fresh water from the streams running through the village.[32]

Settlement names

None of the maps and charts reveal a specific name for the main village by Mingulay Bay. Buxton suggests that there may have been another three sites which show evidence of human habitation.[33] The area around Skipisdale, a valley in the south-west of Mingulay, contains clusters of ruins, and land close by still shows remnants of lazy-beds, used for growing food. As suggested by the name Skipisdale, from ON *skip* ('ship') and ON *dalr* ('valley'), there is a landing place for boats.

On Dòmhnall Bàn's map of Mingulay, the river running through Skipisdale appears as *Abhainn Sumhsabaist,* and is listed as *Abhainn Sûsabost* or *-bast* in the handwritten additions on John Lorne Campbell's map. A local contributor pronounced this name as [ãũiN 'husabƐʃt] in an interview with the author in 1998. This name contains the Gaelic generic *abhainn* ('stream') and a specific, almost certainly of ON origin, possibly a settlement name.[34] As the Gaelic generic *abhainn* is feminine, it would require lenition of the following word, even if this

---

31. Local folklore mentions a water horse, believed to have lived in a well in a hollow near the top of MacPhee's Hill. See Buxton 1995: 46.
32. I am grateful to Mingulay ranger Jonathan Grant for this information.
33. Buxton 1995: 35.
34. Ian A. Fraser observed a similar case in Illeray, where the river name, containing a settlement name, survived, even as the original habitative name had been lost. See Fraser 1973: 155; Branigan and Foster 2000: 307 identify a settlement on either side of this stream.

word is not of Gaelic origin. Lenition, a form of softening of consonants, can occur with twelve consonants in the Gaelic alphabet. Phonologically, lenition can affect the consonants b, c, d, f, g, l, m, n, p, r, s, and t. However, in orthography, only nine require the insertion of the letter 'h' after the lenited consonant, with l, n, and r remaining unaltered. In many cases, the lenition of ON names makes it difficult to trace their meaning because the initial sound of the original name can be obscured.

Figure 10: Lazy-beds near Skipisdale on the slopes of Hecla.
Photo: Anke-Beate Stahl.

With *Abhainn Sumhsabaist* or *Abhainn Sûsabost*, it is at this point not possible to establish if *sumhsa* or *sûsa* is derived from ON *hús* ('house') or from the ON adj. *sunnr* ('south')[35] or noun *suðr* ('the south'). *Abhainn Sumhsabaist* is indeed located on the southern shore of Mingulay. This part of the specific, *Sumhsa-*, *Sûsa-*, or potentially *Husa-*, requires further investigation. The second part

---

35. Mentioned in correspondence with Ben Buxton.

of the specific may be derived from ON *bólstaðr* ('farm', 'settlement').[36] In relation to other place-names containing the element *bólstaðr*, this site would potentially be the most southerly one in the Outer Hebrides.[37]. Alternatively, the name may point to *Sūinsibost* (1903), a name recorded on Fr Allan's list. The specific of this name may be derived from the ON personal name *Sveinn*, which was used frequently in ON place-names.[38] This possible use of personal names as specifics is reflected in other places in the vicinity, examples being Arnamul, Gunamul, and Geirum.[39]

Another name from Fr Allan's list is *Sheōw-a-dal*. At this point in time, the location of the name is not known. The name may potentially function as settlement name.

Conclusion

The commissioning of maps and charts was mainly driven by social and political interests. Providing safe navigation for ships to facilitate trade was as important a use of maps as documenting land ownership, establishing if an area was agriculturally viable, and to help with taxation. Mingulay's earliest place-names date back to Norse times, being actively used in oral tradition for many hundreds of years before being officially recorded. The first meaningful depictions of Mingulay took place in the sixteenth century. Five hundred years later, even the remotest areas of the island can be explored digitally with the help of OS data and modern satellite images.

36. See Gammeltoft 2001; Jennings 1994: 27 for an in-depth discussion of the element *bólstaðr*.

37. The name *Abhainn Sumhsabaist/Abhainn Sûsabost* is not mentioned in Gammeltoft 2001.

38. See Gammeltoft 2001: 153.

39. For an extensive discussion of ON personal names in place-names within a Hebridean context, see Evemalm 2018.

Coining and using place-names, however, remains a very human endeavour. On its journey from collection to depiction on a map, a name passes through many hands. As such, a place-name is subject to potential error by surveyors, cartographers, local informants, sappers, engravers, and officials who decide on the inclusion or omission of the place-name, its exact location, and its spelling.

The place-names collected on lists by Finlayson (1892) and Fr Allan (1903) add a new dimension to the heritage of the island. Compiled out of interest in local history and linguistics, the names depict places that were of no interest to official cartographers but were meaningful and relevant to the people who contributed them. The short explanations for various features mentioned by Finlayson, and the attempt at phonetic spelling by Fr Allan, are valuable resources for toponymic research and go beyond what is normally found in maps or charts. The work of Finlayson, Fr Allan, Dòmhnall Bàn, and the locals who volunteered their knowledge of the land and shore illustrates the importance of individuals in preserving history. In doing so, they pave the way for onomastic research and for international comparative studies.

Mingulay's last permanent residents left in 1912, and in 2000, the island was sold to the National Trust for Scotland. Access to the island is regulated, but it still sees a steady stream of visitors attracted to adventure tourism activities, such as rock climbing and extreme swimming. Sheep are no longer kept on the island, and gradually, nature is claiming back its territory. Interest in the island has never ceased.

Acknowledgements

I would like to thank Ben Buxton for allowing me access to Donald MacPhee's unpublished map. Many thanks to

Jonathan Grant, ranger of Mingulay and Barra, who never tired of answering my questions. I am also grateful to Dr Simon Taylor who made thoughtful and valuable comments. Last but not least, I would like to thank my contributors from Barra and Vatersay: Donald MacNeil (Dogain), Joseph Sinclair (Jaw), Roderick MacLeod (Roddy Dhòmhnall Uilleim), John MacLeod (Iagan an Dot), Domhnall Dhunnchaidh Campbell (DD), Peigi Anna Campbell, and Malcolm MacNeil (Calum a Chal), who kindly scrutinised my maps and filled them with their expert knowledge. All remaining errors and inaccuracies are entirely my own.

Bibliography

Maps and place-name lists of Mingulay

1546. Lily, George. *Britanniæ Insulæ*. Rome: Anglorum studio & diligentia.

1654. Blaeu, Joan. 'Vistus Insula, vulgo Viist cum aliis minoribus ex *æbudarum n*umero ei ad meridiem adjacentibus'. In *Theatrum orbis terrarum sive Atlas novus*, vol. V. Amsterdam: Joan Blaeu.

1714. Moll, Herman. *The North Part of Britain Called Scotland*. London: Bowles, King.

1776. Mackenzie, Murdoch. 'The south part of Long Island from Bara Head to Benbecula I.' In *A maratim survey of Ireland and the west of Great Britain*, vol. II. London: Mackenzie, Plate XXVIII.

1794. Huddart, Joseph. *A New Chart of the West Coast of Scotland from the Point of Ardnamurchan to Cape Wrath*. London: Laurie & Whittle.

1804. Heather, William. *A new and improved chart of the Hebrides or Lewis Islands*. London: William Heather.

1807. Arrowsmith, Aaron. *Map of Scotland constructed from original materials*. London: A. Arrowsmith.

1827. Lothian, John. 'Western Isles'. In *Lothian's Counties of Scotland*, vol. III. Edinburgh: John Lothian.

1832. Thomson, John. 'Western Isles'. In *John Thomson's Atlas of Scotland*. Edinburgh: John Thomson & Co.

1850 (approx.). Black, A. and Black. C. *Scotland*. Edinburgh: A. and C. Black.

1865. 'Scotland – west coast – sheet 5 – Hebrides or Western Isles from Barra Head to Scarpa Island'. Admiralty Chart no. 2474 [corrections in 1872], surveyed by Otter, Thomas, Edye. London: Hydrographic Office.

1880. Ordnance Survey. 'Inverness-shire (Hebrides)'. Sheets LXX and LXVIII (1880). First edition. 1:10,560 (six-inch to the mile).

1892. Finlayson, John. Letter to J. Harvie-Brown, 9 March 1892. J.A. Harvie-Brown Papers, 20/329, Special Collections, National Museums of Scotland Library.

1903. McDonald, Fr Allan. 'A List of Non-Gaelic Place-Names in the Island of Mingulay, Near Barra-Head'. Appendix of 'The Norsemen in Uist Folklore'. *Saga-Book of the Viking Club* III [1901-1903], 413–433.

1931. Mingulay place-names as located by Donald MacPhee. Hand-drawn map with hand-drawn entries. Location of original map unknown.

Map of the West coast of Mingulay. Photocopy. Note in pencil: 'Sent by Hugh Cheape, Dec 99. From Canna House Library. J.L. Campbell's additions from Barra informants. This is the only section of the map'.

Additional Sources

Borgstrøm, C.Hj. 1936. 'The Norse Place-Names of Barra'. In J.L. Campbell (ed.), *The Book of Barra*. London: Routledge, 287–295.

Branigan, K. and Foster, P. 2000. *From Barra to Berneray: Archaeological Survey and Excavation in the Southern Isles of the Outer Hebrides*. Sheffield Environmental and Archaeological Research Campaign in the Hebrides (SEARCH) V. Sheffield: Sheffield Academic Press.

Bruford, A. (ed.). 1983. 'Nan MacKinnon'. *Tocher* 38, 2–47.

Buxton, B. 1995. *Mingulay: An Island and Its People*. Edinburgh: Birlinn.

Campbell, J.L. (ed.). 1936. *The Book of Barra*. London: Routledge and Sons.

Carmichael, A.A. (ed.). 1900. *Carmina Gadelica: Hymns and Incantations*, 2 vols. Edinburgh: T. and A. Constable.

Cleasby, R. and Vigfússon, G. 1874. *An Icelandic–English Dictionary*. Oxford: Clarendon. https://old-norse.net/search.php. Accessed 19 May 2022.

Collectanea de Rebus Albanicis. 1839. W.F. Skene and D. Gregory (eds). Edinburgh: Iona Club.

Cox, R.A.V. 1989. 'Questioning the value and validity of the term "hybrid" in a Hebridean place-name study'. *Nomina* 12, 1–9.

Evemalm, S. 2018. 'Theory and practice in the coining and transmission of place-names: a study of the Norse and Gaelic anthropo-toponyms of Lewis'. PhD thesis. University of Glasgow.

Fraser, I.A. 1973. 'Place-names of Illeray'. *Scottish Studies* 17, 155–166.

————. 1985. 'The Place-Names of a Deserted Island – Eilean nan Ron'. *Scottish Studies* 22, 83–90.

Gammeltoft, P. 2001. 'The place-name element *bólstaðr* in the North Atlantic area'. PhD thesis. University of Copenhagen.

'Geirum Mór, Mingulay', *Canmore: National Record of the Historic Environment*. https://canmore.org.uk/site/21381/geirum-mr-mingulay. Accessed 19 May 2022.

Jennings, A. 1994. 'Historical study of the Gael and Norse in Western Scotland from c. 795 to c. 1000'. PhD thesis. University of Edinburgh.

————. 1996. 'Historic and linguistic evidence for Gall-Gaidheil and Norse in Western Scotland'. In P. Sture Ureland and I. Clarkson (eds), *Language Contact across the North Atlantic*. Tübingen: Max Niemeyer Verlag, 61–74.

Martin, M. 1703. *A Description of the Western Isles of Scotland*. London: Andrew Bell.

'Mingulay, Dun Mingulay', *Canmore: National Record of the Historic Environment*. https://canmore.org.uk/site/272187/mingulay-dun-mingulay. Accessed 19 May 2022.

Nicolaisen, W.F.H. 2001. *Scottish Place-Names*. Edinburgh: John Donald.

Ordnance Survey Name Books. 1878. Inverness-shire, Outer Hebrides, vol. II (Barra Parish, OS1/18/2). https://scotlandsplaces.gov.uk/digital-volumes/ordnance-survey-name-books/

inverness-shire-os-name-books-1876-1878/inverness-shire-outer-hebrides-volume-02. Accessed 19 May 2022.

Stahl, A.-B. 2000. 'Place-names of Barra in the Outer Hebrides'. PhD thesis. University of Edinburgh. https://era.ed.ac.uk/handle/1842/15754.

Whyte, A.C. 2017. 'Settlement-Names and Society: analysis of the medieval districts of Forsa and Moloros in the parish of Torosay, Mull'. PhD thesis. University of Glasgow.

Withers, C.W.J. 2000. 'Authorising Landscape: "Authority", Naming and the Ordnance Survey's Mapping of the Scottish Highlands in the Nineteenth Century'. *Journal of Historical Geography* 26:4, 532–554.

· X ·

After the Vikings: Language Shift in Scotland and the Irish Sea World

Pavel Iosad

What was the sociolinguistic situation in the North Atlantic in the Viking Age and its aftermath? In the near-total absence of reliable, contemporary historical sources, enquiry into language maintenance and shift in the Northern Isles, the Hebrides, and the Irish Sea basin is a fascinating, multidisciplinary enterprise, to which Arne Kruse has made very significant contributions. In this chapter, I consider how the Western Norse vernacular of the Scandinavian settlers in much of this region was ultimately replaced by the Gaelic languages. My perspective is grounded in historical sociolinguistics: I will interrogate what interplay between the sociohistorical context and specific types of contact-induced change could be expected in this region in the medieval period, and try to match these predictions against what is known about Norse-Gaelic contact.

Britain and Ireland in the North Atlantic

Our discussion begins during the Viking Age. It is uncontroversial that the rise of 'Norse' polities was associated with both population movement and cultural diffusion, including the introduction of North Germanic as the vernacular of a large, sometimes overwhelming proportion of the population. We cannot recap the debates around whether Viking-Age settlement was associated with a degree of continuity or resulted in a 'blank slate' situation.[1] Ultimately, we must reckon with a situation in which Western Norse was the first language of both a political and cultural elite plugged into the wider North Atlantic world and much of the local population working the land.

It is, of course, important not to erase the heterogeneity of the interactions across the region. Norse settlement in the Danelaw was different from its counterparts in Ireland, the Hebrides, the Northern Isles, or the Isle of Man. We can reconstruct differences in the number of Norse-speaking settlers, their proportion within the local population, the aim of their migration, and their social position within the resulting communities. All these factors would remain in flux across time, with the same region subject to raiding, hostile takeover, relatively peaceful settlement, and language shift to and away from Norse at different stages of the 'Viking expansion'. In particular, we need to distinguish between areas with a preponderance of Norse speakers and those that were within the Scandinavian political and cultural ambit, but where the Norse language co-existed with other vernaculars, or where significant settlement may not have lasted for too long.

The precise role of the Norse population is at the heart of the distinction between the 'inner' and the 'outer' zone of settlement in Scotland postulated by Arne Kruse and Andrew Jennings.[2] Local studies for parts of the 'inner' zone, such as Bute[3] and

---

1. Barrett 2003; Kruse 2005; Jennings and Kruse 2005; Macniven 2015.
2. Jennings 1996; Jennings and Kruse 2009a; 2009b.
3. Márkus 2012.

south-eastern Mull,[4] have confirmed the basic correctness of this division, even though some controversy remains about the precise status of individual localities (such as Islay).[5]

Ultimately, Norse ceased to be spoken in both the 'inner' and the 'outer' zones by the early modern period. Only in Caithness and the Northern Isles did it take longer, with Scots (and eventually English) taking over. Unfortunately, historical sources are very largely silent about the sociolinguistics of Gaelic (re)expansion. Evidence for the mechanism of language shift and relationship between the communities is mostly circumstantial. Apart from what can be recovered from political history, it comes from literary sources, archaeology, onomastics, and linguistics.

Here, I concentrate on the linguistic arguments. Language contact in the North Atlantic sphere has left an imprint on both Norse[6] and Gaelic.[7] This influence is observed in the lexicon (including the onomasticon) and the grammatical systems. In particular, Scottish Gaelic sound patterns such as preaspiration and tonal accents have often been treated as unusual and ascribed to influence from Norse.

The narrowly linguistic arguments for and against the proposition have been litigated quite extensively; I refer the reader to Iosad (in preparation) for an up-to-date overview. Here, I would like to focus on the sociohistorical context by addressing the following question: how plausible is it that the situation in the Norse-Gaelic world would give rise to contact-induced change in Gaelic?

---

4. Whyte 2017.
5. Macniven 2015.
6. Gammeltoft 2004; 2007; Lindqvist 2015.
7. Marstrander 1932; Borgstrøm 1974; R.W. McDonald 2015.

Mechanisms of contact-induced change

Current understanding in historical sociolinguistics[8] builds on insights that relate the outcomes of contact-induced change to an interplay of the sociohistorical context, mechanisms of language learning, and the different impacts of these factors on different areas of grammar.

The key notion here is *agency*.[9] From a cognitive perspective, the most relevant distinction is between *borrowing* (L1 agency) and *imposition* (L2 agency). In the former, the contact-induced feature comes into the target language via those users who have acquired it by mechanisms of first-language acquisition. This is the pathway engaged where the agents are multilingual. They have L1 command of both systems, but the coexistence of the two grammars also results in convergence in the usage of such speakers. Under these conditions, there are essentially no limits to *what* can and cannot be borrowed. Certain tendencies in the 'borrowability' of individual features can be identified, but in the right social conditions, almost any feature can be subject to transfer.

Conversely, in situations of L2 agency, the contact feature appears first among those who have acquired the target language via second-language acquisition mechanisms, usually as adults, and often 'incompletely' or 'imperfectly' compared to L1 users. Such contact can involve the transfer of specific kinds of structures, or a more general 'simplification' of grammatical structure that does not directly build on models in the putative 'source'. Interestingly, large-scale borrowing of general lexical items is often avoided in such situations.

---

8. See, for instance, Thomason and Kaufman 1988; Trudgill 2011; Matras 2020.
9. Winford 2005.

A second important dimension for the reconstruction of historical contact situations is social. For a contact-induced feature of multilinguals' language to become more widely established, they need to form a significant proportion of the relevant speech community. Leaving aside the precise definition of 'significant' (this can, but perhaps does not have to, refer to numerical preponderance), we should note that in L1 agency ('borrowing') situations, wide-ranging contact-induced change is facilitated when bilingualism is widespread within the community and persists over long periods of time. Such communities can remain multilingual for many generations, with a stable situation not characterised by asymmetries of status that drive language shift. In such communities, we can expect quite profound contact-induced change affecting all levels of structure – including, crucially for our purposes, sound patterns.

L2 agency ('imposition'), on the other hand, commonly occurs under conditions of rapid language shift, when adult learners of the target language come to constitute a large proportion of the speech community. The change propagates when a contact-influenced variety becomes the L1 of the next generation of users. Here, the ultimate outcome of contact depends strongly on the social circumstances. Sometimes, the community of 'language shifters' can maintain a distinct identity within the larger population, in which case their variety can be considered an 'ethnolect'. At other times, their language loses its ethnic connotation. However, since rapid language shift is often driven by status asymmetries, the association of this contact-influenced variety with lower-status groups can persist, which will hinder the wider spread of originally contact-induced features (or at least their attestation in higher-status written varieties). Alternatively, of course, it is also possible that, despite their contact origins, such features can enter the pool of variants within the target language community, and eventually spread to those groups who originally lacked any ties to the users of the source language. All these scenarios are viable, and they are of interest to us because sound patterns are widely recognised as a kind of linguistic feature that is especially prone to transfer in an L2 agency context.

Grammatical change in the transition from Old Gaelic to the Classical Modern Gaelic system that became established by the end of the twelfth century is rarely ascribed to contact with Norse or any other language. Granted, the grammatical system was simplified, with a drastic decrease in the complexity of verbal morphology and a reduced system of nominal inflection. However, this trend is in evidence across all of the Gaelic-speaking world, including areas with no history of significant Viking influence, and language contact does not appear necessary to explain it. Consequently, scholars' attention has focused on the lexicon and on sound patterns. It is particularly interesting to note that at least two phonetic/phonological features linking Gaelic and Norse – preaspiration[10] and tonal accents[11] – are relatively rare cross-linguistically and appear to have an areal concentration in Northern Europe.

Having thus identified the phenomena of interest, we will now evaluate the likelihood of each conceivable contact scenario for the origin of these features in the Gaelic languages.

Norse-Gaelic contacts and sociolinguistic typology

Lexical evidence

The influence of Norse on the Gaelic lexicon is undeniable. The evidence of onomastic contacts has been extensively

---

10. Wagner 1964.
11. Jakobson 1931; Ternes 1980.

considered in previous work.[12] Here, I focus on the appellative lexicon: as noted earlier, lexical borrowings are often avoided in L2-agency situations, and so their presence could be diagnostic of an L1-agency mechanism.

Unfortunately, the evidence is more equivocal than it is often given credit for. Although Norse borrowings are no doubt attested in the Gaelic languages,[13] a careful consideration of the nature of these borrowings shows them to be primarily cultural vocabulary, related to the economy and natural environment of the Atlantic littoral.[14] Such vocabulary is far less diagnostic of the general situation with respect to bilingualism.

Furthermore, although the lexical geography of the *Gàidhealtachd* remains understudied,[15] it is acknowledged that northern dialects corresponding to the 'outer' zone show a greater Norse impact;[16] one well-known example is *nàbaidh* for 'neighbour' (Norse *nábúi*), which is restricted to northern dialects in contrast to *comhairsneachd* (Old Gaelic *comarsanach*), the normal word in 'inner zone' regions.[17] Thus, the lexical evidence does not support an especially strong role for Norse influence on Gaelic outwith the area of the most intensive Scandinavian settlement.

Phonetic and phonological evidence

Assume for the sake of the argument that linguistic arguments can support the proposition that Gaelic underwent phonetic and phonological influence from Norse in the post-Viking Age

12. Cf. Clancy 2011; Fellows-Jensen 2015.
13. See Marstrander 1915, and more recently, Schulze-Thulin 1996; R.W. McDonald 2021.
14. See especially R.W. McDonald 2015.
15. Ó Maolalaigh 2010.
16. Gillies 2007.
17. Ó Dochartaigh 1996.

period. Phonetic influence is consistent with both L1 and L2 agency in language contact. In the former case, it is effected via convergence in the speech of multilingual users; in the latter, it occurs initially as a kind of 'foreigner accent' during language shift before becoming established among a community of L1 users. Can either of these scenarios be sustained?

Both options are certainly *a priori* plausible. First, we could envisage Gaelicisation as rapid language shift, where phonetic influence would have come about via L2 agency and the imposition of Norse phonetic and phonological patterns as part of an 'imperfect learning' process. However, there is little evidence for any phonological patterns being introduced into Gaelic under Norse influence. Thomas Stewart[18] discusses a case of 'imposition' related to transfer of lexical items beginning with certain consonant clusters such as *sp-* and *st-*, which are overrepresented in the set of words borrowed from Norse. However, whatever the reason behind this numerical skew, such structures had been present in the Gaelic vocabulary even prior to contact with Norse, and are not diagnostic of an L2-driven scenario.[19]

More widespread in the literature is a somewhat more complex scenario relying on a combination of convergence under L1 agency and later propagation. In his influential paper,[20] Carl Marstrander envisaged a period of prolonged bilingualism in high-contact areas, leading to the formation of a Norse-influenced (*norskstemplet*) variety of Gaelic, followed by an expansion of such originally Norse features into the rest of the *Gàidhealtachd*. Carl Hj. Borgstrøm also considered this course

---

18. Stewart 2004.
19. I would like to thank an anonymous peer reviewer for helpful discussion on this point.
20. Marstrander 1932.

of events plausible.[21] The existence of high-contact varieties of both Norse and Gaelic in Scotland is also posited by Christer Lindqvist.[22] The existence of such a 'hybrid' community is almost assured given the widely recognised presence of individuals with links to Gaelic-speaking regions of Britain and Ireland in other North Atlantic communities, most notably Iceland.[23]

I suggest, however, that the key problem, presenting insurmountable difficulties for either scenario, is propagation. Why would an L2 variety of Gaelic formed in high-contact areas become particularly influential throughout the *Gàidhealtachd*? There are at least three possibilities.

One is sheer weight of numbers, if speakers of such a variety were to be a majority of Gaelic speakers. This is unlikely: much of the Gaelic-speaking world remained little affected by Viking settlement, especially on the mainland, or lay in the 'inner zone', where Norse political and cultural influence was combined with the maintenance of a large, primarily Gaelic-speaking population.

The second possibility is the spread of features from the outer zone driven by internal dynamics of the Gaelic-speaking world. Such a scenario, however, is difficult to motivate. We need to ask ourselves whether the high-contact variety of Gaelic would be a plausible source for innovation.

One possible scenario for such 'secondary' spread involves the formation of an ethnolect, when the contact variety remains strongly associated with a 'post-Viking' identity. This is certainly possible, but the very existence of a language shift away from Norse and cultural Gaelicisation rather suggest that this identity would not be associated with a particularly high status.

---

21. Borgstrøm 1974.
22. Lindqvist 2015.
23. Hermann Pálsson 1996; Gísli Sigurðsson 2000. See also, more generally, the discussion of the 'Viking diaspora' in Jesch 2015.

Alternatively, the loss of Norse political power did *not* lead to loss of status, perhaps because of a de-ethnolectalisation effect.[24] Here, we can profitably draw on the Icelandic parallel: it is clear that, by the later medieval period, individuals could bear Gaelic names or evince other links to Britain and Ireland without being strongly identified as in any way other than fully integrated into Icelandic society. Once again, although this option is not inconceivable, what evidence we have seems to speak against it.

It is no surprise that the Outer Hebrides or the north-west mainland do not figure prominently in our written sources. Nominally, they were subject to the Hiberno-Norse polities before coming into the Gaelic ambit. Economically, politically, and culturally, this world was focused around the Irish Sea and the inner seas of Scotland, including Dublin, the Isle of Man, Argyll, and Galloway.[25] We also need to remember that, although today the Gaelic 'centre of gravity' is tilted towards the areas of historically heavy Viking settlement in the north and west, Gaelic ecclesiastical, political, and cultural power – until well into the early modern era – was concentrated in Argyll and further east, including areas such as Perthshire, near to the interface with Lowland Scotland.[26] There is very little contemporaneous evidence that suggests the north and west as an important centre of innovation within the Gaelic world in the immediate 'post-Viking' era.

What, then, is the most likely scenario for the Norse to Gaelic language shift in medieval Scotland? A significant degree of bilingualism is widely agreed on,[27] possibly lasting until as late as the thirteenth century. However, we need to ask ourselves what the role of the bilingual group was within the larger speech community. We have already referred to findings

24. See especially Lindqvist 2015: 176–177.
25. R.A. McDonald 1997; 2021.
26. For discussion, see Mac Aonghuis 1990; Meek 1996.
27. Gillies 2007; Jennings and Kruse 2009b; Clancy 2011.

from the inner zone that suggest that the Norse cultural and
political intrusion may not have led to long-lasting linguistic
disruption. Especially instructive is the case of Man. A major
centre of Norse political and cultural power, it may nevertheless
have preserved some continuity alongside heavy Scandinavian
settlement.[28] This surely leads us to expect a similar prolonged
period of 'twilight'. Nevertheless, the evidence discussed by
Michael Barnes[29] suggests that, even in this stronghold of vernacular Norse, it was on the way out if not extinct by the end of
the thirteenth century. In fact, it was already under pressure in
the 900s and isolated from the rest of the West Norse speech
community by the mid-1000s. As a result, Norse influence on
Manx, outwith the lexicon, is negligible or absent.[30]

Conclusion

Overall, we undoubtedly need to reckon with a community speaking a high-contact variety of Gaelic with some Norse-induced
features. It is likely that, in some areas, a stable bilingual situation
could have resulted in convergence led by L1 speakers and the
formation of an ethnolectal (regional) variety, whilst in others,
L2 agency would be the more important mechanism. In either
case, however, this community would not be especially influential,
and would, over time, gradually shift to the linguistic norms of
the wider *Gàidhealtachd*. Critically, under this scenario, we cannot
expect much in the way of structural influence of Norse on Gaelic,
because there is no viable vector for such a transfer.

This conclusion can be supported by at least three plausible
parallels from instances of language shift to English, namely in

28. Thomson 2015; Fellows-Jensen 2015; Steinforth 2015.
29. Barnes 2004.
30. Lewin 2017; *pace* Williams 1996; R.W. McDonald 2021.

Cornwall,[31] the Isle of Man,[32] and Ulster.[33] In all of these cases, gradual language shift has not resulted in extensive (if, indeed, any) contact-induced phonetic or phonological change, whilst leaving traces in areas such as the lexicon.

In view of these parallels, I conclude that historical sociolinguistics cannot support the proposition that Norse exerted phonetic and phonological influence on the Gaelic varieties of Scotland. It is certainly possible that the Norse vernacular, and maybe Norse-influenced Gaelic dialects, remained spoken in parts of the *Gàidhealtachd* until late in the medieval period. It would, nevertheless, be wise not to overstate their role in the subsequent development of the Gaelic languages.[34]

Bibliography

Barnes, Michael P. 2004. 'The Scandinavian Languages in the British Isles: The Runic Evidence'. In Jonathan Adams and Katherine Holman (eds), *Scandinavia and Europe 800–1350: Contact, Conflict, and Coexistence*. Medieval Texts and Cultures of Northern Europe 4. Turnhout: Brepols, 121–136.

Barrett, James H. 2003. 'Culture Contact in Viking Age Scotland'. In James H. Barrett (ed.), *Contact, Continuity, and Collapse: The Norse Colonization of the North Atlantic*. Studies in the Early Middle Ages 5. Turnhout: Brepols, 73–112.

Borgstrøm, Carl Hjalmar. 1974. 'On the influence of Norse on Scottish Gaelic: Preaspiration of stops and pitch patterns'. *Lochlann* 6, 91–107.

---

31. Wakelin 1975.
32. Lewin 2017.
33. Maguire 2020.
34. Thanks are due to Christopher Lewin and to an anonymous peer reviewer for clarifying discussion and important literature suggestions. All errors of fact and judgement remain my own.

Clancy, Thomas Owen. 2011. 'Gaelic in medieval Scotland: Advent and expansion'. *Proceedings of the British Academy* 167, 349–392.

Fellows-Jensen, Gillian. 2015. 'The Manx place-name evidence'. In Seán Duffy and Harold Mytum (eds), *A New History of the Isle of Man*, vol. III. Liverpool: Liverpool University Press, 257–280.

Gammeltoft, Peder. 2004. 'Scandinavian-Gaelic contacts: Can Place-Names and Place-Name Elements be Used as a Source for Contact-Linguistic Research?' *North-West European Language Evolution (NOWELE)* 44, 51–90.

———. 2007. 'Scandinavian Naming-Systems in the Hebrides: A Way of Understanding how the Scandinavians were in Contact with Gaels and Picts?' In Beverley Ballin Smith et al. (eds), *West over Sea: Studies in Scandinavian Sea-Borne Expansion and Settlement before 1300. A Festschrift in Honour of Dr Barbara E. Crawford.* The Northern World 31. Leiden; Boston: Brill, 479–496.

Gillies, William. 2007. 'The Lion's Tongues: Languages of Scotland to 1314'. In Thomas Owen Clancy et al. (eds), *The Edinburgh History of Scottish Literature*, vol. I. Edinburgh: Edinburgh University Press, 52–62.

Iosad, Pavel. In preparation. *Phonological Drift and Language Contact: The Northern European Phonological Area.* Cambridge: Cambridge University Press.

Jakobson, Roman. 1931. 'Über die phonologischen Sprachbünde'. *Réunion phonologique internationale tenue à Prague (18–21/XII 1930).* Travaux du Cercle Linguistique de Prague 4. Prague: Jednota československých matematiků a fysiků, 164–183.

Jennings, Andrew. 1996. 'Historical and linguistic evidence for Gall-Gaidheil and Norse in Western Scotland'. In P. Sture Ureland and Iain Clarkson (eds), *Language Contact across the North Atlantic.* Linguistische Arbeiten 359. Tübingen: Max Niemeyer Verlag, 61–74.

Jennings, Andrew and Kruse, Arne. 2005. 'An Ethnic Enigma: Norse, Pict and Gael in the Western Isles'. In Andras Mortensen and Símun V. Arge (eds), *Viking and Norse in the North Atlantic: Selected papers from the Proceedings of the Fourteenth Viking Congress, Tórshavn, 19–30 July 2001*. Tórshavn: Føroya Fróðskaparfelag, 284–296.

———. 2009a. 'From Dál Riata to the Gall-Ghàidheil'. *Viking and Medieval Scandinavia* 5, 123–149.

———. 2009b. 'One coast – three peoples: Names and ethnicity in the Scottish west during the early Viking period'. In Alex Woolf (ed.), *Scandinavian Scotland Twenty Years after: Proceedings of a Day Conference Held on 19 February 2007*. St John's House Papers 12. St Andrews: University of St Andrews Committee for Dark Age Studies, 75–102.

Jesch, Judith. 2015. *The Viking Diaspora*. London: Routledge.

Kruse, Arne. 2005. 'Explorers, raiders, and settlers: The Norse impact upon Hebridean place-names'. In Peder Gammeltoft et al. (eds), *Cultural Contacts in the North Atlantic Region: The Evidence of Names*. NORNA; Scottish Place-Name Society; Society for Name Studies of Britain and Ireland, 141–156.

Lewin, Christopher. 2017. '"Manx hardly deserved to live": Perspectives on language contact and language shift'. *Zeitschrift für celtische Philologie* 64, 141–206.

Lindqvist, Christer. 2015. *Norn im keltischen Kontext*. Amsterdam: John Benjamins.

Mac Aonghuis, Iain. 1990. 'Cainnt is cànan'. *An Tarbh* 1, 23–25.

Macniven, Alan. 2015. *The Vikings in Islay: The Place of Names in Hebridean Settlement History*. Edinburgh: Birlinn.

Maguire, Warren. 2020. *Language and Dialect Contact in Ireland: The Phonological Origins of Mid-Ulster English*. Edinburgh: Edinburgh University Press.

Márkus, Gilbert. 2012. *The Place-Names of Bute*. Donington: Shaun Tyas.

Marstrander, Carl J.S. 1915. *Bidrag til det norske sprogs historie i Irland*. Videnskabs-Selskabets Skrifter. II. Hist.-Filos. Klasse 5. Kristiania: I kommission hos Jacob Dybwad.

———. 1932. 'Okklusiver og substrater'. *Norsk tidsskrift for sprogvidenskap* 5, 258–304.

Matras, Yaron. 2020. *Language Contact*, 2nd edition. Cambridge: Cambridge University Press.

McDonald, R. Andrew. 1997. *The Kingdom of the Isles: Scotland's Western Seaboard, c. 1100–c. 1136*. Scottish Historical Review Monographs 4. East Linton: Tuckwell Press.

———. 2021. *The Sea Kings: The Late Norse Kingdoms of Man and the Isles*. Edinburgh: John Donald.

McDonald, Roderick W. 2015. 'Vikings in the Hebridean economy: Methodology and Gaelic language evidence of Scandinavian influence'. *Zeitschrift für celtische Philologie* 62, 97–182.

———. 2021. 'The problem of Manx: Norse linguistic evidence for the survival of Manx Gaelic in the Scandinavian period'. In Dirk H. Steinforth and Charles C. Rozier (eds), *Britain and its Neighbours: Cultural Contacts and Exchanges in Medieval and Early Modern Europe*. London: Routledge, 87–104.

Meek, Donald E. 1996. 'The Scots-Gaelic scribes on late medieval Perthshire: An overview of the orthography and contents of the Book of the Dean of Lismore'. In Janet Hadley Williams (ed.), *Stewart Style, 1513–1542: Essays on the Court of James V*. East Linton: Tuckwell Press.

Ó Dochartaigh, Cathair. 1996. 'Two loans in Scottish Gaelic'. *Scottish Gaelic Studies* 17, 305–313.

Ó Maolalaigh, Roibeard. 2010. 'Caochlaidheachd leicseachail agus "snowflakes" sa Ghàidhlig'. In Gillian Munro and Richard A.V. Cox (eds), *Cànan & Cultar / Language & Culture: Rannsachadh na Gàidhlig 4*. Edinburgh: Dunedin Academic Press, 7–21.

Pálsson, Hermann. 1996. *Keltar á Íslandi*. Reykjavík: Háskólaútgáfan.

Schulze-Thulin, Britta. 1996. 'Old Norse in Ireland'. In P. Sture Ureland and Iain Clarkson (eds), *Language Contact across the North Atlantic*. Linguistische Arbeiten 359. Tübingen: Max Niemeyer Verlag, 83–114.

Sigurðsson, Gísli. 2000. *Gaelic Influence in Iceland: Historical and Literary Contacts. A Survey of Research*, 2nd edition. Reykjavík: University of Iceland Press.

Steinforth, Dirk H. 2015. *Die skandinavische Besiedlung auf der Isle of Man: Eine archäologische und historische Untersuchung zur frühen Wikingerzeit in der Irischen See*. Ergänzungsbände zum Reallexikon der Germanischen Altertumskunde 92. Berlin; New York: De Gruyter.

Stewart, Jr, Thomas W. 2004. 'Lexical imposition: Old Norse vocabulary in Scottish Gaelic'. *Diachronica* 21:2, 393–420.

Ternes, Elmar. 1980. 'Scottish Gaelic phonemics viewed in a typological perspective'. *Lingua* 52:1-2, 73–88.

Thomason, Sarah G. and Kaufman, Terrence. 1988. *Language Contact, Creolization, and Genetic Linguistics*. Berkeley: University of California Press.

Thomson, R.L. 2015. 'Language in Man: Prehistory to literacy'. In Seán Duffy and Harold Mytum (eds), *A New History of the Isle of Man*, vol. III. Liverpool: Liverpool University Press, 241–256.

Trudgill, Peter. 2011. *Sociolinguistic Typology: Social Determinants of Linguistic Complexity*. Oxford: Oxford University Press.

Wagner, Heinrich. 1964. 'Nordeuropäische Lautgeographie'. *Zeitschrift für celtische Philologie* 29, 225–298.

Wakelin, Martyn F. 1975. *Language and History in Cornwall*. Leicester: Leicester University Press.

Whyte, Alasdair C. 2017. 'Settlement-Names and Society: Analysis of the medieval districts of Forsa and Moloros in the parish of Torosay, Mull'. PhD thesis. University of Glasgow.

Williams, Nicholas. 1996. 'An Mhanannais'. In Liam Breatnach et al. (eds), *Stair na Gaeilge: In ómós do Phádraig Ó Fiannachta*. Maynooth: Department of Old Irish, 703–744.

Winford, Donald. 2005. 'Contact-induced changes: Classification and processes'. *Diachronica* 22:2, 373–427.

· XI ·

Assigned to Favourable Sites? What Spatial Analyses Can Reveal about Place-Names Ending in *-bólstaðr* and *-staðir*

Peder Gammeltoft

Introduction

Place-name research is, at the outset, a linguistic discipline of profound interdisciplinarity. To be able to interpret a place-name and understand the context in which it was coined, the name researcher must be a jack of all trades. Albeit specialised in linguistics, the name researcher also needs to have a broad insight into history, archaeology, history of administration, geography, biology, etc. Interdisciplinary interaction is always present in toponymic research, with new insights from relevant disciplines needing to be considered in an onomastic light. This makes place-name research ever dynamic in nature.

Over the past many years, Norwegian place-name research has mainly focused on securing the country's rich treasure trove of minor names before they vanished. Part of the reason can be found in the fact that Oluf Rygh's *Norske Gaardnavne* (Norwegian Farm Names), in having dealt with most settlement names, gave little reason for national and systematic research into settlement names and corresponding name types.

One notable exception is the handbook *Norsk stadnamnleksikon* ('Norwegian Place-name Lexicon'),[1] which provides a general overview of the Norwegian place-name stock, from regional names to the names of municipalities, cities, towns, settlements, and natural features. However, *Norske Gaardnavne* remains the main Norwegian source for settlement names.

The nineteen volumes of *Norske Gaardnavne* were published from 1897 to 1936 (and reprinted twice).[2] The series was then digitised around the turn of the millennium and has now been georeferenced as part of its digital relaunch. When the place-name archive, alongside the other constituents of the Norwegian Language Collections, was transferred from the University of Oslo to the University of Bergen, the digitised *Norske Gaardnavne* was singled out for upgrading and georeferencing. This effort has made it possible to see and research place-names and place-name types in their spatial context and to link these to information about cultural and natural phenomena, archaeological finds, as well as cadastral, statistical, and administrative data.

The obvious advantage of a georeferenced *Norske Gaardnavne* is the possibility of making distribution maps to show such things as period-specific settlement name distributions, as well as distributions of typologically and semantically similar place-name types. However, to illustrate the full potential of this work, the dataset from the new digital *Norske Gaardnavne* will be coupled to cadastral and land-resource information. The aim is to demonstrate how the digitisation and georeferencing of *Norske Gaardnavne* can be used in advancing place-name research and other research fields. The focus will be on showing the relevance of spatially enabled place-name resources,

---

1. Stemshaug and Sandnes 1997.
2. Rygh 1897–1936.

and how to combine these with modern cadastral data and resource-management data to make retrogressive analyses[3] of two Viking Age place-name types, *bólstaðr* and *staðir* (m.), in order to gauge their status and significance.

The basis for the study: *Norske Gaardnavne*

The place-name series *Norske Gaardnavne* is based on the place-name standardisation work carried out in connection with a cadastral revision.[4] In 1863, the Norwegian parliament commissioned a general revision of the Norwegian cadastre of public and private lands to allow for consistent land-ownership records, and to revise land taxation in Norway. Another intention of this work was to correct inconsistencies and errors in the spelling of place-names from earlier cadastres.

In 1878, Professor of Archaeology Oluf Rygh, Professor of Linguistics Sophus Bugge, and the Old Norse expert Johan Fritzner were appointed members of a commission to do this spelling revision of the cadastre. At the time, there was no officially sanctioned standard of written Norwegian. This caused challenges to the standardisation effort. Rygh, Bugge, and Fritzner realised that, since most Norwegians spoke their own dialect, the best way to establish a correct spelling of a place-name was through the local, inherited pronunciation. To accomplish this, the commission recorded place-name pronunciations used among ordinary people in everyday conversations.

---

3. The retrogressive method provides a means of studying spatial-historical phenomena by using data or evidence from a younger time period to analyse earlier spatial conditions. Cf. e.g. Antonson 2018.

4. In Norway, all real estate must be registered in *Norges Matrikkel* (the Norwegian Cadastre), the official property register. The cadastre provides an overview of properties, property boundaries, addresses, and buildings that are necessary for planning, development, use, and protection of real estate.

Differences were observed regionally as well as between urban and remote areas.[5] Through this effort, they found consistent relationships between current oral forms of place-names and the original names as found in both the current parish records and in historical sources.

The main tool for establishing the origin and etymology was to record the names found in historical sources. The commission reviewed several sources, such as *Diplomatarium Norvegicum* and old land records like *Aslak Bolts jordebok*, *Biskop Øysteins jordebok* (*Røde bok*), *Oslo Kapitels Gods jordebok*, *Olaf Engelbrektsens jordebok*, *Bergens kalvskinn*, and the cadastral works from 1665 and 1723.

This monumental work was completed in 1882, in time for the new cadastre to be published in 1886. However, realising the potential of the work and methodology of the linguistic revision of the cadastre, the parliament allocated funding in 1896 to publish the revised place-names in an academic series. The first volume of the series *Norske Gaardnavne* was published in 1897. The series is published in county (*amt*) volumes and is structured according to local government areas (*herred*), thus mirroring the structural framework of the 1886 cadastre. There is a further subdivision into parishes, although this division is not directly relevant to the cadastre. Each cadastral unit of significance – farm settlement areas (*gard*) as well as many individual farm holdings (*bruk*) – features a section preceded by their cadastral number, followed by the standardised place-name as section heading. This, in turn, is followed by pronunciation information, source forms, and an etymological

---

5. Cf. University of Bergen, Norwegian Language Collections: The Place-Name Archive, SPR/A-0003/O/Oa/L0001, an original manuscript by Oluf Rygh submitted to the Cadastral Commission, 10 June 1882. https://www. arkivportalen.no/entity/no_SPR_arkiv000000028351. Accessed 16 May 2022.

description. In this way, *Norske Gaardnavne* documents almost 61,000 settlement names.[6]

Norske Gaardnavne had a monumental significance for place-name research in north-western Europe, as its etymological interpretations originated in scientific linguistic principles based on pronunciation and a detailed compilation of written records on land ownership. Not only did this establish a standard for scientific and systematic place-name research, but the concept also became the inspiration for similar studies in e.g. Denmark (*Danmarks stednavne*), England (*Survey of English Place-Names*), Scotland (*The Survey of Scottish Place-Names*), and Sweden (*Sveriges ortnamn*).

The next step: digitising *Norske Gaardnavne*

Norway has been at the forefront of digitising central historical sources. As early as 1981, the Registration Centre for Historical Data was established at the University of Tromsø, with the aim of creating a national population register. One of their digitisations was the 1886 Cadastre (*Matrikkelen av 1886*). A few years later, in the mid-1990s, the *Dokumentasjonsprosjektet* (the Norwegian Documentation Project)[7] began mass-digitising central sources, including *Norske Gaardnavne*, which has been digitally available for almost twenty years. So far, no attempt has been made to link these digitised sources together or to link historical cadastres to the modern, spatially enabled cadastre. The main reason for this is that the Norwegian cadastral

---

6. The digitised volumes of *Norske Gaardnavne* are freely available at the *Nasjonalbiblioteket* (Norwegian National Library). https://www.nb.no s.v. Norske Gaardnavne. Accessed 15 May 2022.
7. 'Dokumentasjonsprosjektet', https://www.dokpro.uio.no. Accessed 15 May 2022.

code system is dynamic,[8] which poses a serious limitation on historical-administrative research. Even though the current cadastral system was only introduced in 1886, the consequence is that interlinking or merging with modern cadastral data or modern coordinate data has been nigh on impossible – until now.

With the transfer of the Norwegian Language Collections from the University of Oslo to the University of Bergen in 2016, the opportunity arose to reorient the Norwegian Place-Name Archive and to upgrade and modernise the collections. Having established an overview, the decision was made to begin the modernisation with the cadastre and related works. However, to be able to furnish the cadastre with coordinates, it was necessary to introduce a means of managing cadastral information over time. In 2018, Kåre Bævre, of the *Folkehelseinstituttet* (Institute of Public Health) in Oslo, provided the Language Collections with a copy of his work on the historical cadastre, which made it possible to combine cadastres over time. I have subsequently upgraded the historical cadastre and assigned precise coordinates to cadastral records. Thus, it has been possible to georeference the 1886 Cadastre, as well as all the other digital historical cadastres from 1838 to 2010. All other historical and administrative resources that make use of the cadastral system, such as censuses and statistical accounts – and *Norske Gaardnavne* – were also able to be georeferenced according to the same principles.[9]

The work was undertaken in several stages. Since the cadastre documents property history, it was necessary to first

---

8. The Norwegian cadastre code is based on the current local government code. Hence, as the local government system has undergone both reforms and individual revisions, each cadastral number has, on average, been amended three times since the establishment of the current cadastral numbering system in 1886.

9. Gammeltoft 2021: 81.

introduce a unique cross-historical cadastral code (*historisk matrikkelnummer*) at the level of individual farm holdings (*bruk*), as well as a code to manage the cadastral farm (*gard*) or township (*historisk gardsnummer*). This was then applied to each historical cadastre since 1838. The historical cadastral code ID is composed of a twelve-digit code system, i.e. four digits for the *kommunenummer* (local government code) + four digits for *gardsnummer* (cadastral farm code) + four digits for *bruksnummer* (individual farm holding/cadastral code). The higher farm-level ID consists only of eight digits for the *kommunenummer* + *gardsnummer*.

After the 1886 Cadastre and *Norske Gaardnavne* had been coded with historical cadastral and farm codes, all farms and single holdings could be assigned point coordinates harvested from the modern cadastre. The point coordinate deposition was quite complicated. However, it was possible to designate coordinates to some 99.2% of the cadastral units treated in *Norske Gaardnavne*.

The result, as shown in Figure 1, is a complete and full localisation of Norwegian farm names in all of Norway, apart from Finnmark (which did not have the same cadastral system as the rest of Norway until the second half of the twentieth century). As the figure also shows, the concentrations vary considerably from region to region. The greatest concentrations are found in the Viken area around the Oslofjord, the Mjøsa region north of Oslo, as well as on the southern tip of Norway between Kristiansand and Flekkefjord. Lower concentrations can be found along the entire coast and fjords of Vestlandet, Telemark, central Trøndelag, and – to a lesser degree – in southern Nordland. These concentration areas correspond to the main agricultural areas of Norway.[10]

---

10. OECD 2021: 37.

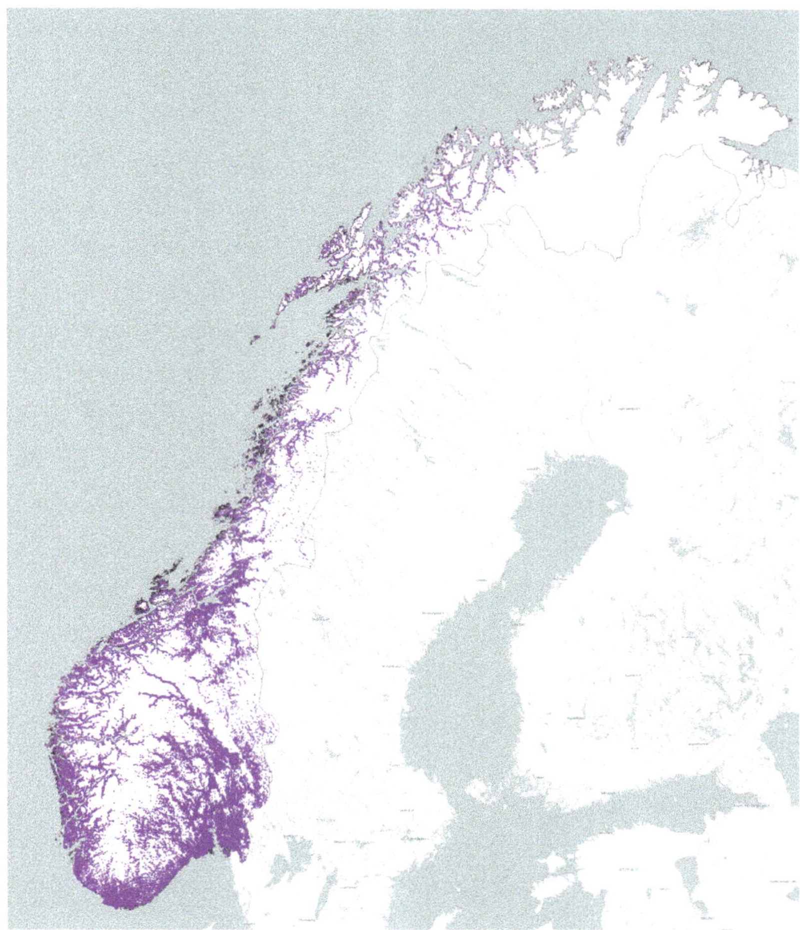

Figure 1: Point map of place-names in Oluf Rygh's *Norske Gaardnavne* (1897–1936), except for Finnmark. This volume has not been digitised. In addition, this county did not have the same cadastral system as the rest of Norway, making georeferencing very difficult. Basemap: Carto Positron, CartoDB (CC-BY). Overlay: Peder Gammeltoft.

The new, spatially enabled digital *Norske Gaardnavne*[11] differs somewhat from the printed series, as well as the initial digital version of *Norske Gaardnavne* of the *Dokumentasjonsprosjektet*.

11. *Norske stadnamn – Norske stedsnavn*, https://toponymi.spraksamlingane. no. Accessed 15 May 2022.

The printed volumes contained roughly 60,800 entries, consisting of farm names (c. 40,000), single holdings (c. 15,600), settlements no longer in existence (c. 4,200), as well as administrative names, such as parish (*sogn*) and local government area (*herred*) names (c. 1,000). In the online version of *Dokumentasjonsprosjektet*, however, only farm names and single holdings are searchable, that is, a total of 55,600 items.

The new digital *Norske Gaardnavne* has one entry per place-name unit. Some 3,600 entries in *Norske Gaardnavne* cover several cadastral units, the so-called *navnegard* (multiple cadastral units with the same place-name origin, resulting from an early splitting up of a parent farm into two or more independent farm units). In the printed version, these are distinguished by having more than one cadastral farm number. This means that an additional 8,100 farm-name entries have been added to the dataset. In total, the new digital *Norske Gaardnavne* has c. 69,000 entries with cadastral information and coordinates.

How to determine the typical size of a Norwegian farm area (*gard*)

Today, the Norwegian cadastre is managed by the Norwegian Mapping Agency (*Statens kartverk*) as a digital cadastre. The cadastre is entirely managed as a system for individual land holdings. It is thus only possible to use the cadastre in unchanged form on individual cadastral units (*bruk*). There are no datasets or thematic GIS layers for higher-level *gard* cadastral units, thus making analyses at the farm level of *Norske Gaardnavne* impossible. To create a higher-level thematic cadastral layer, it was necessary to dissolve the 2.5 million cadastral *bruk* units into the 47,000 higher-level *gard* cadastral farm units of Norway. Needless to say, this was a monumental task, but one

which enabled not only the georeferencing of the Norwegian
cadastre and *Norske Gaardnavne*, but also quantitative studies
of farm-unit sizes and name types. The potential of this dataset is considerable, as it will enable the study of Norwegian
place-names from different angles – and align these closer to
computational onomastic studies, such as those carried out in
Denmark.[12]

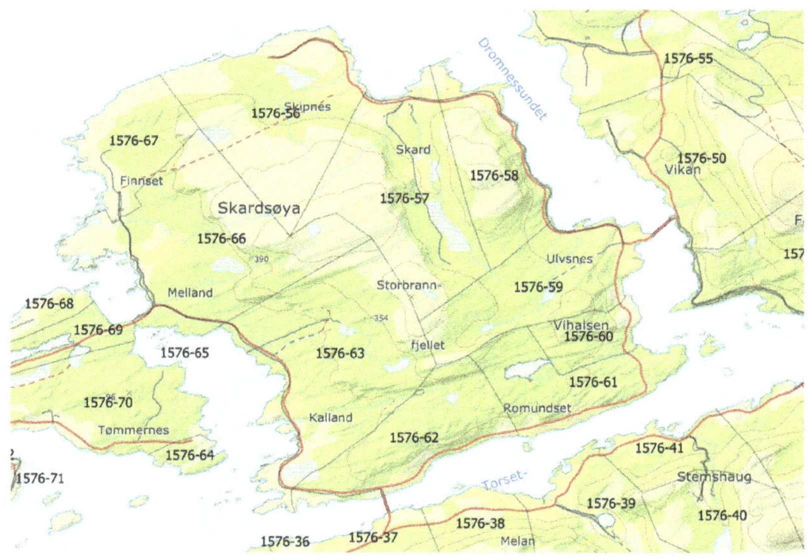

Figure 2: Map of section of Aure *kommune* in Møre and Romsdal. The grey lines
represent cadastral farm-unit (*gard*) borders. The numbers represent the current
farm-unit codes (*gardsnummer*). Basemap: Topografisk norgeskart, *Statens kartverk*
(CC-BY). Overlay: Peder Gammeltoft.

This project is very much a work in progress, and the figures
of the analyses may change slightly as the material gets pro-
gressively quality assured. To eliminate 'noise' resulting from
aggregation errors and individual cadastral changes, the figures
are calculated using the so-called Gaussian distribution model,

12. Cf. Jakobsen 2004, as well as Dam 2015, albeit with a slightly different
focus.

also called a normal distribution model. The model is mainly used in social sciences and natural sciences to calculate the general, typical distribution of independent, randomly generated variables from a central distribution range constituting 68% of the material. The distribution provides a parameterised mathematical function that can be used to calculate the probability for any individual observation from the sample to be within this range.[13]

This study operates only with national figures, although figures can, naturally, be calculated for any administrative level, from county level (*fylke*) through to local-government level (*kommune*). The national average *gard* cadastral farm-area size for Norway is 173 hectares (ha) – see grey column in Figure 3. However, the Gaussian distribution range is relatively broad, from 26 to 517 ha. The average resides in the lower half of the distribution range, signalling that the general size is more often under 173 ha than over.

The 'average farm' serves as the median by which to judge any place-name type regardless of number and distribution. The place-name types have been collated by consulting the individual place-name interpretations in *Norske Gaardnavne*. The interpretations have been aggregated from the general index volume of *Norske Gaardnavne* from 1936, individual textual interpretations, and from spellings. These still need to be independently verified, so final figures may vary slightly with time.

For this study, the focus will be on the place-name elements *bólstaðr* and *staðir*. However, to place them in a wider context, several place-name types have been analysed for comparison.

---

13. 'Normal distribution', *Encyclopædia Britannica*, https://www.britannica.com/topic/normal-distribution. Accessed 15 May 2022.

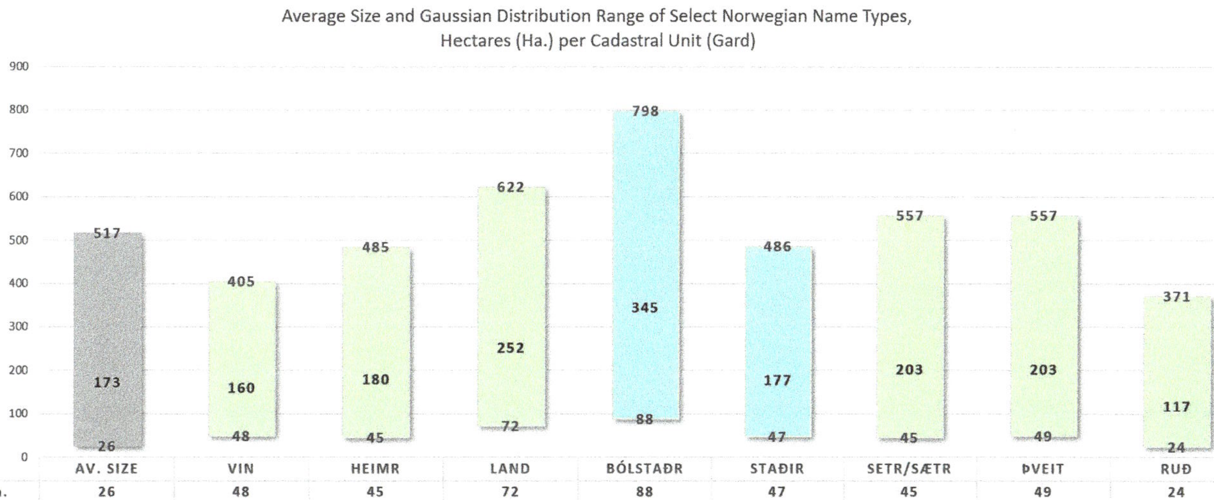

	AV. SIZE	VIN	HEIMR	LAND	BÓLSTAÐR	STAÐIR	SETR/SÆTR	ÞVEIT	RUÐ
Min.	26	48	45	72	88	47	45	49	24
Average	173	160	180	252	345	177	203	203	117
Max.	517	405	485	622	798	486	557	557	371

Figure 3: Diagram of selected Norwegian place-name types showing average and Gaussian distribution range of the overall size of the top-level *gard* cadastral farm units. The grey column represents the national average and distribution range. The blue columns constitutes the place-name types ON *bólstaðr* and *staðir* (m.), which are focused on in this study. The green columns are name types chosen for comparison. Diagram: Peder Gammeltoft.

The examples have been chosen to represent place-name types considered to belong to different time periods. In addition, ON *setr/sætr* (n.) has been chosen as an example of a place-name type in which the named localities were seemingly established with a greater focus on shieling economy. All elements are also found in the Scottish Viking Age colonies, although ON *vin* (f.) and *heimr* (m.) are only represented in limited numbers in the Northern Isles.

The elements ON *vin* (f.) and *heimr* (m.) represent typical pre-Viking Age settlement types. As such, it is only *heimr* (m.) that can be called a settlement name type, although it is questionable what the general meaning of the word 'home' really covers.[14] Is it the living quarters, the farm itself, or the resource area? ON *vin* (f.) originally designated a topographical feature, most likely some sort of grassland meadow or similar. At some time, these place-name types consolidated into farm settlements, akin to today's situation. The elements ON *land* (n.), *bólstaðr* (m.), and *staðir* (m.) represent the archetypal Viking Age settlement types. ON *land* (n.) is, like *vin* (f.), not really a settlement name type as such, but rather a topographical feature designating an area suitable for agriculture.[15] The name types ON *bólstaðr* and *staðir* (m.) are usually considered to be settlement name types, although the base meaning of the word ON *staðr* (m.), in a topographical sense, literally just means 'place' or 'place for permanent occupation'.[16] Again, it is a rather diffuse way of describing the type of settlement and its means of sustenance.

---

14. Cf. 'heimr m.', https://oda.uib.no/ordbok/?men=norrone s.v. heimr. Accessed 15 May 2022.

15. Cf. 'land n.⁴', https://oda.uib.no/ordbok/?men=norrone s.v. land. Accessed 15 May 2022.

16. Cf. 'staðr m.', https://oda.uib.no/ordbok/?men=norrone s.v. staðr. Accessed 15 May 2022.

The remaining elements ON *þveit* (f.), *setr/sætr* (n.), and *ruð* (n.) represent chronologically later settlement types than the above-mentioned ones. Of these, only ON *setr/sætr* (n.) has any settlement connotation, again with a rather vague core meaning of 'seat, place to stay', which developed into the known meaning of 'shieling, mountain pastures'.[17] The meaning of the elements ON *þveit* (f.) and *ruð* (n.) imply some sort of sectioning-off or development from a main settlement, as the core meaning of the word ON *þveit* (f.) is 'cut off'[18] and ON *ruð* (n.) carries the meaning of 'cleared place in a forest'.[19] All three elements would probably have been present in the Viking Age but mainly in the latter part, and ON *ruð* (n.), in particular, is associated more with medieval settlement development.

The application of the name elements at the time of name-formation may thus not necessarily have been the same as the historically known farm unit. They may reflect earlier and different settlement structures,[20] if these were settlements at all at the time of naming. However, from the earliest sources, it seems that both the application of meaning and type of locality were firmly placed in the settlement category. It should, therefore, be possible to say something about the type of settlement by examining the size of the settlement and its arable. For instance, if a place-name type is large in overall farm unit size but comparatively small in its size of arable, it may suggest a greater focus on extensive farming and non-agrarian sources of income. On the other hand, a relatively large proportion of a farm unit's overall size dedicated to farmland indicates

---

17. Cf. 'setr n.', https://oda.uib.no/ordbok/?men=norrone s.v. setr; 'sætr n.', https://oda.uib.no/ s.v. sætr. Both accessed 15 May 2022.

18. Cf. 'þveit f.', https://oda.uib.no/ordbok/?men=norrone s.v þveit. Accessed 15 May 2022.

19. Cf. 'ruð n.', https://oda.uib.no/ordbok/?men=norrone s.v. ruð. Accessed 15 May 2022.

20. Cf. Pilø 2005: 261–265; Gjerpe 2014: 68–69.

that the place-name type is oriented towards the cultivation of land.

With a baseline of 173 hectares in average size and a Gaussian distribution range of 26 to 517 ha, we can compare this to sizes of name types. It is generally assumed – and clearly suggested by studies from Denmark[21] – that the older the settlements are, the larger they are – especially in terms of value based on production capacity.[22] From the Norwegian material, however, the picture looks a bit more blurred. At the same time, it must be said that Norway has large regional differences in agricultural potential and capacity from region to region. Such differences may well lie behind any inconclusive results. For instance, the early name type *vin* (f.) is generally smaller than the national average, at 160 ha. The Gaussian distribution range does show that the name type's lower typical size is larger than the average range, although the typical larger size falls some 20% shy of the national average. ON *heimr* (m.) and *land* (n.), on the other hand, exceed the national average at 180 ha and 252 ha, respectively. In particular, *land* (n.) has a higher than baseline Gaussian distribution range.

Of the chronologically young place-name types, ON *setr/sætr* (n.) and ON *þveit* (f.) are surprisingly close to the national Gaussian distribution range, albeit slightly above average – typologically representing relatively solid settlements. ON *ruð* (n.) is, unsurprisingly, well below both the national average as well as the Gaussian distribution range. ON *ruð* (n.) is especially applied to small and later farm units. Working from the assumption that 'older equals larger', this is the expected distribution for this name type. It is a surprise, however, that the name types ON *setr/sætr* (n.) and ON *þveit* (f.) exceed the sizes

---

21. Jakobsen 2004: 74–80.
22. Cf. Dam 2015.

and Gaussian distribution range of the older place-name types. So 'older equals larger' does not seem to work for Norway, not when using overall size of the farm unit as the sole parameter.

The two central place-name types of this study, ON *bólstaðr* and *staðir* (m.), display some rather interesting and surprising characteristics. Sizewise, ON *staðir* (m.), as a place-name type, is almost identical in Gaussian distribution to the older name type ON *heimr (*m.), although the average of *staðir*-farms is a little lower. This name type can generally be seen to be relatively akin to the national average. The average of farm units in ON *bólstaðr* (m.) is, however, double that of the national average. But with a Gaussian distribution range of 88–798, this settlement name type is far greater than the average. Why ON *bólstaðr* (m.) displays such a deviation from the norm is not clear from the farm size alone, but it is suggestive of a farming economy differing from the norm or of a difference in farming management.

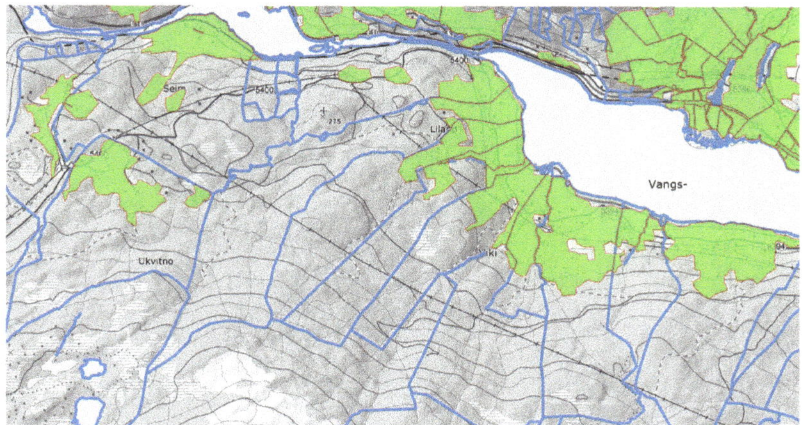

Figure 4: Map of section of Voss *kommune* in Vestland. The blue lines represent cadastral farm unit (*gard*) borders, and the green areas are farmland areas (NIBIO AR50 types settlement and farmland combined). Each farmland area is divided into units falling within cadastral farm unit areas. Basemap: Topografisk norgeskart gråtone, *Statens kartverk* (CC-BY). Overlays: Peder Gammeltoft.

Calculating the amount of arable per farm unit

Sheer size is not everything, though, and a better parameter to measure cadastral farm units may well be to look at the amount of arable in each of the 47,000 Norwegian *gard* units. There is no such data readily available for Norway, and no attempt at conducting research into this at a national level has ever been attempted. However, with the availability of area resource GIS themes from the Norwegian Institute of Bioeconomy Research (NIBIO), it has been possible to create a bespoke dataset for the purpose of researching amounts of arable per cadastral farm unit. This process is not easy, however, as it entails dividing the resource map into areas matching that of the cadastral farm units, which includes several stages of dataset modification before it is usable for such a purpose. The dataset used for this was the NIBIO AR50 dataset,[23] which is a generalised area resource map for Norway at the scale of 1:50,000. There are eight main resource classification themes, from which *Agriculture* (code 20) was chosen. It encompasses fully cultivated land, surface cultivated land, and infield pasture.

One of the major changes to the Norwegian landscape is settlement encroachment on agricultural land, so to be able to produce a more historically correct farmland theme per cadastral unit, the theme *Built-up areas* (code 10) – comprising residential areas, towns, cities, transport, industrial areas, etc. – was also included. There is a danger that this theme will inflate the numbers, as not just arable land is given over to settlement and industry. Every retrogressive geographical study operates with the problem of aligning historical phenomena

---

23. 'Dokumentasjon av AR50', *NIBIO*, https://www.nibio.no/tjenester/nedlasting-av-kartdata. Accessed 15 May 2022.

with later statistical information, and figures are never going to fully match former conditions – they can only act as a guiding figure for statistical purposes. The current agricultural state of Norway is definitely not the same as in earlier time periods, but since Norway's topography leaves the country with no more than 3% agricultural land available, these figures cannot be significantly different now from then – there simply is nowhere to expand into.

For any type of standard Norwegian farm, the arable has traditionally been the main source of income, with outfield pasture an important addition to the economy. Thus, arable resource information will be relevant to the evaluation of the significance of place-name types. As Figure 5 shows, the average arable of an average *gard* cadastral unit for Norway is a mere 23 ha, with a Gaussian distribution range of 3 to 56 ha. If the overall farm-unit size did not show the expected 'older equals bigger' distribution known from Denmark, the arable gives a somewhat clearer overall picture of larger sizes for older name types and lower for younger.

For instance, place-names of the *vin*-type are almost double in average size as compared with the chronologically later ON *setr/sætr* (n.), *þveit* (f.), and *ruð* (n.) place-name types. Generally, the pre-Viking and Viking Age types have larger averages and Gaussian distributions, and only the later name types are close or lower than the average-size farm unit. This generally speaks to the agricultural focus of these place-name types, and that these constituted important and high-status name types in their time. ON *vin* (f.) is the one with the highest average of 42 ha and a Gaussian distribution range of 17–80 ha. The name type ON *heimr* (m.) is not far behind, with an average of 35 ha and a Gaussian distribution range of 11–73 ha.

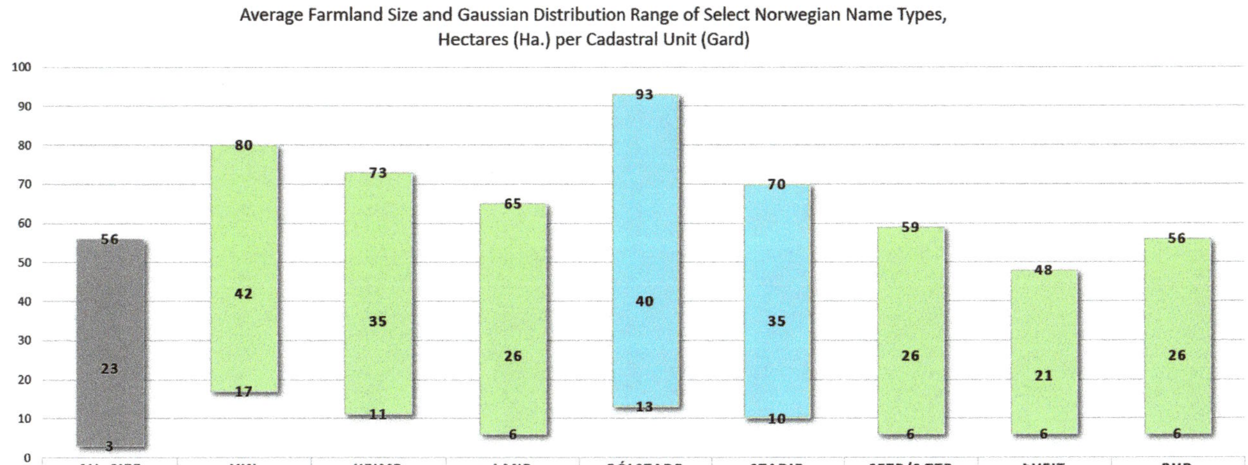

Average Farmland Size and Gaussian Distribution Range of Select Norwegian Name Types, Hectares (Ha.) per Cadastral Unit (Gard)

	AV. SIZE	VIN	HEIMR	LAND	BÓLSTAÐR	STAÐIR	SETR/SÆTR	ÞVEIT	RUÐ
Min.	3	17	11	6	13	10	6	6	6
Average	23	42	35	26	40	35	26	21	26
Max.	56	80	73	65	93	70	59	48	56

Figure 5: Diagram of select Norwegian place-name types showing average and Gaussian distribution range of farmland sizes of top-level *gard* cadastral farm units. The grey column represents the national average and distribution range. The blue columns constitute the place-name types ON *bólstaðr* and *staðir* (m.) focused on in this study. The green columns are name types chosen for comparison. Diagram: Peder Gammeltoft.

It is surprising that ON *bólstaðr* and *staðir* (m.) almost match the averages of their pre-Viking counterparts at 40 and 35 ha, respectively. ON *bólstaðr* (m.) has a Gaussian distribution range of almost double that of the farm-unit average, and at 13–93 ha, it clearly supersedes ON *vin* (f.) in the top of the distribution range. The Gaussian distribution range of ON *staðir* (m.), on the other hand, is like that of the pre-Viking name types. ON *land* (n.), which sported the largest overall size average and one of the highest Gaussian distribution ranges, is exhibiting relatively low figures when it comes to available agricultural land. The average of 25 ha and Gaussian distribution of 7–65 ha for ON *land* (n.) aligns it closer to the agricultural potentials displayed in later name types than to its contemporaries. This seems to signal a focus on extensive farming in addition to cultivation.

Again, ON *bólstaðr* and *staðir* (m.) demonstrate that they are important settlement types that must have been high-status at the time of their establishment. It is, however, surprising that they match or exceed their pre-Viking counterparts. How this is the case is uncertain, and cannot be solved without further study. However, with two different geographical parameters to judge settlement types on, it is possible to look at the percentage of agricultural land compared to overall size. If the percentage is high, then the agricultural focus is clearly on cultivation, whereas a low percentage will signal a greater reliance on extensive farming, pastoral activities, and hunting.

Figure 6 shows that the average farm unit agricultural resource percentage is 16% and the Gaussian distribution range runs from 1% to 50% (grey column), meaning that the typical average cadastral farm unit in Norway only has about one sixth agricultural land, the remainder being too hilly, mountainous, wet, or with too shallow a soil cover to be viable for cultivation. The normal percentage range is quite large, but a cadastral farm unit does typically not have half of its total area under cultivation.

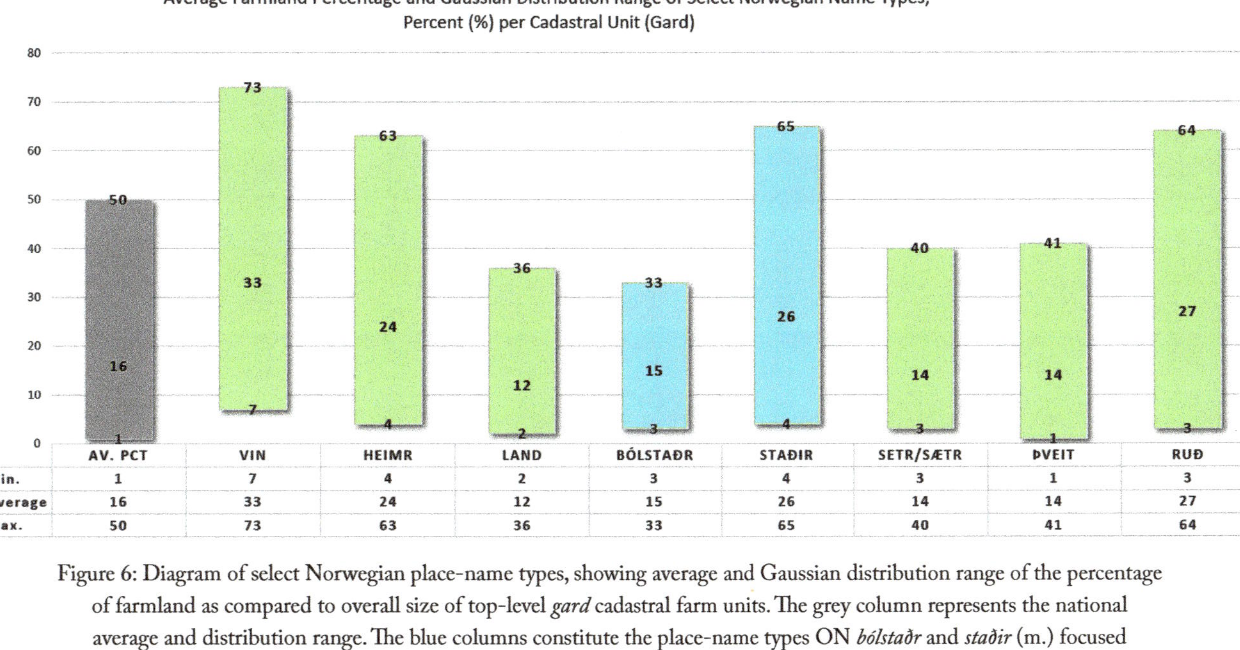

	AV. PCT	VIN	HEIMR	LAND	BÓLSTAÐR	STAÐIR	SETR/SÆTR	ÞVEIT	RUÐ
Min.	1	7	4	2	3	4	3	1	3
Average	16	33	24	12	15	26	14	14	27
Max.	50	73	63	36	33	65	40	41	64

Figure 6: Diagram of select Norwegian place-name types, showing average and Gaussian distribution range of the percentage of farmland as compared to overall size of top-level *gard* cadastral farm units. The grey column represents the national average and distribution range. The blue columns constitute the place-name types ON *bólstaðr* and *staðir* (m.) focused on in this study. The green columns are name types chosen for comparison. Diagram: Peder Gammeltoft.

In comparison, the pre-Viking Age ON *vin* (f.) and *heimr* (m.) by far exceed both the average and the Gaussian distribution range percentages. On average, a *vin*-settlement has a third of its total land under cultivation, and although the size range varies a lot, it may be as high as 73% within the normal distribution. ON *heimr* (m.) does not have figures quite as prominent as those of ON *vin* (f.), but around a quarter of the total size taken up by the arable is average, even though the arable can take up anything from 4% to 63%. Of the Viking Age name types, ON *staðir* (m.) features almost identical figures to ON *heimr* (m.), albeit with a percent or two higher in average and in normal distribution. By comparison, ON *land* (n.) and ON *bólstaðr* (m.) have rather poor farmland averages, below that of the national average for cadastral farm units, at 12% and 15% respectively. And within the Gaussian distribution range, they never exceed more than 36% and 33% of the total. For the name type ON *land* (n.), this is not very surprising, given their generally large overall size and low farmland figures. Yet for ON *bólstaðr* (m.), this is rather unexpected, as not only does it have a high overall size average, but it also has high farmland features. This suggests that this name type relies on a dual intensive-extensive farming economy, possibly even to the extent that these sites were originally laid out according to a certain farmland to size ratio.

The chronologically later place-name types ON *setr/sætr* (n.) and ON *þveit* (f.) share almost identical average and Gaussian distribution range percentages, being generally below the national cadastral farm unit average, as would be expected by later settlement types. ON *ruð* (n.), on the other hand, is almost on par with ON *staðir* (m.). This, however, is owed to the generally low overall size of the name type and comparatively large farmland size average.

What can we use this knowledge for?

Previous research into Norwegian place-name types have focussed on etymology and to some extent on post-medieval taxation (*landskyld*). There were no other means of subjecting place-name types to comparative studies. With the introduction of geographical information systems (GIS) to the humanities, spatial analyses of place-name types have gained popularity.[24] They are, however, still difficult to undertake due to a lack of availability of basic spatial GIS themes that can be used and adapted for this kind of research. This chapter has demonstrated how adaptation of datasets can yield new information which can be used in future analyses.

Although ON *bólstaðr* and *staðir* (m.) share the same word – ON *staðr* (m. 'place' or 'place for permanent occupation') – they perform quite differently when compared spatially. Both place-name types are above the average farm size, but ON *bólstaðr* (m.) has the highest overall size Gaussian distribution range (88–798 ha; average sized farm: 26–517 ha), showing that this name type can occupy very large tracts of land as cadastral farm units. However, the average *bólstaðr*-farm size (345 ha) is double that of the national average (173 ha). The amount of arable farmland (13–93 ha; average 40 ha) is almost double the national cadastral farm unit average (3–56 ha; average 23 ha), signalling that cultivation must have figured as a central element.

More surprisingly, however, the percentage of farmland in relation to overall size is only average and of a very limited Gaussian distribution range of 3–33% of a farm's entire size. This means that *bólstaðr*-farms have a stable ratio between

---

24. Cf. e.g. Foster 2020: 371–385.

farmland and overall size. Regardless of the size of the arable, the overall size is proportionally similar: on average four to five times larger than that of the arable. So although there was a cultivation focus, extensive sustenance activities must also have played a significant role. This name-type trait may relate to the first element of the name type compound, ON *ból* (n.). This word has several meanings, one being 'land of a certain size, yielding a certain amount in rent'.[25] It is not inconceivable that as a farm rent unit, the value was assessed based on a farming potential where extensive farming sustenance figures on par with intensive farming.

ON *staðir* (m.), on the other hand, has a more restricted overall Gaussian distribution range (47–486 ha) than the average cadastral farm unit (26–517 ha). It is roughly similar in size to the contemporary name types ON *setr/sætr* (n.) and *þveit* (f.), and seems to reflect the 'standard' Viking Age size needed for a farm unit. However, the average arable farmland size (35 ha vs 25 and 21 ha, respectively) and generous Gaussian distribution range of ON *staðir* (10–70 ha) is considerably higher than for ON *setr/sætr* (6–59 ha) and *þveit* (6–48 ha), and is also well above that of the average (3–56 ha; average 23 ha). It is thus not surprising that the name type has a higher than normal farmland-to-overall-size ratio. In fact, it is comparable to that of older settlement types like ON *heimr* (m.) and, to some extent, ON *vin* (f.) The high percentage of arable of the total size (4–65%; average 26%) as compared to the average sized farm (1–50%; average 16%) strongly indicates that the farming focus must generally have been on cultivation and to a lesser extent on extensive farming.

---

25. 'ból n.', https://oda.uib.no/ordbok/?men=norrone s.v. ból. Accessed 15 May 2022.

Conclusion

This study has shown that both place-name types were used for high-status settlements, which may help us understand the popularity of the name types in the Viking Age colonies in Britain and Ireland. Whether their original meanings were carried over and applied to similar types of farms in the Scottish Viking Age colonies is unknown. Lindsey Macgregor's studies of the taxation and value of the place-name types in Shetland demonstrated that ON *staðir* (m.) was definitely applied to high-status secondary farms on very productive land.[26] However, for *bólstaðr*-farms, she concluded that they were generally of a much more restricted nature and established as secondary farms on cultivated fields. Their valuation was also generally lower than for *staðir*-farms.[27] This seems somewhat at odds with what this study finds for Norway, but outfield extensive farming may perhaps not have been factored in in the same way within the later Shetland taxation valuations. Either that, or the settlements may have experienced subsequent splitting up, thus blurring the later picture.

Concerns can be raised over applying modern material retrogressively to historical names. This is, indeed, a valid concern. A retrogressive analysis can only be indicative of past conditions. However, where the Norwegian natural and topographical conditions determine agricultural activity and sustenance, current conditions will not be significantly different to past ones. Without this type of analysis, we will still be forced to describe place-name types in the broadest possible terms without any quantifiable evidence. In a spatial analysis, the measurements

---

26. Macgregor 1986: 92–93.
27. Ibid.: 96.

are precise and quantifiable. And with a constant set of measurable parameters, quantitative statistics are enabled across any place-name type at any number and distribution.

Creating the datasets behind this analysis has not been straightforward, but is now proven to be possible. It is my hope that this will be the first of several forays into quantitative analyses of place-names, to attain a better understanding of our onomastic past. Arne Kruse, to whom this edited volume is dedicated, has worked tirelessly on improving our knowledge of place-names and putting them into context. This chapter has been written with the above aim, and it is therefore appropriate to dedicate it to Arne and his work!

Bibliography

Antonson, H. 2018. 'Revisiting the "Reading Landscape Backwards" Approach: Advantages, Disadvantages, and Use of the Retrogressive Method'. *Rural Landscapes: Society, Environment, History*, 5:1, 1–15.

Cleasby, R. and Vigfússon, G. 1874. *An Icelandic–English Dictionary*, 2nd edition. Oxford: The Clarendon Press. https://oda.uib.no/ordbok/?men=norrone. Accessed 15 May 2022.

Dam, P. 2015. *Bebyggelser og stednavnetyper*. Navnestudier 44. Copenhagen: Museum Tusculanum.

Danmarks Stednavne, 1922–2022. 27 vols. Copenhagen: Københavns Universitets Arkiv for Navneforskning.

'Dokumentasjon av AR50', *NIBIO*. https://www.nibio.no/tjenester/nedlasting-av-kartdata. Accessed 15 May 2022.

Encyclopædia Britannica. https://www.britannica.com. Accessed 15 May 2022.

English Place-Name Society. 1924–2012. *Survey of English Place-Names*, 89 vols. Cambridge: Cambridge University Press.

Foster, R. 2020. 'Viking shieling names and Scandinavian settlement in Scotland'. In A. Pedersen and S. Sindbæk (eds), *Viking Encounters:*

Proceedings of the 18th Viking Congress. Aarhus: Aarhus University Press, 371–385.

Fritzner, J. 1886–1896. *Ordbog over det gamle norske Sprog*. Kristiania: Den norske Forlagsforening. https://oda.uib.no/ordbok/?men=norrone. Accessed 15 May 2022.

Gammeltoft, P. 2001. *The place-name element bólstaðr in the North Atlantic area*. Copenhagen: Reitzel.

————. 2021. 'De norske historiske matrikler'. In P. Dam et al. (eds), *Brugen af historiske kort – fag for fag*. Geoforum Perspektiv 38. Aalborg: Geoforum Danmark, 77–86. doi: 10.5278/ojs.perspektiv. v20i38.6588. Accessed 22 May 2021.

Gjerpe, L.E. 2014. 'Kontinuitet i jernalderens bosetning. Et utdatert postulat arvet fra 1814-generasjonen?' *Viking – Norsk arkeologisk årbok* 77, 55–75.

Jakobsen, J. 2004. 'Middelalderens landbrug og bebyggelse. En statistisk-geografisk undersøgelse af landbrugs- og bebyggelsesforhold i NV-Sjælland gennem vikingetid, middelalder og tidlig moderne tid'. MA thesis. University of Roskilde.

Macgregor, L. 1986. 'Norse Naming Elements in Shetland and Faroe: A Comparative Study'. *Northern Studies* 23, 84–101.

Norske stadnamn – Norske stedsnavn. https://toponymi.spraksamlingane. no. Accessed 15 May 2022.

OECD (Organisation for Economic Co-operation and Development). 2021. *Policies for the Future of Farming and Food in Norway, OECD Agriculture and Food Policy Reviews*. Paris: OECD Publishing. doi: 10.1787/20b14991-en. Accessed 11 November 2021.

Pilø, L. 2005. *Bosted – urgård – enkeltgård: en analyse av premissene i den norske bosetningshistoriske forskningstradisjon på bakgrunn av bebyggelsesarkeologisk feltarbeid på Hedemarken*. Oslo archaeological series, 3. Oslo: University of Oslo.

Rygh, O. 1897–1936. *Norske Gaardnavne: Oplysninger samlede til brug ved Matrikelens Revision*. Kristiania/Oslo: Fabritius, 1–19.

Scottish Place Name Society. 2006–2020. *The Survey of Scottish place-names,* 8 vols. Donnington: Shaun Tyas.

Stemshaug, O. and Sandnes, J. 1997. *Norsk stadnamnleksikon*, 4th edition. Oslo: Samlaget.

Sveriges ortnamn, 1906–2014. 85 vols. Uppsala: Kungl. Ortnamnskommissionen.

University of Bergen, Norwegian Language Collections: The Place-Name Archive. SPR/A-0003/O/Oa/L0001. An original manuscript by Oluf Rygh submitted to the Cadastral Commission, 10 June 1882. https://www.arkivportalen.no/entity/no_SPR_arkiv000000028351. Accessed 16 May 2022.

· XII ·

When Herring Was King? Boom and Recession in Shetland, 1880–1893

Linda Riddell

I know Arne mainly through the Scottish Society for Northern Studies; I was secretary when he was president from 2012 to 2015. But we have more in common than that. We are both from fishing backgrounds, he from Veiholmen, a small island community in the municipality of Smøla, in the western part of Norway – even further north than my hometown, Lerwick in Shetland. Before he became an academic, Arne was a fisherman, as were my Shetland-based male ancestors. My chapter recognises that connection and explores a time when Scotland and Norway were competitors in the herring trade.

Introduction

That herring was the king of fish is an ancient, widespread, and popular idea. This metaphor has been used about Shetland to imply that herring, the most important fish, ruled as the economic mainstay in the late nineteenth and early twentieth centuries.[1] The boom in the herring fishery is also well known;

---

1. E.g. Halcrow 1994: 146; Fenton 1978: 603–615; Irvine 1985: 151–163.

in 'one of the most spectacular episodes in the whole history of fisheries in Britain', it escalated from the late 1870s to a peak in 1905 and ended abruptly, though temporarily, with the First World War.[2] The effects were far-reaching: 'the herring fishery in Shetland after 1880 [...] permeated into every aspect of the life of the islands'.[3] This period has been portrayed as when Shetland emerged from economic backwardness and deprivation into the modern world. Herring has often been cast as the catalyst and financier of this development – for example, 'the herring boom [...] was a major event in Shetland and did much to change and modernise the islands; and most important it lifted living standards to a new and higher level'.[4]

But it was not a story of continuous prosperity: 'Though history tends to show the period from 1880 onwards as a time of unbroken success [...] there were numerous downs as well as ups [...] It was far from being the universal bonanza which history tends to imply'.[5] Six hectic years of phenomenal growth were followed by a longer recession (Figure 1).

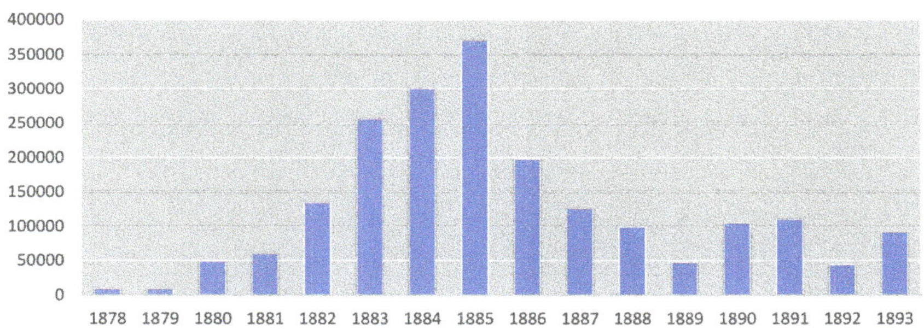

Figure 1: Herring cured in Shetland (barrels). Source: Fishery Board for Scotland.

2. Coull 2007: 114.
3. Goodlad 1971: 196.
4. Coull 2006: 17. See also Halcrow 1994: 146; Nicolson 1978: 122–123; Irvine 1985: 151; Coull 2007: 119.
5. Irvine 1985: 154, 162.

Writers have been unsure how significant this was. Goodlad did not mention it at all; Halcrow merely hinted that 'lean times were to come'; Nicolson reported 'a serious decline', although 'the slump [...] was no more than a temporary setback it had a serious effect on Shetland's economy'.[6] Hance Smith referred impassively to 'a certain lack of adjustment' and 'periodic crises in the balance of supply and demand in the herring industry', though also to 'the great slump between 1886 and 1894'.[7] Coull saw it as part of a general picture: 'one of the downward fluctuations that is included in the experience of every herring fishery', though it hit Shetland particularly hard.[8] Brian Smith referred to it in the context of land-tenure legislation, but Gray gave the longest account.[9] In 1884, over-production caused a sudden drop in market prices, and in 1885 and 1886, rates to fishermen diminished. In 1887, banks foreclosed on some curers – the businesses which bought herring from fishermen, salted, sold, and shipped them – and the scale of fishing began to be curtailed. Fleets, landings, and prices remained well below the levels of the early 1880s, and differences developed both between parts of Scotland and even between parts of Shetland.

With hindsight, therefore, these years have been perceived as a blip in the upward curve of the herring industry, but of course, at the time, people did not have that perspective. Analysing the effects on Shetland's economy and society in the context of other contemporary events, this chapter shows how Shetlanders reacted, how they viewed their situation, and how they survived the recession.

---

6. Halcrow 1994: 139; Nicolson 1987: 31, 44.
7. Smith 1984: 177, 196.
8. Coull 2007: 120; Coull 1988: 28.
9. Smith 2000: 78; Gray 1978: 206–207.

Exploiting the boom

Herring had been caught around Shetland for centuries, but commercially mainly by Dutch fishermen. A local fishery from the 1820s, using half-decked boats, declined rapidly from 1839, and continued only as 'a pale reflection' with sixerns, the local six-oared boats which usually fished with longlines for ling and cod at the 'haaf' (i.e. the deep or open sea fishery).[10] In contrast, on the east coast of Scotland, the herring fishery had grown by the 1870s into a significant industry, using larger boats and drift nets.

Shetlanders doubted the suitability of these vessels for local waters.[11] But in 1875, some Orcadian crews tried their luck.[12] In the next few years, more boats and curers arrived, and Shetlanders joined in.[13] Expansion was swift – in 1879, over 200 boats landed herring in Shetland, 1880 was 'a year of bonanza', and in 1881, the average catch per boat was the highest in Scotland.[14] The Fishery Board commented that, in 1882, 'the prosperity which attended the herring fishing in the Shetland district [...] was extraordinary'.[15] The catches rocketed, as did the number of boats involved (Figure 2). Shetland offered many suitable sheltered anchorages for 'stations', where

---

10. Goodlad 1971: 171–177; Halcrow 1994: 130–133; Smith 1984: 109, 113–114.
11. Gray 1978: 201; Tudor 1883: 139–140.
12. Coull 2007: 114.
13. Ibid.: 115.
14. Ibid.: 116–117; *The Shetland Times* [hereafter *ST*], 17 September 1881, 2. Average catches per boat were often quoted. The statistics were problematic due to varying fleet numbers and different types of boat, but were useful for comparisons between time periods.
15. Parliamentary Papers [hereafter PP]. 1883. XVIII. Annual Report of the Fishery Board for Scotland [hereafter FBS] 1882. xxvi.

fish were gutted, salted, and packed into barrels; by 1884, there were 123.[16]

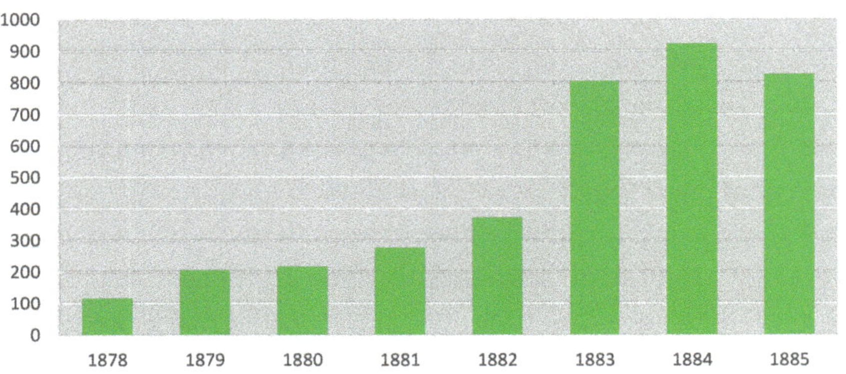

Figure 2: The number of boats at the Shetland herring fishing (in one sample week).
Source: Fishery Board for Scotland.

The fishing and curing methods and the Eastern European markets were already well developed. Shetland became 'part of a great seasonal migration of activity around the British coasts', filling a gap between the west and east coast fisheries.[17] The season was divided into two parts. The first, in May and June, to the west and north, attracted the widest participation from 'strangers'; the second, on the east and south, involved mainly local boats. Shetlanders participated with alacrity. In 1885, there were nearly 400 Shetland-owned decked drifters.[18] Some fishermen were able to buy them outright, showing a new willingness and ability to risk the capital.[19] Many other people bought shares; traders hired or financed them through

---

16. PP. 1884–85. XVI. FBS 1884. xvii.

17. Goodlad 1971: 178.

18. *The Shetland News* [hereafter *SN*], 26 September 1885, 5.

19. The *SN* 1887 Calendar shows over seventy out of 360 boats owned by the crew, but the owners of over eighty others were unknown.

the half-catch system.[20] Sheriff Rampini described it: 'a spirit of enterprise, almost approaching rashness, has seized all classes [...] All Shetland thinks, talks, smells of nothing but fish'.[21]

The number of local fishermen did not increase significantly; generally, they transferred from other fisheries as the potential earnings could be much greater.[22] The practice, called an 'engagement', was for a crew to agree with a curer to deliver their catch, often to a maximum or 'complement', for a set period at an agreed price.[23] The fishermen were probably also attracted by the greater comfort and safety: the fishing was generally nearer shore, less onerous, and allowed weekends at home. Some sixerns fished herring in the late season.

Not only fishermen benefited; there were unprecedented employment opportunities (Figure 3). Ships were, of course, used to transport people, equipment, barrels, and salt, though foreign vessels generally carried the cured herring. Barrels, initially imported, were later made in Shetland, and decked boats were built. Stations entailed the construction of piers, stores, and accommodation. Gutting and packing provided, perhaps for the first time, cash payments for women. Many came from outside Shetland, but a growing number of locals were employed, often working and living away from home in a new social environment. In 1881, *The Shetland Times* welcomed the increased money in circulation and increased prosperity.[24]

---

20. 'Half-catch' refers to the process of dividing the proceeds after deducting expenses, half for the owner and half for the crew.
21. Rampini 1884: 68.
22. Halcrow 1994: 139; PP. 1884. XXIV. Report of Her Majesty's Commissioners of Inquiry into the Condition of the Crofters and Cottars in the Highlands and Islands of Scotland [hereafter Napier Commission]. 1206.
23. Coull 1987; 2007: 121–128.
24. *ST*, 31 December 1881, 2.

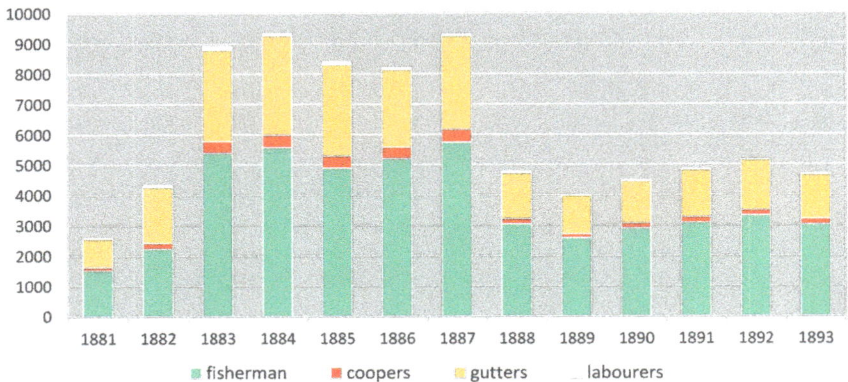

Figure 3: People employed in the Shetland herring fishing (in one sample week).
Source: Fishery Board for Scotland.

The ancillary effects were widespread:

> Curing stations and piers have to be provided, houses for
> coopers and gutters have to be erected, provisions of all kinds
> have to be imported [...] Every kind of farm produce in
> great demand [...] Merchants have had their business greatly
> increased, and the demand for workpeople has been largely
> in excess of the supply. All classes have got a share.[25]

Landlords benefited from fishermen being able to pay their
rents, while some 'have reaped a rich harvest in letting building
stances and ground for the prosecution of the fishing'.[26]

The Shetland Times claimed '[t]he trade of the Islands has
received a great impetus [...] much to the benefit of the poorer
classes both in town and country'.[27] Lerwick experienced a
great boost with many stations and incoming workers; business

---

25. Russell 1887: 111.
26. Ibid.
27. *ST*, 30 September 1882, 2.

premises, houses, and an ambitious harbour scheme were built.[28] But stations were established in many places with the early and late seasons concentrated in different areas. Baltasound in Unst was described as 'an infant herringopolis' with 'station after station, pier after pier'.[29]

While the fishery was significant on a national scale, it was of outstanding local importance. Commentators then and now have no doubt that it 'ushered in a period of prosperity in the islands', at least in comparative terms.[30] In 1880, the Fishery Officer wrote: 'This development of the herring fishing has raised these islands to a height of material prosperity hitherto unknown in their history'.[31] According to *The People's Journal*, Shetlanders believed a great future was in store.[32] The Fishery Board Report for 1884 observed 'the great development of the herring fishery in Shetland has had a marked effect in improving the condition of the people'.[33] But in 1883, the Napier Commission had been warned: 'Were it coming an unsuccessful season, the effect and consequence to the people [...] would be very serious'.[34] This prediction was soon to be tested.

Suffering the recession

In Scotland, the plentiful 1884 catch was composed mainly of small, immature fish. High engagement prices had encouraged an early start, and curers struggled to process the surfeit; the

---

28. Irvine 1985: 166–167, 170–177; Nicolson 1987: 27–28.
29. *ST*, 26 May 1883, 2.
30. Coull 1988: 25.
31. Coull 2007: 119.
32. *ST*, 10 February 1883, 3.
33. PP. 1885. XVI. FBS 1884. xii–xiii.
34. PP. 1884. XXIV. Napier Commission. 1204.

market was glutted. In Shetland, the total catch also increased again, and the quality of herring was the best in Scotland.[35] But, with a larger fleet, the average catch decreased; while some boats prospered, others could hardly pay expenses. For curers, the results were 'almost disastrous, heavy losses being universal'.[36]

In 1885, fishing started later to avoid repetition.[37] But the number of curers was exceeded with three new stations, and the even greater catch was again sometimes too much for the curers; some made little or no profit.[38] With fewer boats, the average catch, though variable, was the highest ever, and despite lower prices, the season was generally very successful for fishermen.[39] For the Scottish trade, however, it was a catastrophe. The curers were short of capital, and market prices fell again, a substantial proportion of the catch being small, unsellable herring.[40] The Fishery Board commented that no year had ever proved as disastrous as the last two.[41]

The causes seemed clear – too many fish, poor quality, some disputes about duties and with agents, competition from the Netherlands and Scandinavia, and payments to fishermen which did not reflect demand. For the next decade, Scottish production was smaller, but only at most reduced to 65%, while Shetland's plunged to 13% in 1889, recovered to nearly 30% in 1890 and 1891, before falling again to 8.5% in 1892 (Figure 4). The continued recession in Shetland, therefore, was on a different scale and had different causes from the shorter-lived market problem.

---

35. PP. 1885. XVI. FBS 1884. xiv.
36. *ST*, 27 December 1884, 2.
37. *ST*, 26 September 1885, 2.
38. Ibid.
39. Ibid.
40. PP. 1886. XV. FBS 1885. xi–xii.
41. Ibid.: xii.

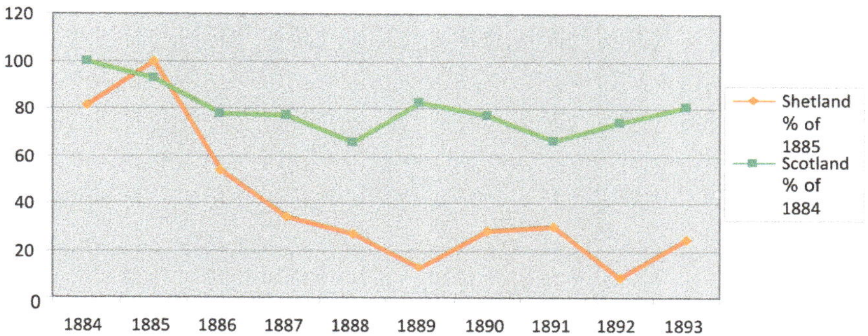

Figure 4: Herring cured as a percentage of maximum.
Source: Fishery Board for Scotland.

Bad weather was sometimes a problem, as in 1886. Herring was scarcer, which fishermen blamed on the prevalence of dogfish; they ate herring and destroyed nets by becoming entangled in them.

The effects of the varying catches and prices were not straightforward, since the proceeds were split between the fishermen and curers, and between locals and 'strangers'. Curers bore the brunt of the market collapse because, when catches were small, they still had to pay costs for rents, transport, and labour, or, as in 1890, despite improved catches, quality was poor and market prices low.[42] Many went bankrupt.[43] The number of stations reduced by half from 1885 to 1891, and sometimes external curers left early.[44]

While fishermen suffered most when curers defaulted, the obvious way to reduce costs was to pay fishermen less. But they also incurred costs, and in 1886 and 1887, they threatened to stay ashore until the curers caved in.[45] Later, they were

42. *ST*, 13 September 1890, 2.
43. Gray 1978: 148.
44. *ST*, 13 September 1890, 2.
45. *ST*, 18 September 1886, 3; *SN*, 11 June 1887, 4; PP. 1888. XXVIII. FBS 1887. xx.

reluctant to fish without engagements.[46] But prices fell and
'complements' were reduced. The total value, therefore, fell even
more than the catch (Figures 5 and 1).

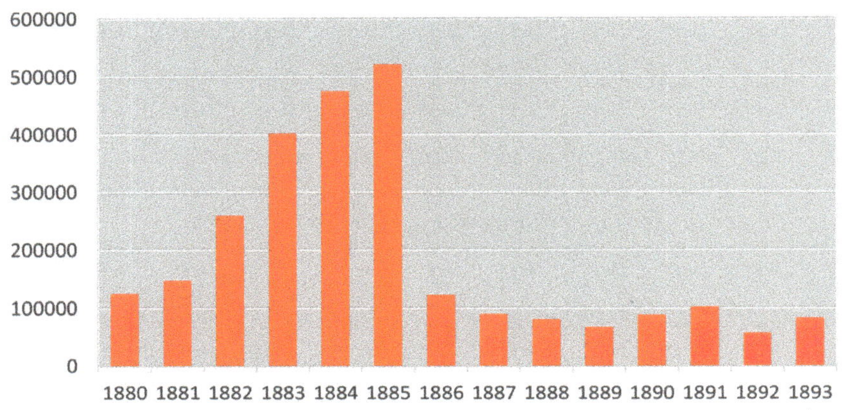

Figure 5: Value (to fishermen) of all fishing (£). Source: *Shetland Times*, *Shetland
News*, Fishery Board for Scotland.

It took some time to sink in that the problems were not short-lived,
and in 1887, even more boats and men participated. Thereafter,
activity was influenced both by the prevailing circumstances and
the previous year's fishing. For example, 1889's poor earnings
discouraged fishermen and curers in 1890. In several years, the
east coast boats left as soon as dogfish appeared, meaning the
Fishery Board's statistics for boats fishing around Shetland
(based on a single week) could be misleadingly high. The average
catch per boat dwindled until 1889, recovered well in 1890, only
to fall steeply again in the next two years (Figure 6).

But these numbers concealed great discrepancies; in 1887,
catches per boat varied from 440 to 1.25 crans; in 1889,
'three-quarters had not seen a herring'; and in 1892, over twenty
boats landed nothing in the early season, only two landed over 200

---

46. E.g. *ST*, 15 September 1988, 2; 31 December 1889, 2.

crans, and most under fifty.[47] The 'stranger' crews were thought to be more successful, as they persevered despite low catches and were more likely to update their gear than the undercapitalised Shetlanders.[48] Then again, although the early fishing lasted barely two weeks in 1890, prices improved later; so, with fewer external boats, more of the income stayed in Shetland.[49] Some fishermen who had taken out loans on boats under a government scheme struggled to repay. By 1893, 25% were still outstanding, and two boats had been returned; the local fleet of first-class boats was reduced by a quarter, and there were thirty not in use.[50]

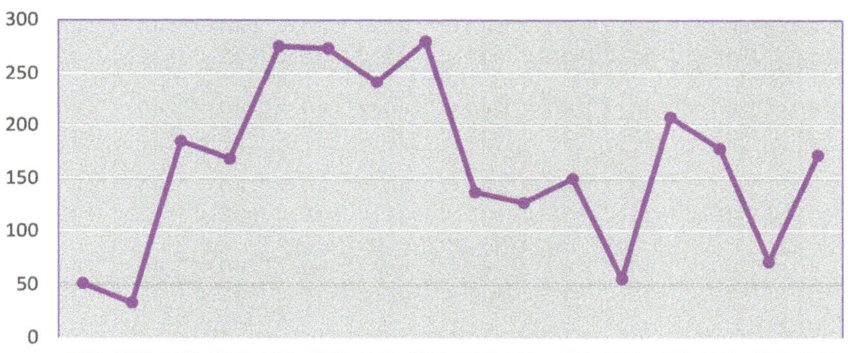

Figure 6: Average catch per boat (crans). Source: *Shetland Times, Shetland News.*

In Lerwick, trade was depressed. By 1887, construction of new buildings had stopped, and employment opportunities reduced.[51] No more decked boats were built, and during some winters, the coopers had little work.[52] In 1890, however, *The*

---

47. Fresh herring was measured in crans, a volume measurement roughly equivalent to 37.5 imperial gallons. *SN*, 17 September 1887, 4; *ST*, 14 September 1889, 2; 10 September 1892, 2.
48. *ST*, 15 September 1888, 2.
49. *SN*, 27 December 1890, 4.
50. PP. 1894. III. FBS. 1893. 44, 130.
51. *SN*, 31 December 1887, 4.
52. *ST*, 27 December 1890, 2; 28 December 1889, 2.

Shetland News reported: 'Workers of all kinds have been busily employed, a good deal of money has been put into circulation, and on all hands there had been a feeling that better times had come at last'.[53]

But this was a fleeting recovery. The catch rose again in 1891, but prices fell, and this season was not a success.[54] In 1892, the fishing hit rock bottom. The combined failure of fishing and crops threatened to push the economy over the edge. In early 1893, seed corn was scarce and was provided by government grants and the Society of Friends.[55]

Then, the herring catch improved and, despite fluctuations, generally continued to do so until 1905. Shetland had come through this recession. What, however, was contemporary opinion of the fickle fortunes of herring fishing?

The voice of the people

The best source for what ordinary people thought about their conditions is the evidence given at the hearings in 1889 and 1892 of the Crofters Commission, established by the 1886 Crofters Holdings (Scotland) Act. This was primarily about land issues such as rent rises and other charges, housing conditions, and the confiscation of the common grazing. A large percentage of crofters had applied for assessment.[56] Fishing was an essential part of the context and, just as the boom had enabled many people to pay their rent, reductions had now become more critical. Unsurprisingly, the Commission heard of 'exceptionally disastrous fishing failures', how in recent years

---

53. *SN*, 13 September 1890, 4.
54. *ST*, 10 September 1891, 2.
55. *ST*, 18 March 1893, 3; 22 July 1893, 3.
56. PP. 1890. LVIII. Report by the Crofters Commission for 1889. 256.

the fishing had not paid well, how some who had bought shares in boats were in debt, and how others were not likely to be paid as curers had gone bankrupt.[57] Although non-payment of rent may have been due to the expectation of the cancellation of arrears and even to collusion and intimidation, many maintained they could not afford it. The claims succeeded: in 1889, 1,330 rents were reduced by an average of 28%, and 60% of arrears were cancelled, followed in 1892 by another 706 reductions by an average of 30% and cancellation of 78% of arrears.[58]

What is striking is not so much what was said as the attitude of the applicants. This evidence provides a better indication of the views of ordinary people than the Truck or Napier Commissions in 1872 and 1883. Then, landlords could still evict, and few crofters were willing to speak out.[59] Now, hearings were crowded, and witnesses were encouraged. Most clearly enjoyed the opportunity to decry their landlords or factors in public; stories were told of injustices, mostly in times when fishing tenures still applied. There were more active manifestations of this new confidence – for example, in disputes and court cases with John Bruce, one of the most reactionary and unpopular landlords.[60]

Security of tenure had made the most difference to these attitudes, but other aspects of recent experience also mattered. Witnesses to the Napier Commission had been treated with respect, and legislation had been the outcome. The franchise had been extended in 1885.[61] Newspapers had also contributed by reporting the Crofters Commission's operations, visits

---

57. *SN*, 31 August 1889, 5; 14 September 1889, 5.
58. PP. 1893–94. LXXI. Report by the Crofters Commission for 1892. 109.
59. Irvine 1985: 33, 60; Tudor 1883: 177; Smith 2000: 76.
60. Renwantz 1980; Sutherland 1989; Smith 2003.
61. Tindley 2002: 95–96.

by crofters' leaders, and debates about the circumstances; *The Shetland Times* had encouraged crofters to make applications.[62]

But the herring boom had also been influential. It boosted confidence to be free from debt or just to know the price for fish in advance, perhaps bargaining for higher prices, and to choose to sell fish to someone who was not connected with land tenure. As early as 1883, it was reported that 'the men are fast achieving a position which will enable them to dictate their own terms to the curers', and fishermen held their first public meeting about prices and bounties.[63] This challenged out-of-date views: 'that this immeasurably poor and down-trodden thrall should be practically dictating his own terms to his quondam masters' would give rise to incredulity.[64] Remarkably, this continued in the recession. The men who 'went on strike' in 1891 had learned about organising resistance, having a spokesman and a committee representative of different areas, and the importance of communication – using the bellman to drum up support.[65] A branch of the Sailors' and Firemen's Union was established the same month.[66] A similar 'strike' followed next spring in Whalsay, when fishermen's refusal to accept prices for cod and ling led to the despatch of a gunboat by the overreacting authorities.[67]

While incoming curers were credited with raising prices and other benefits, there had also been other increased contacts with the outside world.[68] Shetland became known as a principal location of the fishing economy, not just a backward society of antiquarian interest.

---

62. Ibid.: 96–97; *ST*, 31 July 1886, 2; *SN*, 3 September 1887, 4.
63. *ST*, 10 February 1883, 3 (from *The People's Journal*); *ST*, 27 October 1883, 2.
64. Rampini 1984: 65.
65. Ratter 1983.
66. *SN*, 22 August 1891, 4.
67. *ST*, 23 April 1892, 2.
68. PP. 1884. XXIV. Napier Commission. 1219, 1282, 1287.

Both visits of the Crofters Commission coincided with the nadirs of the herring recession. Nevertheless, a lawyer representing crofters predicted: 'today is the dawn of a new order of things, and henceforth a spirit of independence and a sense of security and freedom, will spring up among the crofters in Shetland'.[69] The herring industry, by providing new opportunities and increasing earnings, had facilitated this transformation. It is perhaps too much to say that Shetland society became 'vociferous in demanding its rights and expressing its views'.[70] Nevertheless, the change in a short period was remarkable.

The debate in the newspapers

The main sources of contemporary views are the two local newspapers, which provided both reports on events and commentary. *The Shetland Times*, launched in 1872, published local news, letters, and reports from Scottish and national newspapers, as did *The Shetland News* from 1885. Both are rich sources for social and economic conditions, particularly in their year-end summaries. For fishing, there were weekly reports, and a longer one at the end of the summer season, also covering mainland ports and European markets.

As a source, newspapers are complex. 'A text, a record of historical events, a representation of society and a chronicle of contemporary opinions, aspirations and debates [...] also a business enterprise, a professional organization, a platform for advertisements and itself a commodity', their content should not be accepted without scrutiny.[71] Here they reflected different political views: *The Shetland Times* was liberal, *The*

69. *SN*, 31 August 1889, 5.
70. Fryer 1995: 96.
71. Vella 2009: 93–94.

Shetland News conservative. The competition provides a check on the accuracy of information, though there were rarely major discrepancies on news. Despite overlap, both newspapers were supported, but, while it is very likely that most people were aware of the content, it cannot be assumed that they reflected the views of the entire population. They carried reports from rural districts but were published in Lerwick, and had a certain bias towards the town.

During the early 1880s, they were upbeat and enthusiastic about the herring boom. In the 1885 year-end review, however, *The Shetland Times* assessed the situation:

> The two great elements in the material prosperity of Shetland – the crops and the fishings – have been undoubtedly failures in the bygone year […]. The several previous fortunate seasons ought to have left so much in hand everywhere in our islands, that one bad season should be tided over without much difficulty and without rendering it necessary to appeal for that charitable aid which is the last resort of every community with proper notions of self-support and independence.[72]

This introduced recurring themes: both fishing and crops were required to sustain the population, the boom had provided enough surplus to cover a poor season, and seeking outside aid was to be discouraged. Another, agreed by both newspapers, was the interdependence of social classes: 'in the body social as well as in the body individual – if one member suffer, all the others suffer with it. If curers are ruined – there's an end of our fishing industries'.[73] Unfortunately, there was not just one poor season, and *The Shetland News* saw 1886 as 'one of the most trying periods our

---

72. *ST*, 4 January 1886, 2.
73. Ibid.

Islands have ever passed through [...] the result is that the bulk of the population has had to endure much privation and many hardships'.[74] But the newspapers conceded that 'few if any have been reduced to absolute want'.[75] By 1887, however, there were reports of impoverishment. 'Our fishermen came up with a bound', lamented *The Shetland News*, 'and they are apparently going down as fast'.[76]

Fishermen were encouraged not to depend on the short herring season.[77] The newspapers disagreed, however, on the scale of the hardship and how people could cope. *The Shetland News* tended to minimise deprivation and thought people could work their way out of difficulty. *The Shetland Times* painted a bleaker picture; crofters had small landholdings and faced high rents as well as unprofitable fishing.

There was a lively discussion in 1888. *The Shetland News* asserted that, with hard work, fishing and a croft could adequately sustain a family; crops would produce food for most of the year; and the sale of a pony would pay rent and taxes, allowing the fishing income to buy a small amount of 'luxuries'.[78] *The Shetland Times* was adamant: 'No one can visit the country districts just now and fail to recognise the state of poverty in which the crofters are situated'.[79] Having collected information on income, it summarised: 'the bulk of the crofting population of Shetland are neither well fed nor well clothed, and the less said about their house accommodation the better'.[80] *The Shetland News*, producing its own examples,

---

74. *SN*, 1 January 1887, 4.
75. *ST*, 1 January 1887, 2; *SN*, 1 January 1887, 4.
76. *SN*, 17 September 1887, 4.
77. *SN*, 14 August 1886, 4.
78. *SN*, 22 September 1888, 4.
79. *ST*, 6 October 1888, 2.
80. *ST*, 13 October 1888, 2.

maintained that 'the condition of the people is not as near pauperism as *The Shetland Times* would have us believe'.[81] *The Shetland Times* argued that many crofters lived on poor land and that the herring had left more in debt; potentially over 40% would be bankrupt if pressed for payment.[82] *The Shetland News* countered that crofters had a multiplicity of sources of income and now security of tenure, and that *The Shetland Times* was backward-looking and preaching 'a gospel of despair'.[83]

In their year-end reports, both newspapers modified their stance. *The Shetland News* acknowledged: 'there has been such a constant run of ill-luck lately, that every effort has been required to make ends meet'.[84] Meanwhile, *The Shetland Times* admitted: 'However, the cry of "hard times" is not so loud, nor so general as it was last year at this time'.[85]

The newspapers' ideological differences help balance perspective, but they could be so engrossed in argument that it clouded the picture. They were also inconsistent. Although they denied 'absolute want', they admitted poverty, hardship, and even 'destitution'.[86] There was an aversion to creating a bad impression and a pride in Shetland's survival.[87] *The Shetland News* contrasted the Shetlanders' willingness to seek external employment with the apathy of the Irish and Western Highlanders.[88] *The Leeds Mercury*'s claim that Shetlanders had 'nothing but starvation staring them in the face' was deemed 'a most astounding statement'.[89]

81. *SN*, 20 October 1888, 4; 3 November 1888, 4.
82. *ST*, 27 October 1888, 2; 10 November 1888, 2.
83. *SN*, 3 November 1888, 4; 17 November 1888, 4.
84. *SN*, 29 December 1888, 4.
85. *ST*, 29 December 1888, 2.
86. *SN*, 31 December 1887, 4.
87. *SN*, 6 October 1888, 2.
88. *SN*, 31 December 1887, 4.
89. *SN*, 3 December 1892, 4.

Both newspapers referred to the psychological effect of the herring fishing. The bustle and optimism of the boom gave way to disillusionment: 'when that time is recalled, few but will regret that all these expectations were doomed to disappointment, and that the golden hopes then formed should have been completely blasted'.[90] The recession brought discouragement: 'the trade seemed to be devoid of the energy and life which formerly characterised it', and the fishermen 'pursued the late fishing in a half-hearted, apathetic, "dűless" [slothful] fashion'.[91] In contrast, the improvement in 1890, *The Shetland News* claimed, 'has put new life into everything. Shetland was beginning to look as though it were plague-stricken'.[92] More prosaically, *The Shetland Times* reported 'everyone seemed to rejoice in the prosperous turn events had taken [...] Matters are assuming a more hopeful tone all round'.[93] Of course, newspapers can influence as well as reflect popular views.

The Shetland Times suggested that 'it is always darkest before the dawn'; but unfortunately that was in 1891, just before 1892 showed how dark it could get.[94] Then, it summarised: 'Men have hoped and persevered; persevered until now it is almost hopeless; and there seems little but ruin and destitution ahead'.[95] *The Shetland News*, though stressing 'anything like starvation among the people as a class is fortunately a stretch of the imagination', admitted 'misfortunes have told heavily on the bulk of the population'.[96]

---

90. *ST*, 28 December 1889, 2.
91. *ST*, 15 September 1888, 2; *SN*, 15 September 1888, 4.
92. *SN*, 9 August 1890, 4.
93. *ST*, 13 September 1890, 2.
94. *ST*, 26 December 1891, 2.
95. *ST*, 27 August 1892, 2.
96. *SN*, 3 December 1892, 4; 31 December 1892, 2.

The higher catches in 1893 brought new hope. *The Shetland News* decided: 'The result is to leave the county in a very much better condition than it was at the close of 1892', while *The Shetland Times* thought: 'All things considered, the county of Shetland is fairly well off' and 'The pinch of "hard times" is still felt, but it is not so general as it was two or three years back'.[97]

Means of survival

Given that commentators claimed the herring fishery was the mainstay of the economy, how did Shetlanders survive the recession? An assessment in *The Shetland News* provides clues:

> When we consider all the things that can be done to support a Shetland family – farming, fishing, sailing, and knitting – [...] the toiler in the far north has many things to be thankful for [...] Forty or sixty years ago, the failure of one branch was sufficient to cause desolation and famine [...] This is not the case now-a-days.[98]

Even in the worst year, the herring catch was four times the 1879 total (Figure 1), and this was still the most valuable fishery. The statistics must be treated with caution. Since many of the curers and fishermen came from outside, most of the revenue generated directly left Shetland.[99] The total catch and value were unreliable indicators of the profitability for local fishermen, who were partly protected by the engagement system and benefitted most if the late fishing was successful.

---

97. *SN*, 30 December 1893, 4; *ST*, 18 November 1893, 2; 30 December 1893, 2.
98. *SN*, 27 December 1890, 4.
99. Coull 1988: 37.

The curers bore initial costs and the risks involved in selling the fish, and prices were determined by various factors, including the quantity and quality of fish on the market and conditions in consumer countries. The recession, however, affected other employment and general trade. But the boom had been short-lived, and the habits and resources of the past remained.

Herring was never the only fishing. Participation in the haaf had declined especially after fifty-eight men died in a storm in 1881, but sixerns returned briefly to favour with new boats built in 1889 and a large fleet in 1892.[100] The introduction of decked boats had initiated a cod and ling fishing from March until June that also encouraged a longer season for sixerns. The 'smack' fishing in Faroese and Icelandic waters had already been on the decline before the boom had attracted manpower away, but it revived with about twenty vessels and new grounds.[101] Despite transport difficulties, the inshore winter fishing expanded for haddocks to be sold fresh.[102] So commercial fishing was becoming more of a year-round activity. Nevertheless, the best indicator of the prosperity of fishing was the combined value, and it dropped immensely (Figure 5).

And fishing was never the only occupation. Whaling had greatly declined, but – despite being rarely quantified in the newspapers – the contribution to the economy of employment in the Merchant Navy was substantial.[103] Though hard and dangerous, it was not seasonal, paid a guaranteed wage, and could be combined with other work. Perhaps the majority of Shetland men served some time at sea, although this was not fully visible in the censuses. Numbers dropped during the boom

---

100. Halcrow 1994: 75–80; *ST*, 30 July 1881, 2; *SN*, 28 December 1889, 4; 31 December 1892, 4.
101. Goodlad 2017: 38–40.
102. Smith 1884: 168.
103. Smith 1984: 158–159.

years, but *The Shetland Times* reckoned 20% of crofters went
to sea in the winter of 1888 to 1889.[104] Opportunities were
not always limitless. Foreign seamen were being employed at
low wages, and trade union activity, with strikes in 1889 and
1892, caused disruption. In early 1893 – a very critical time for
Shetland – 500 British ships were not in use.[105]

Another sometimes underappreciated source of income was
knitting. Nearly all women, except the affluent, knitted for sale,
and more so when there was no gutting.[106] *The Shetland News*
asserted in 1892 that 'it would be not too much to say that their
industry comes in to stave off what would otherwise often be a
state of absolute want'.[107]

Most Shetlanders still lived in agricultural communities with
subsistence crops and some stock for sale, though not all had
land. The recession was always worst when crops, particularly
corn and potatoes, failed – as, for example, in 1885, when *The
Shetland Times* reported: 'Thus both strings of our bow gave
way'.[108] In 1886 and 1888, although the corn was poor, potatoes did well; 1887's crops were good; and 1889's fine summer
produced the best yields for a long time, stock prices rose, and
the condition of crofters improved. From 1890, however, poor
harvests culminated in 1892 with the loss of many sheep and
the failure of both grain and potatoes. This was the lowest point.

It is difficult to evaluate the significance of the crofters' rent
reductions, although they were doubtless welcome. The removal
of the threat of eviction was also a great relief, but tenants had
already been free from tenures that compelled them to fish for
their landlord before the herring boom; otherwise, it could not

---

104. Halcrow 1994: 137; *ST*, 6 April 1889, 2.
105. *SN*, 6 July 1889, 4; *ST*, 14 January 1893, 2.
106. Fryer 1995.
107. *SN*, 31 December 1892, 4.
108. *ST*, 2 January 1886, 2.

have occurred. In 1883, the Napier Commission was told of only a few cases where compulsion still existed.[109] Russell, a minister, credited this partly to public opinion and partly to improvements in fishing.[110] The change has not been entirely explained; Brian Smith wrote: 'It thus becomes a mystery how it disappeared as rapidly as it did'.[111]

One effect of the boom, however, was a decrease in the form of truck enforced by landlords and factors.[112] Although the Truck Commission of 1872 did not result in relevant legislation, the publicity seems to have had some effect. The Napier Commission reported that truck was disappearing 'before the forces of increasing intelligence, public opinion and commercial competition'.[113] Hance Smith also considered that the increasing mobility of labour during the herring boom was a major cause.[114]

Nevertheless, truck did not disappear overnight. Tudor reported that, despite new shops, the fact that 'many evils arising from the system still survive is undoubted'.[115] Herring fishermen were still not paid until after the season: curers and merchants still provided boats and goods on credit.[116] If a curer owned or part-owned a boat, the crew would have to sell their catch to that particular curer.[117] In some places, there

---

109. PP. 1884. XXIV. Napier Commission. 1224, 1434, 1320.
110. Russell 1887: 144.
111. Smith 2000: 77.
112. In this form of truck, tenants, as a condition of landholding, might have to sell fish and other produce exclusively to the landlord or his nominee and buy boats, fishing gear, and other goods from him. Rent might also be included in the arrangement, which was sometimes enforced by threats of eviction. Smith 2000: 65–80.
113. PP. 1884. XXII. Napier Commission. 48.
114. Smith 1984: 156–158; Irvine 2005: 162. See also Coull 1998: 34; Gray 1978: 1, 200.
115. Tudor 1883: 131.
116. Halcrow 1994: 137; PP. 1884. XXIV. Napier Commission. 1283, 1238.
117. Ibid.: 1205, 1238, 1282–1283.

was no choice, as a curer or merchant was able to prevent the establishment of competitive businesses.[118] The difference now was that fishermen knew the price for fish in advance and, provided proceeds exceeded debts, received cash.[119] Men who owned their boat outright were free to fish for whomever they wished, and might get better prices, though they did not vary by much and were reported in the newspapers.[120] Curers from outside Shetland were less likely to be interested in long-term economic ties to fishermen. But the practice of maintaining integrated boat and family accounts with merchants endured. Credit was still supporting those who were struggling.

Some people, however, found the struggle too difficult or envisaged better opportunities elsewhere and chose to leave. This had been the case for some time, but had been retarded by the boom; Russell thought that 'economic causes have stopped the tide of emigration from Shetland'.[121] In 1883, an Australian emigration agent found his task very difficult.[122] The net loss between the 1881 and 1891 censuses has been calculated at 10%, less than in the previous decade but probably concentrated in the last four years.[123] Then, the newspapers frequently referred to people emigrating, mainly young men. The external opportunities – the Merchant Navy and emigration – were seen as the saviours of Shetland.

This period in Shetland's history saw many changes, some related to the herring fishery and some not. One outcome was recognition of the potential of government assistance. Another commission enquiring into conditions was lobbied by the

---

118. Ibid.: 1355–1362, 1392.
119. Ibid.: 1223–1224, 1283, 1286–1287, 1322.
120. Ibid.: 1284, 1222–1223, 1238.
121. Russell 1887: 112.
122. *ST*, 5 August 1882, 2.
123. Barclay 1967: 53.

County Council with a list of requirements relating, for example, to steamer services, roads, harbours, and telegraph facilities, many of which were recommended.[124] The Western Highlands and Islands (Scotland) Works Acts 1891 was of limited value, but some government grants were also forthcoming in 1893.[125]

There was, therefore, some flexibility in the Shetland economy. The range of sources of income, though none were lucrative, made an overall evaluation difficult. Even then, there were differences of opinion, evident in the newspapers. Shetland had experienced poor fisheries many times before and so the expectation was that catches would pick up again. Even in the worst years, there were good catches, and some crews did well, but there was nearly a decade of generally hard times. Rent reductions in 1889 and 1890's expanded herring catch improved the situation temporarily, but another year like 1892 could have been catastrophic.

Conclusion

In 1891, *The Shetland Times* described the herring boom and recession: 'the wave of prosperity which reached Shetland recently [...] receded, and [...] left wrack and confusion in its train'.[126] The boom was a major upheaval, and the recession seemed all the more acute because it followed this unparalleled widespread success. It accelerated change which contemporaries attributed to herring. The recession retarded some of

---

124. *SN*, 27 December 1890, 4; *ST*, 27 December 1890, 2; Irvine 1985: 194; PP 1890–91. XLIV. Second Report of the Commissioners Appointed to Inquire into Certain Matters affecting the interests of the Western Highlands and Islands, 5, 10; Tindley 2002: 59–63.
125. Ibid.: 63–64; *SN*, 30 December 1893, 4.
126. *ST*, 1 August 1891, 2.

these changes, such as the decline of truck and the haaf fishery. However, other influences were in play, and Shetland did not merely return to previous circumstances. Ordinary people had seen new possibilities, and attitudes had changed, due also to other factors, particularly security of tenure and more contact with the outside world. This transformation can be seen in the evidence to the Crofters Commission and negotiations between fishermen and curers.

The enthusiasm with which the local press and other commentators greeted the boom shows how it was perceived as a huge increase in economic activity and a vast improvement. Besides higher earnings for fishermen, there were opportunities for other employment, a seasonal influx of people, and increased trade, dispersed throughout the islands. The recession dashed hopes of consistent expansion and brought a partial retreat to other means of livelihood, other fisheries, agriculture, knitwear, and the Merchant Navy.

An assessment of the overall severity of the effects is problematic, as circumstances, individual experience, and opinions varied. The herring fishing never moved past the boom to a steady state operation before the recession. If we consider it not as a blip in the triumphal progress of King Herring, but recognise the boom as a temporary peak of prosperity, we see the precarious nature of the Shetland economy. Operating in a tough geographical environment, its fishing was hampered by underdeveloped technology and transport difficulties from selling in a market beginning to prefer fresh fish to cured; and its agriculture was limited by small holdings and out-of-date methods. It was flexible, but much of that flexibility was provided by external opportunities.

The immediate aftermath, however, was that catches of herring in Shetland waters increased again, bringing a return to high levels of activity, comparative affluence and optimism, and rising with fluctuations to a peak in 1905. The low catches from 1886 to 1892 faded from popular memory, with nostalgia playing its part.[127] In contemporary accounts, there was probably an understandable measure of hyperbole, in descriptions both of the boom and of the recession. A more balanced review described this time as part of a 'period of oscillating and intermittent progress towards a modern Shetland' with 'a modestly prosperous economy emerging'.[128]

Bibliography

Newspapers

The Shetland News. 1885–94.

The Shetland Times. 1872–94.

Parliamentary Papers

PP. 1884. XXII and XXXIV. Royal Commission of Inquiry into the Condition of Crofters and Cottars in the Highlands and Islands of Scotland.

PP. 1890. LVIII. Report by the Crofters Commission for the year from 31 December 1888 to 31 December 1889 to the Secretary for Scotland.

PP. 1890–91. XLIV. Second Report of the Commissioners Appointed to Inquire into Certain Matters affecting the interests of the Western Highlands and Islands.

PP. 1893–94. LXXI. Report by the Crofters Commission for the year from 31 December 1891 to 31 December 1892 to the Secretary for Scotland.

Reports of the Commissioners of the Fishery Board for Scotland, 1878–1881, and Annual Reports of the Fishery Board for Scotland, 1882–1893.

---

127. E.g. Halcrow 1994: 137.
128. Fryer 1995: 93.

Additional Sources

Barclay, R.S. 1967. 'The Population of the Parishes and Islands of Shetland 1755–1961'. In A.T. Cluness (ed.), *The Shetland Book*. Lerwick: Zetland Education Committee, 44–56.

Coull, James R. 1987. 'The Engagement System during the Shetland Herring Boom, 1880–1914'. *Scottish Economic and Social History* 7, 55–65.

———. 1988. 'The Boom in the Herring Fishery in the Shetland Islands 1880–1914'. *Northern Scotland* 8, 25–38.

———. 2006. *Fishing in Unst*. Scotland: James Coull.

———. 2007. *Fishing, Fishermen, Fish Merchants and Curers in Shetland*. Lerwick: Shetland Amenity Trust.

Fenton, Alexander. 1978. *The Northern Isles: Orkney and Shetland*. Edinburgh: John Donald.

Fryer, Linda G. 1995. *Knitting by the Fireside and on the Hillside: A History of the Shetland Hand Knitting Industry, c. 1600–1950*. Lerwick: Shetland Times.

Goodlad, C.A. 1971. *Shetland Fishing Saga*. Lerwick: Shetland Times.

Goodlad, John. 2017. *The Cod Hunters*. Lerwick: Shetland Heritage Publications.

Gray, Malcolm. 1978. *The Fishing Industries of Scotland, 1790–1914: A Study in Regional Adaptation*. Oxford: Oxford University Press.

Halcrow, A. 1994. *The Sail Fishermen of Shetland*. Lerwick: Shetland Times.

Irvine, James W. 1985. *Lerwick: The Birth and Growth of an Island Town*. Lerwick: Lerwick Community Council.

Nicolson, James R. 1978. *Traditional Life in Shetland*. London: Hale.

———. 1987. *Lerwick Harbour*. Lerwick: Lerwick Harbour Trust.

Rampini, C.J.C. 1884. *Shetland and the Shetlanders*. Kirkwall: W. Peace & Son.

Ratter, Drew. 1983. 'Herring Strike'. *Shetland Life* 33, 8–9, 11.

Renwantz, Marsha Elizabeth. 1980. 'From Crofters to Shetlanders: The Social History of a Shetland Island Community's Self-Image'. PhD thesis. Stanford University.

Russell, John. 1887. *Three Years in Shetland*. Paisley: Alexander Gardner.

Smith, B. 2000. *Toons and Tenants: Settlement and Society in Shetland, 1299–1899*. Lerwick: Shetland Times.

———. 2003. 'Pilot Whales, Udal Law and Custom in Shetland'. *Northern Scotland* 23, 85–97.

Smith, Hance D. 1984. *Shetland Life and Trade, 1550–1914*. Edinburgh: John Donald.

Sutherland, Stella. 1989. 'The Hoswick Whale Case'. *Shetland Life* 108, 9–11.

Tindley, Anne Marie. 2002. 'Orkney and Shetland: Land Reform, Government Policy and Politics c. 1870–1914'. MSc dissertation. University of Edinburgh.

Tudor, John R. 1883. *The Orkneys and Shetland: Their Past and Present State*. London: Edward Stanford.

Vella, Stephen. 2009. 'Newspapers'. In Miriam Dobson and Benjamin Ziemann (eds). *Reading Primary Sources: The Interpretation of Texts from Nineteenth- and Twentieth-Century History*. London: Routledge, 192–208.

$\cdot$ XIII $\cdot$

Language and Landscape: Focalisation and the Arne Kruse Method

Liv Helene Willumsen

Introduction

The title of this chapter reflects Arne Kruse's lifelong scholarly work, from his 1983 master's thesis ('Médnamn frå Smøla') to the present day.[1] I have had the honour of working together with him, writing two articles collaboratively in recent years, and I have learned a great deal from him. This article pays tribute to his qualities as a scholar and researcher.

One of Arne's strongest qualities is his combination between a down-to-earth attitude, a very theoretical interest, and an interdisciplinary approach. This combination is on display throughout his research efforts: on the one hand, he is a practical and pragmatic scholar within the field of place-names, with both feet firmly on the ground, be that the deck of a Norwegian fishing boat or an East Lothian field. On the other hand, he is a very theoretical and intellectual scholar of linguistics, phonetics, grammar, etymology, and history, working on a highly abstract level. I will refer to this as 'the Arne Kruse Method'.

---

1. Kruse 1983.

The aim of this chapter is twofold. Initially, I would like to illuminate the journey from Arne's first research work on Norwegian fishing *méd* (1983) to a quest ending in an East Lothian field in 2015 – the Bara Kirk experience. Secondly, I would like to demonstrate Arne's interdisciplinary competence by presenting research findings we have obtained together over the last few years, particularly those related to language.

The Bara Kirk experience

This chapter takes an expedition to the kirk of Bara as its starting point, representing a journey I made together with Arne in 2015. I am a historian and a witchcraft scholar, with a master's thesis[2] on the Finnmark witchcraft trials in Northern Norway, and a PhD in history on both Scottish and Finnmark witchcraft trials.[3]

In 2015, I was on one of my research trips to Edinburgh, working on the North Berwick witchcraft trials, which took place in 1590–91.[4] These trials were the first ones of their kind in Scotland for which learned European demonological ideas are documented, including the ideas of a woman or man entering into a pact with the devil and participation at witchcraft gatherings.[5] The trials were held in Edinburgh but are named after an alleged witchcraft convention in North Berwick. They are famous because of their scale – resulting from a witchcraft panic with many people accused – but also because of their demonological content, and because King James VI took part in the interrogation of the accused persons at Holyrood Palace.

---

2. Willumsen 1984.
3. Willumsen 2008.
4. Normand and Roberts 2000.
5. Willumsen 2020.

One of the first people accused, imprisoned, and interrogated during the North Berwick trials was Agnes Sampson from Nether Keith. She was interrogated by King James VI on 4–5 December 1590, and confessed to participation at the North Berwick convention, as well as participation at other witches' gatherings: 'She confesses that she was at the convention of Bara where Meg Steel, Kate Gray, and Janet Campbell was with her, and another who is dead sensine [since], being altogether five in number. They convened by east the kirk [east of the kirk] at the burn side'.[6] Here, the convention at Bara is mentioned, as well as the location of the convention, by the kirk.

As part of my research, in order to get closer to an understanding of the sources, I wanted to visit all the places of witches' conventions in East Lothian mentioned in the confession of Agnes Sampson. Among others, Bara Kirk was on my agenda. I asked Arne to go with me on this trip, due to his considerable knowledge of place-names. He answered in the affirmative, and planning commenced.

Straight away, Arne's focus on landscape came to the fore when we started planning the trip. Beforehand, I had found a description of Bara Kirk and sent it to Arne. The building is situated in Haddington, in the county of East Lothian.[7] Subsequently, I found another description of Bara Kirk from 1627, part of a report on parishes in Scotland sent to the authorities, and forwarded this to Arne as well.[8] He answered:

Takk for skildringa av Barakyrkja. Eg kan visualisere kor ho ligg ut ifrå det du skriv. Det at ho ligg så høgt i landskapet blir reflektert i namnet som betyr på gælisk, 'høgde, spiss'.

6. Normand and Roberts 2000: 146.
7. Martine 1883.
8. Reports on Parishes in Scotland 1627.

Thanks for the description of the Bara Kirk. I can visualise where it lies from what you are writing. The fact that it is situated that high in the landscape is reflected in the name, which in Gaelic means 'height, edge'.

Thus, Arne's first thought when he saw the name was to connect it to Gaelic, and to interpret the place-name in relation to its position in the landscape.

Then came the importance of the map. As part of the planning, Arne sent me two maps: one of Haddingtonshire and one of Bara Kirk's location.[9] In addition, he planned for a comfortable outing: *Eg skal ta med kart og kamera og kaffe* ('I will bring along a map, a camera, and coffee').

When examining the map and the description in the court records before we started the trip, Arne was sceptical with regard to the possibilities to find water near Bara Kirk:

Figure 1: Location of Bara Kirk. © OpenStreetMap.

---

9. On one of the map images, the name Bara is interchanged with 'Baro'.

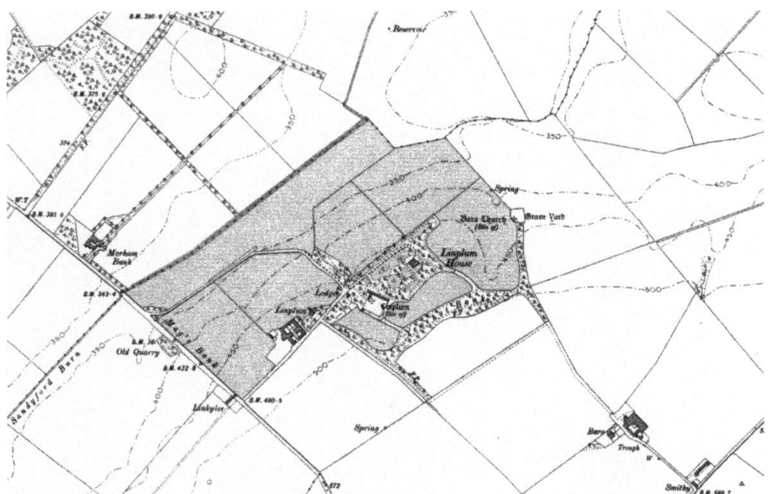

Figure 2: Bara as featured on the 1908 edition of the Ordnance Survey Map
('Haddingtonshire Sheet X. SE'). Reproduced with permission of
the National Library of Scotland.

Her er eit par kart som fortel kvar kyrkja låg. Det er snakk om eit høgdedrag og langt frå vatn. Det nærmaste vatnet er temmeleg langt i sør, som du ser av øvste kartet. Det er markert 'spring' like ved kyrkja, men er det nok?

Here are a couple of maps that report where the kirk was placed. We are talking about a 'height' or 'ridge', far from water. The nearest water is rather far to the south, as you can see on the map at the top. There is a site marked 'spring' next to the kirk, but is that enough?

We set out for the adventure, arrived at Bara, and approached 'by east the kirk at the burn side', following the accurate description from the court records of the North Berwick trials. Standing at the east corner of the kirk, we looked down and saw the enbankment and a field next to it. At that moment, both of us knew that this might have been the place for the alleged witches' convention described in the confession of

Agnes Sampson. Whilst I am usually a very grounded person, I remarked: 'I got a scary feeling – do you feel anything?' Arne answered: 'No, I do not feel anything'.

So here, a difference in temperament between us was revealed. I was carried away by the sight of the enbankment and the field next to it, struck by the amazement that the mystery of a 400-year-old description was still valid. Arne found it natural that such an accurate description of a place could be conveyed over the centuries. In fact, he trusted the historical source – and what the language can convey – more than me. We were both standing at the same corner of the kirk and saw the same landscape.

Arne Kruse's first scholarly work

In order to understand Arne's particular method of looking at the landscape and to incorporate this observation into his interpretation, I would like to go back to his first research work: his master's thesis. This work deals with *médnamn* – names of good fishing places triangulated using multiple surrounding landscape features when at sea. When the direct lines towards two landmarks would cross one another, a good fishing place was marked. A fisherman knew how to use these *méd* in order to find the best fishing places.

At the very beginning of Arne Kruse's master's thesis, the map below (Figure 3) is shown. His study deals with the island of Smøla, on the west coast of Norway, and its surroundings, including inlets, straits, and smaller islands. The map provides the framework for the study, which explores the fisherman's view from various positions at sea towards the landscape of Smøla and its surroundings. Likewise, when Arne sent me the map of Bara before our trip started, it was a signal that we needed a similar framework, and that framework was the information about the landscape as could be discerned from a map. For him, starting with a map was a given in both 1983 and 2015 – a basic requirement.

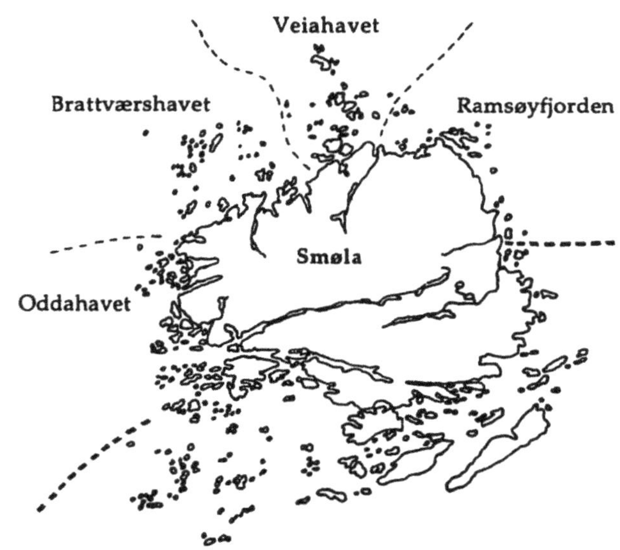

Figure 3: Map of Smøla (after Kruse 1983: 5).

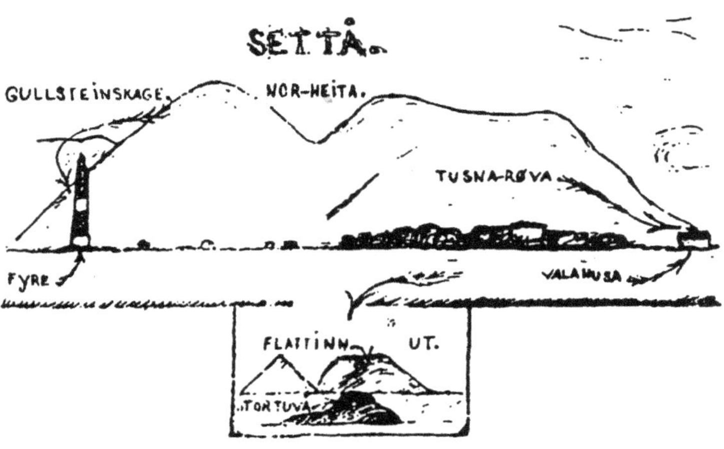

Figure 4: The *médnamn* Settå. Drawing by Ole Jakobsen Oterholm (from Kruse 1983: 207).

Figure 4 provides an illustration of how a *méd* is found. The fisherman looks towards land to find orientation points in various directions. For Settå, a lighthouse (*fyre*) is also used as a marking point. Thus, profiles of the landscape, mountains, and inlets make it possible to draw lines in several directions, and in their convergence, the favourable fishing place is found. Arne's analyses of *médnamn* include diligent work on phonetics, paying attention to the range of pronunciations present in his source material, with most of his informants providing oral interviews. His research into landscape is characterised by examining every single word, before combining this with the map, the landscape, and other textual sources. It is a detailed and elaborate approach, wherein considerable interests in both landscape and language are merged.

Returning to the Bara experience, a parallel to finding *méd* may be found in the lines drawn from the textual directions (i.e. east side of the kirk) and the burn. Like a fisherman looking at the landscape in order to find the location of a *méd*, the place we were after – i.e. the location of the witches' convention – was spotted when a 'crossroads' was established.

Thus, using a moving focal point in the landscape – the visual impression taken in by a person when changing positions – has been part of the Arne Kruse Method for decades. In combining what we can factually see in the landscape with information from other sources, locating a certain place is possible, whether at sea or on land. In Arne's research from Smøla, the information from landscape formation and other visual markers was exploited to draw lines and, in the crossing of these lines, find fishing places. In the Bara experience, the information that enabled us to draw lines through the landscape was obtained from written sources, but permitted a similar technique to spot a location – the crossing of the lines. In both cases, physically standing in the landscape was key to finding the crossroads in question. 'Focalisation', from the point where one is observing, is decisive to find this intersection. It is a term previously employed by Gérard Genette in his work on narratology, a methodological approach for analyses of texts with a narrative structure, such as historical sources like court records.[10] In Smøla, obtaining the required information depended on a fisherman who could move the focal point – his field of vision – and take measurements in order for several directional lines to meet. In Bara, it was necessary to stand at one definite point to be able to find the field. 'Focalisation' is thus an important concept to denote the Arne Kruse Method.

Interdisciplinary approaches are another characteristic of Arne's work, identifiable from his master's thesis to the research he carried out thirty years later. His thesis demonstrates a diligent researcher, who, through his analyses of phonetical and grammatical elements of *médnamn*, worked in a clearly interdisciplinary fashion. The same interdisciplinary approach is seen in the Bara experience through his interest in language: close reading and interpretation of a historical source, as well as the etymological interpretation of the name Bara.

Place-names are of particular interest to Arne. This was where he started, using place-names to denote fishing places, and this is a constant path he has continually travelled along in his later studies. There are more elements to his scholarly work, however. The examples above demonstrate that, even in his master's thesis, Arne was a researcher who heeded landscape in his analyses of place-names, yet inserted many other threads of interpretation into his scholarly work – particularly linguistics, championing interdisciplinarity from the very beginning of his career.

Interdisciplinarity is a keyword of Arne's research, and involves intersections between (comparative) linguistics, history,

---

10. Genette 1980; 1988; 1993, 55-56.

geography, archaeology, etymology, international transmission, and *histoire croisée*. He is always searching for etymological explanations, whether from a Nordic perspective (Old Norse, Icelandic) or a Scottish one (Gaelic, Old Norse). Bringing in etymology is a compulsory part of Arne's research in order to find the appropriate origin and time period of place-names.

Arne Kruse's mentor

I would like to say a few words about a person who has certainly motivated and influenced Arne Kruse as a scholar – Nils Hallan, who was Arne's supervisor during his master's thesis.[11] Hallan, based at the University of Trondheim, was one of Norway's most renowned experts on place-names. For a number of years, from 1976 onwards, he was a *statsstipendiat*, a scholarly position appointed by the Norwegian state.

Hallan always stuck to a down-to-earth interpretation of place-names. He argued that a simple, common-sense interpretation of a place-name was often the most likely one – a fact I will return to below – and he made an impact on a generation of students from the University of Trondheim in arguing for a down-to-earth interpretation of place-names. According to him, if there was a logical interpretation for the name related to landscape, language, and/or culture in the local area, this option should be preferred.

I think that Hallan, as Arne's mentor and supervisor, strengthened not just one approach of Arne Kruse's

---

11. Nils Hallan (1926–1997), Norwegian historian and *statsstipendiat*. Educated as teacher; worked as teacher, journalist and director of museum in Mo i Rana until 1976, when he was appointed *statsstipendiat,* and connected to the Department of History and Department of Nordic Studies at the University of Trondheim.

interpretations of place-names, but has also, in a broader sense, paved the way for a basic pragmatic nuance that is included in the Arne Kruse Method. The methodology applied by Arne never enters into the esoteric or speculative. Instead, it is firmly grounded and relies, for part of its argumentation, on common people's knowledge over the course of generations. The practical act of standing in a landscape is echoed in this approach.

Exploration of language

I have titled this chapter 'Language and Landscape', and have already pointed to landscape as a long-lasting field of research in Arne's work. In what follows, I would like to demonstrate the role of language in the two research articles I have written together with Arne Kruse in recent years. Both articles are based on court records from the witchcraft trials in Finnmark, an area in northern Norway which suffered a severe persecution of witches in the period 1600–1692.

The first article we authored together focused on the interpretation of the place-name Ballvollen, allegedly the site of witches' gatherings on the island of Vardø, in Finnmark.[12] The name featured in confessions in witchcraft trials during the period 1621–1624, but not before and not after these years. It is not known as a place-name in Vardø.[13] The article deals with the exploration of the name as related to the transmission of particular demonological ideas.

The name Ballvollen has a corresponding name in Scotland: Ball Ley, located in Orkney, which also occurs in witchcraft records as a place for witches' gatherings. It is argued that John

---

12. Kruse and Willumsen 2014.
13. Ibid.: 407–424.

Cunningham, a Scotsman who entered the service of the Danish king and was appointed district governor in Finnmark, brought with him demonological ideas from Scotland to Finnmark.[14] As Cunningham knew about the Scottish notion of the Ball Ley, and was versed in the Danish language, he was able to introduce the name Ballvollen in Finnmark. During interrogation in witchcraft trials in a Vardø courtroom, he translated the Scottish name Ball Ley into the Norwegian name Ballvollen. The possibility of connecting linguistic markers to the transfer of ideas and to identifiable persons provides a strong argument for transfer of ideas.

The place-name Ballvollen was of special interest for us as authors, because it was so short-lived and only related to witches' gatherings. Arne's great competence in place-name research, as well as his sharp analysis of courtroom discourse, contributed valuable insights into a possible linguistic transfer during the interrogation. Interesting discussions arose between Arne and myself, related to how the interrogation might have taken place and the impact of John Cunningham's bilingual competence, leading to an ad hoc translation.

The interpretation of the two language elements in Ballvollen and Ball Ley clearly pointed in the same direction as Nils Hallan's understanding – namely, the first part interpreted as a ball, the second part interpreted as a field. It later turned out that Hallan himself had written an article on Ballvollen, arguing for the same interpretation Arne and I reached on an independent basis.[15] Hallan must also have found the name Ballvollen very special. Exactly where on the island of Vardø this field was situated is not known, so there remains an enigma connected to this place-name.

---

14. Willumsen 2013; Willumsen and Baptie 2013.
15. Hallan 1975: 276–287.

During our work on the article on the place-name Ballvollen, I learned of Arne's interest and love of language. His need to scrutinise linguistic expressions in order to find new explanations, to ask challenging questions, is characteristic of his attitude. This courage leads to posing new research questions, finding new explanations, and suggesting new explanatory paradigms. His need to turn another stone, to look for possibilities that have not been scrutinised before, is a wonderful quality to possess as a scholar.

The aim of our next joint article was to map out a fascinating transnational path regarding the transfer of ideas on witch-craft.[16] The article demonstrates how language has the ability to carry and transport an ideological doctrine across national and linguistic borders – in this case, knowledge directly related to the learned European doctrine of demonology, which influenced witchcraft persecution in Finnmark.

By tracing certain linguistic markers, which can be associated with the ideology of the demonologists, cognate words can be found in the source material on both sides of the North Sea in the late sixteenth and early seventeenth centuries. These findings offer direct evidence for transmission of certain ideas linked to them. Through concrete examples from Scotland and Finnmark, it is argued that a direct oral transmission is evident, and that the transmission revolved around two individuals: King James VI of Scotland and the 'king' of Vardøhus, district governor John Cunningham. The article is a continuation of the research questions posed in the paper on Ballvollen, and includes source material from both Finnmark and Scotland. The linguistic arguments offered in the article are new, highlighting the possibility of connecting linguistic markers to the transfer of ideas and to identifiable persons.

---

16. Kruse and Willumsen 2020.

As for linguistic analysis, particular attention is paid to the phrase 'master and admiral'. This expression occurs during the North Berwick trials in the interrogation of Euphame MacCalzean (1591),[17] and in the trial of Kirsten Sørensdatter in Finnmark (1621).[18] During the former interrogation, she is led to admit that there is truth in the accusation that Robert Greirsoun is 'youre [her] admerall and maister man'.[19] Throughout the entire panic of 1620–1621 in Finnmark, the word 'admiral' and the extended phrase *mester och Admiral* ('master and admiral') were in use. When the trial of Kirsten Sørensdatter started, seven trials were already finished, and seven accused women had confessed that Kirsten was their 'master and admiral'. Threatened with both torture and the water ordeal, Kirsten confessed a couple of days later, this time likewise 'in the very own presence of the illustrious Hans Køningh',[20] that she had practised witchcraft and that she was guilty in several of the accusations 'except that she was not their Admiral'.[21]

The article includes reflections on linguistic context. In the phrase 'master and admiral', the command structure is emphasised. The fact that the metaphor is sourced from a naval setting is initially surprising, as those charged are accused of witchcraft. It has the effect, however, of strengthening the aspect of an urgent and absolute institution: in a fleet and on a ship, there are no questions of authority and obedience. Further, features of orality are paid attention to. As a doublet, wherein the two words both indicate authority, it is an example of a semantic repetition

---

17. National Record Office of Scotland, Circuit Court Books, JC2/2, f. 224a.
18. Regional State Archives of Tromsø, The Archive of Finnmark District Magistrate, 6, ff. 10v–12v.
19. National Record Office of Scotland, Circuit Court Books, JC2/2, f. 224a.
20. Regional State Archives of Tromsø, The Archive of Finnmark District Magistrate, 6, f. 28r.
21. Ibid.: f. 29r.

or pleonasm, whose the first word of provides an expectation that another word with more or less similar meaning will follow suit. This is a significant feature of oral culture, where semantic redundancy functions as an aid to keep both the speaker and the listener on track.[22] It also has a function of a mnemonic tool.

Through accurate linguistic analysis, the article argues that a linguistic phrase is able to convey meaning. The linguistic argument is that the joining of the two words 'master' and 'admiral' – as a *meme* – can convey a notion, carry a whole dogma in three words, and relate to a doctrine of leadership, one being in charge of a group performing collective witchcraft. Not 'master' alone, not 'admiral' alone, but the joining of the two words.

When we read the court records from Finnmark aloud, it was Arne who observed that the same joining of words took place in Scotland and in Finnmark – I had not noticed this before. This moment of revelation made us both understand something about transference of ideas through linguistic expressions. One of the words had not been enough to prove a conveyance of the same ideas, but both words in a string in two countries is a proof of transference – it is not haphazard that these three words are expressed. Although the word order in the Scottish court records is reversed – i.e. 'admerall and maister man' – the doublet 'master and admiral' or more common 'master and commander', has become set in a fixed and non-reversible word order in Modern English and Scots, and this seems to be the most usual word order in Older Scots as well.[23] This way of scrutinising linguistic expressions, to observe and examine not only every word but also the linguistic surroundings and the context of the expression, is a quality that Arne has as a scholar. It was also Arne's suggestion to title the article 'Magic Language'.

---

22. Ong 1989: 39–41.
23. Kruse and Willumsen 2020: 22.

Conclusion

I would like to thank Arne Kruse for his insightful contributions to the study of landscape and language – wherein research threads of pragmatic, empirical, theoretical, methodical, and interdisciplinary character are interwoven in 'the Arne Kruse Method'.

Figure 5: Arne Kruse and Liv Helene Willumsen in East Lothian.
Photo: Brigitte Guenier-Kruse, used with kind permission.

Bibliography

Primary Sources

National Record Office of Scotland, Circuit Court Books, JC2/2, f. 224a.

Regional State Archives of Tromsø, The Archive of Finnmark District Magistrate, 6, ff. 10v–12v, 28r, 29r.

Reports on Parishes in Scotland. 1627.

Secondary Sources

Genette, Gérard. 1980. *Narrative Discourse: An Essay in Method*. Ithaca: Cornell University Press.

———. 1988. *Narrative Discourse Revisited*. Ithaca: Cornell University Press.

———. 1993. *Fiction and Diction*. Ithaca: Cornell University Press.

Hallan, Nils. 1975. 'Balvolden (Balduolden)'. *Håløygminne* 14, 276–287.

Kruse, Arne. 1983. 'Médnamn frå Smøla'. Cand.philol. thesis. University of Trondheim.

Kruse, Arne and Willumsen, Liv Helene. 2014. 'Ordet Ballvollen knytt til transnasjonal overføring av idéar'. *Historisk Tidsskrift* 93:3, 407–424.

———. 2020. 'Magic Language: The Transmission of an Idea over Geographical Distance and Linguistic Barriers'. *Magic, Ritual, and Witchcraft* 15:1, 1–32.

Martine, John. 1883. *Reminiscences of the Royal Burgh of Haddington and Old East Lothian*. Edinburgh: John Menzies.

Normand, Lawrence and Roberts, Gareth (eds). 2000. *Witchcraft in Early Modern Scotland*. Exeter: University of Exeter Press.

Ong, Walter. 1989. *Orality and Literacy*. London: Routledge.

Willumsen, Liv Helene. 1984. 'Trollkvinne i nord'. Cand.philol. thesis. University of Tromsø.

———. 2008. 'Seventeenth-Century Witchcraft Trials in Scotland and Northern Norway'. PhD thesis. University of Edinburgh.

———. 2013. 'Exporting the Devil across the North Sea: John Cunningham and the Finnmark Witch-Hunt'. In Julian Goodare (ed.), *Scottish Witches and Witch-Hunters*. Basingstoke: Palgrave, 49–66.

———. 2020. 'Witchcraft against Royal Danish Ships in 1589 and the Transnational Transfer of Ideas'. *International Review of Scottish Studies* 45, 54–99.

Willumsen, Liv Helene and Baptie, Diane. 2013. 'John Cunninghams karriere og bakgrunn'. *Norsk Slektshistorisk Tidsskrift* 43:3, 159–176.

· XIV ·

Frolics and *Freuteries*: Norse Magic and Norn Words

Andrew Jennings

The origins of this chapter lie in a talk about Norse magical terms inherited by the dialects of Orkney and Shetland, which I delivered at a Scottish Society for Northern Studies day conference held in Edinburgh in 2010. At that time, Arne Kruse was approaching his presidency of the Society, and it seemed that, given his interest in witchcraft trials and in the culture of the Northern Isles, it would be a suitable subject to revisit in this book dedicated to him.

The Northern Isles have long had a reputation for witchcraft. King James VI of Scotland, in his 1597 dissertation on necromancy, *Daemonologie*, singles out Orkney and Shetland as wild parts of the world, which, along with Lapland and Finland, were places where witchcraft was rife, and where 'the Deuill findes greatest ignorance and barbaritie'.[1] This reputation lasted long after the repeal of the Witchcraft Act in 1736. For example, Walter Traill Dennison relates that, around 1830, while visiting Leith, he was taken on the knee of an old sailor who quickly threw him off again when he discovered that Walter came from Orkney, 'where so many cursed witches

---

1. James VI 1597: 55.

dwell'.[2] Belief in witchcraft was endemic in the community too. For example, Edmonston tells us that

> Witchcraft is still believed by the peasantry to exist in Zetland; and some old women live by pretending to be witches, for no one ventures to refuse what they ask. About six years ago [c. 1802] a man entered a prosecution in the sheriff-court at Lerwick, against a woman for witchcraft. He stated that she uniformly assumed the form of a raven, and in that character killed his cattle, and prevented the milk of his cows from yielding butter.[3]

Belief appears to have lasted well into the twentieth century. In 1973, Gideon Isbister of Lerwick told Ernest Marwick about an incident from his boyhood, wherein his mother discovered an old woman pulling grass from the byre roof after having cut some hair from the cow's tail. His mother got very agitated and shouted to her children to hurry and get some water. They quickly collected some and threw it over the old woman, removing her power to do any harm.[4]

It is of great interest, given the connection that James VI appears to be drawing between the Northern Isles and the wider northern world, that in one of the almost contemporary witch trials, there appears to be a reference to a form of Norse magic. In 1633, the Orcadian Marrioun Richart made a water cure for a woman which had been *forespoken*, a Scots word for bewitched. She did this by filling a cup with water into which she put something like salt, spat three times into it, and then

---

2. Marwick 1991: 368.
3. Edmonston 1809: 74.
4. Marwick 1975: 51–52.

Scho <u>aundit in bitt</u> (quilk is ane Nourne terme) to [be] exponit into right language, in alse mikill as scho did blew hir breath thairin.[5]

The term *aundit* comes from the Old Norse verb *anda* ('to breathe') and Norwegian Bokmål *åndet* ('breathed'). Why would she breathe into the water? Her breath is obviously imbued with power, and the explanation is surely that, given that breath and spirit are intimately connected conceptually and linguistically in Old Norse, the noun *andi* means both breath and spirit. By blowing purposefully into the water, she is putting some of her own spirit into it. In his PhD thesis 'Gand, seid og åndevind', Eldar Heide argues that breath or blowing lies behind the Old Norse magical concept of *gandr* and, although it can be translated in a range of ways – from 'monster' to 'magical staff' – it has the essential meaning of breath, i.e. the magical practitioner's spirit, being sent out to do magic.[6]

Aundit is not the only Norn term associated with Marrioun Richart. She was also accused of helping a woman to regain the profit of her cow's milk, which had been taken by witchcraft. The woman was to go to the sea and count nine waves coming in, and then she was to collect the water, take it home, and put it in her churn. The phrase Marrioun uses is *tell nyne beares off the watter* ('count nine waves of the water'); *beares* is from Old Norse *bára* ('wave, billow'). It seems to have a Scots plural -s ending. It is noteworthy that supernatural connotations of the ninth wave are common to both Norse and Gaelic tradition: Ægir, the Norse god of the sea, has nine daughters with his wife Rán, personifying waves, and the Gaelic god Manannán was believed to live beyond the ninth wave.

---

5. Black 1903: 117.
6. Heide 2006a: 250.

The *gandr* or breath sent forth by the magical practitioner could take on animal form[7]. These forms could include sea mammals. In the twelfth century *Historia Norwegie*, in the earliest description of Sámi shamanism, a shaman is killed because his *gandus*, which had taken the form of a whale, collided with an enemy *gandus* that had changed into a sharp spike.[8] In what is surely a direct parallel with this story, in 1645, the Shetlander Marion Pardoun was executed because, amongst other crimes, she had been

> [*t*]*ransformed in the lyknes of an pellack quhaill* [...] *the devil changing your spirit, qlk fled in the same quhaill* [...] *ye did cum under the said boat and overturnit her with ease, and drowned and devourit thame in ye sey.*[9]

Just as spirit can be breathed or blown out, spirits can be breathed or sucked in. Clive Tolley points out that Siberian shamans breathe in spirits,[10] and in Icelandic folklore, according to Jón Árnason, if you want to know the future, you have to catch a *sagnarandi* ('telling spirit') and trap it in a certain way when it enters your mouth.[11] In the legendary *Hrólfs saga kraka*, a *seiðkona* ('sorceress') is asked for hidden information, so she starts to perform the magical practice called *seiðr*.[12] After a while, she yawns heavily, and immediately afterwards she can give some information. Somebody tries to stop the sorceress, albeit unsuccessfully, and she yawns again, giving more information. It seems that it is the yawning which gives the *seiðkona*

---

7. Price 2019: 185
8. Ekrem and Mortensen 2006: 63.
9. Black 1903: 97.
10. Tolley 1995: 58, 71.
11. Árnason 1958–61 [1862–64]: 309.
12. Jónsson 1954: 11–12.

the information. According to Heide, the *seiðkona* yawns in the spirits that give her the information.[13] Again, the witch trial material seems to provide a parallel. Yawning is recorded as a heinous act. In the trial of Katherine Grant in Orkney in 1623, it is recorded that she *gantit* ('yawned') three times at Henry Janies, before giving him the evil eye

> *with a stoup in her hand, with the boddome formest, and sat down right fornent the said Henrie, and gantit* [yawned] *thrice on him:- and going furth he followit her; and being on the brig-stane, sho lukit over her shoulder and turned up the quhyt of her eye, quhair by hir divilrie, their fell ane great weght upoun him, that he was forcit to set his bak to the wall; and when he came in, he thoucht the hous ran about with him; and theirefter lay seik ane lang time.*[14]

What did she believe she was doing? Was she exhaling her spirit, or was she trying to suck in some of Henry's spirit? Maybe she was sucking in some evil spirit to do her bidding? We will never know, but the actual practice of yawning is indicative of Norse magical practice. Katherine *gantit* on another occasion too. After being suspected of infecting a child, she arrived at the house and *gantit* over a cup of water, in which she had put a knife, and into which she spat. Luckily, the child recovered.

Given that, in the Northern Isles, the witchcraft trials appear to show the continuation of Norse magical practices into the seventeenth century – which should come as no surprise, given that the societies were still largely Norse in culture and language – one might expect to see the existence of Norse magical terms in the Scots dialects of Orkney and Shetland, just as one

---

13. Heide 2006b: 352.
14. Dalyell 1834: 7.

sees the presence of Norn farming and fishing terms. Indeed, words associated with the practice of *seiðr*, *varðlokkur* ('a type of magical song'), and *argr* ('unmanliness') do appear, as do a range of words originating from *gandr*.

Jakob Jakobsen, the great Faroese lexicographer, suggested reasonably that the terms *varl* and *verdie* both came from *varðlokkur*.[15] He recorded the phrases *to varl de land*, which meant to take away the profit of a piece of land by witchcraft, which he suggested came from an abbreviated older verb to **varlek* – and *a auld verdie*, an old superstitious formula or custom. In his dictionary, John Graham does not record the survival of *varl*, but he does record a contemporary use of *vaerdi*:

Dey wir a aald vaerdi i da place at da Toogs wal-water wid cure rheumatics.[16]

The *varðlokkur* is compared by Anna-Leena Siikala with sha-manic songs, the purpose of which was to entice the spirits needed by the sorceress to come to her aid.[17] Magnus Olsen argued that the etymology of the word indicates that it was the 'guardian' spirit, or *vörðr*, that was being attracted.[18] This could be the 'guardian' spirit of a person, farm, or kin group.

The belief in the *vord* or *vardøger* ('guardian' spirits) con-tinued in Norway into the nineteenth century. In western Norway, there was a supernatural being which guarded the farm called a *Tunvord* or *Gars-vor*.[19] The *vardøger*, a personal spirit or a reification of a person's spirit, could take animal

---

15. Jakobsen 1985: 1029, 1042.
16. Graham 1979: 94.
17. Siikala 2002: 345
18. Olsen 1916: 4.
19. Ibid.: 7.

shape (note the similarity with the *gandr*). They occur in a number of folktales, for example the story 'Grandmother's Vardøger Scared the Cows', recorded in Buskerud.[20] Similarly, in nineteenth-century Orkney, there was a belief in the *varden*. Walter Traill Dennison described how he had heard from very old people about the *meen o' the Varden* ('moan of the varden'):

> The varden was a spirit which, unseen, and in the shape of some animal, attended every human being. Each individual had a varden of his own, which followed him everywhere [...]. Previous to a man's decease, his varden sees the approaching calamity, though unknown to mortal ken; and the creature gives vent to its sorrow in low moans, dismal groans, or half-suffocated doleful howlings, which all presage the coming death.[21]

The evidence from Old Norse sources suggests that the magical practice of *seiðr* and the singing of *varðlokkur* was conventionally carried out by women. Men who practised it were open to accusations of *ergi*, the state of being *argr*. *Ergi* and *argr* have a number of unpleasant connotations, including lewdness, lustfulness, wickedness, devilry, unmanliness, and cowardliness. Jakobsen found the word *arg* in the dialect.[22] It seems to have retained its connotations of evilness and lustfulness. Its primary meaning was evil or bad as in the expletive *Arga dirt!* but it also meant 'very desirous of something', which hints at the earlier meaning of lustfulness.

Unlike the word *seiðr*, *gandr* has left its mark on the Shetland and Orcadian dialects. For Shetland, Jakobsen collected *gander, ganfer, gandaguster,* and *gandigo*.[23] Marwick recorded *gamfer* in

---

20. Kvideland 1988: 67.
21. Dennison 1995: 147–148.
22. Jakobsen 1985: 17.
23. Ibid.: 210–211.

Orkney.[24] One of the meanings Jakobsen gives for *gander* is a 'sudden feeling of powerlessness, nausea, sickness at heart', as in *der'r a ill gander aboot my heart,* which he is surely correct to interpret as a sickness brought about by witchcraft. For *ganfer,* he says it means a phenomenon in the sky like a mock-sun or a halo around the moon or sun indicating rain, or additionally, an ominous cracking sound in the atmosphere. Jakobsen derived it from **gand-ferð* ('a company of witches or wicked spirits') which could be seen in the sky, and synonymous with ON *gandreið* ('witches' ride'). Given that in Northern Norwegian *gandferd* is a term for the *Wild Hunt,* also known as the *Oskoreidi, jolareidi* in Norway, or *Odens jakt* in Sweden – the storm of spirits sometimes led by Odin – this was probably also the case in Shetland. In his PhD, Heide made a connection between the *ganfer, gandaguster* ('a sudden gust of wind'), and *gandigo* ('squall of wind with rain') and the Old Norse word *gandrekr* ('a storm brought about by witchcraft'). In this wide-ranging and detailed exploration of the relationship between *seiðr* and *gandr,* he explores, amongst other things, the connection between the idea of a magic wind and the practice of magic practitioners sending out their breath to do magic.[25]

Are there other words in the dialects of Orkney and Shetland which have their origins in Old Norse magical terms? In his paper 'The Name of the Witch: Sagas, Sorcery and Social Context', Gísli Pálsson listed a series of concepts associated with Norse witchcraft which occur frequently in the Icelandic family sagas.[26] A number of the concepts translate as 'witchcraft' (*fjölkynngi, fyrnska,* and *forneskja*); others refer to the special knowledge and powers of the witch (*fróðleikur* and *margkunnindi*); while yet others refer to the practice of witchcraft (*galdr* and *seiðr*). As already stated, *seiðr* does not survive

24. Marwick 1929: 51.
25. Heide 2006.
26. Pálsson 1991: 158.

in the dialects; however, a number of these terms have been preserved (*Felkyo, frolik,* and *galder*). The meanings might have changed a little, but their links to Old Norse magical belief and practice are clear.

One of Pálsson's words for witchcraft – *fjölkynngi* – survived in Orkney as a proper noun. Gregor Lamb records the name *Felkyo* from ON *fjölkyngis-kona* ('woman who knows witchcraft'), which – he writes – was the name of a witch who used to live in the Hillside district of Birsay.[27] He also records the word *felkyied*, 'tired looking', which probably originally meant 'bewitched'. This word does not occur in Shetland. Instead, Jakobsen recorded the word *heksi* for witch, which, although it occurs in Norwegian, is a borrowing from Low German or Dutch.[28]

Another word that occurs in both Orkney and Shetland, and which can be regarded as a synonym for witch or sorcerer, is *finn*. In Scandinavia, those seeking magical help or information might visit the Sámi – *finnar* in Old Norse. The aforementioned Sámi shaman in the *Historia Norwegie* is so named. Visiting the Sámi was called *finnför* and was specifically banned in the Norwegian laws. It did not stop the practice though, and in a fifteenth-century Swedish case, a certain *Margit halffstop* learned the spell for bewitching a man at a distance from *Anna finszka*.[29] A parallel would be an old lady in Sanday in Orkney called *Baabie Finn*, who was reputed to have strange powers,[30] and *Finnie* from Unst, who 'could do things we canna name'.[31] According to John Spence, people who were 'supposed to be skilled in the Black Art, were spoke of as Norway Finns'.[32]

---

27. Lamb 1995: 32.
28. Jakobsen 1985: 302.
29. Mitchell 2000: 335–336.
30. Robertson 1991: 336.
31. Saxby 1932: 96.
32. Spence 1899: 26.

One of the words for the special powers of the witch, *fróðleikur* ('knowledge of magic'), appears to survive as *frolik* ('an old, magic rigmarole or formula'), as in the saying *auld froliks*.[33] The word *fron* (a 'superstition, superstitious ceremony, magic formula'), as in *a auld fron*, probably derives from *fróðr* ('well-informed, learned'), the first part of *fróðleikur*.

Galdr, which Price defines as originally 'a specific type of sorcery focusing on a characteristic type of high-pitched singing',[34] has left its mark on the Shetland dialect. Jakobsen recorded the noun *galder*, which he defined as noisy, foolish talk, as in *nane o dy galder*; noisy mirth; a high, roaring wind; or a great tumult in the sea, as in *a galder i de sea*. He also recorded the verb, which he defined as to speak in a loud, foolish manner, to laugh noisily and wildly, of the wind to bluster, and of water to rush. John Graham found that it was still used. He defined *galder* as a noun meaning a loud, boisterous laugh – *Hears du da galders o yun eediot*.[35] In the dialect, the connotations of the noun and the verb are clear – blustery, noisy weather, loud laughter, or noisy, foolish, unintelligible blethers!

It is interesting to note that, in the eddic poem *Grógaldr*, the dead sorceress Gróa describes to her son Svipdag one way of correctly performing the *galdr*:

á jarðföstum steini
stóðk innan dura,
meðan þér galdra gólk

While singing *galdr* songs I stood on an earth-fast stone just inside the doorway.[36]

---

33. Jakobsen 1985: 200.
34. Price 2019: 35.
35. Graham 1979: 28.
36. Munch 1847: 170.

Anna-Leena Siikala reports that later Scandinavian incantations also mention spell-casting on an earth-fast stone.[37] She claims this stone was so powerful because beneath dwelt guardian spirits. Earth-fast stones were also important in Shetland traditional belief. John Nicolson records:

> On the night when the first winter moon was visible, the lasses were wont to 'rin aboot da eart-fast stane'. Selecting a large stone that was firmly embedded in the ground, the performer would go round it three times with the sun and three times against, at the same time repeating:-
>
> *Winter, winter, new mune, welcome an' true mune,*
> *Grant me da first wiss 'at I ax o' dae.*
> (Here she would repeat the name of her favoured wooer).
> *If I ha'e claes frae dee ta wear,*
> *If I ha'e bairns ta de ta bear,*
> *Dan next sight 'at I see o' dee,*
> *May dy face be ta me,*
> *an' dy back to da sea.*[38]

On the island of Foula, the visiting Norwegian Einar Seim recorded, in his diary in 1934, that when the men wanted a sea-breeze or free wind,

> they went to an earthfast stone, laid a silver penny on it (copper would not do) and then went three times round it sunwise, and three times round widder-shins.[39]

---

37. Siikala 2002: 276.
38. Nicolson 1912: 125.
39. Torvanger 2016: 45.

In the traditional Shetland house, there were also earth-fast stones called *bustanes*. It was considered good practice for a *bustane* to be incorporated in the wall of the house and of the byre.[40] Jakobsen records that

> Such bustens (or properly the good fairies which according to old tradition lived under the stones) were supposed to bring good luck to the houses to which they belonged. When milking the cow, some drops of milk were sprinkled on the 'bosten' in the byre; likewise at a private baptism, the 'bosten' was sometimes sprinkled with a few drops of baptismal water.[41]

In Old Norse, the performer of *galdr* could be called a *galdra-maðr* or *galdra-smiðr*. Neither of these words survives in the dialect. However, in his 1821 novel *The Pirate*, Sir Walter Scott uses the word *galdragon* ('a sorceress or witch').[42] It is possible that Scott created the word from the Old Norse *galdrakona* ('sorceress'), which was not outwith his ability. However, Jakobsen gave *galdragon* the benefit of the doubt and suggested it was a Norn word.[43] It is possible that Scott picked it up on his visit to Shetland in the summer of 1814. However, despite the lack of the word *galdra-maðr*, it is hard to think of a better term to describe Old Yacob in George Stewart's late-nineteenth-century Shetland novel *Shetland Fireside Tales*.[44] Stewart appears to have tapped into real tradition about how magic was once practised in Shetland, using an old Shetland saw which included Norn words like *vaana* from *vatn* ('water') with the definite article

---

40. Nicolson 1981: 96.
41. Jakobsen 1985: 89.
42. Scott 1821: 16.
43. Jakobsen 1985: 208.
44. Stewart 1877: 200.

attached. He describes how Old Yacob attempted, unsuccessfully as it turns out, to dampen the winds of a storm:

When they got outside, Yacob placed himself on the 'brig-stane' with his face towards the east, and taking his staff in his left hand, raised his right arm, and pronounced the following incantation, sawing the wind with his arm as he spoke:

Robbin cam ower da vaana
wi' a shü nü;
Twabbie, Toobie, Keelikin,
Kollickin, Palktrick alanks da
robin. Güid sober da wind

But the wind sobered not; the spirit of the storm, as if in mockery of such feeble attempts to propitiate his wrath, raged still more furiously, and drove the clouds of salt spray, hail and sleet, with hurricane force, against the earth, so that old Yacob had to beat a hasty retreat to his cottage.

Price, in his list of Old Norse magical terms, also includes *útiseta*, which was the practice of 'sitting out' in special places like graveyards or burial mounds in order to communicate with the spirits of the dead.[45] This appears to be what Catherine Jonesdochter was accused of doing. She was *hanting and seeing the trowis ryse out of the kirkyeard of Hildiswick and Holiecross Kirk of Eschenes*.[46] *Hanting* means 'haunting or hanging around' and although *trowis* (modern *trows*) is the common Shetland supernatural being, in this context it means 'spirits of the dead'. This was a crime for which she was *wirriet* and burned in 1616.

---

45. Price 2019: 35.
46. Black 1903: 85.

Pálsson suggested there was a conceptual distinction between two kinds of magical practices – between sorcery, which has been described so far, and divination.[47] Whether or not this is the case, there is plenty of evidence for divination in the Northern Isles and for the survival of Norse terminology.

Jakobsen[48] recorded the word *frøtt*, which he defined as 'soothsaying (combined with old phrases and formulas), especially by an old, wise woman, and a superstitious belief, customs or spells, as in *auld frøtts*'. The word comes from Old Norse *frétt* ('questioning'), which includes asking the will of the gods. The collective plural *frootery* occurs in Orkney.[49] Jakobsen also recorded the adjective *frøtti*, as in the phrase *a auld frøtti saying* ('a phrase or formula used in soothsaying').[50] The word was also borrowed into Scots from Old Norse, but there is no reason to believe it did not go into the dialects directly.

Similarly, the Shetland word *spo*, from Old Norse *spá* ('to prophecy'), although also borrowed into Scots as *spae*, must, given its pronunciation, have come directly into the dialect. Jakobsen recorded the word *spoben*, a sheep bone, which was used by an expectant mother to predict the sex of her unborn child. She would ask a friend to drop the bone three times into her lap, each time saying,

Spo ben! Spo ben, whedder my friend is to ha'e a boy or a lass![51]

If the round side turned up twice, it was to be a boy.

Witchcraft was believed to cause an effect, to impose the witch's will, perhaps to bewitch a subject and do them ill, as

---

47. Pálsson 1991: 158.
48. Jakobsen 1985: 202.
49. Marwick 1929: 43.
50. Jakobsen 1985: 202.
51. Jakobsen 1985: 882.

in one of the meanings of *gander* – an illness brought about by witchcraft. These connotations are encapsulated in the word *granderi*, which Jakobsen interprets as 'witchcraft, sorcery or queer behaviour caused by witchcraft'.[52] It is a derivative of another dialect word, *grand* ('to hurt by witchcraft'), as in *hit is no to say, at he was witched, but he was grandet*. In other words, not only was he bewitched, there was absolutely no hope for him! In Old Norse, *að granda* meant to 'damage or destroy'.

Trollaskod, derived from *troll*, which provides a rich vein of Shetland dialect vocabulary, has a similar meaning to *grandet*. Jakobsen explains that, as well as meaning witch, it properly means 'one who has been shot by a troll and has thus become bewitched'.[53] In Scandinavian folklore, words like *trollskot* ('trollshot'), *alvskot* ('elf-shot'), and *finnskot* ('Finn-shot') imply that supernatural beings and magical practitioners could cause sickness by firing a magical shot.[54] Jakobsen also recorded the words *trollet* – which could mean 'having a sickly appearance'; in other words bewitched – and *trolsket* ('indisposed, unwell, or drowsy'), from ON *tryllskr* ('betwitched, being a troll or witch').

As well as the previous examples, Jakobsen also collected and interpreted the following troll words: *trollamist* ('a thick, dark mist'), *trollamog* ('an insignificant person or malicious little fellow'), *trollhotted* ('troll-like'), *trolliplukk* ('a poor feeble, slow-moving creature'), *trollmolet* ('having an ugly mouth or face, like a troll), *trollslaget* ('queer, odd looking, originally troll-struck)', *trolleman* ('a wizard or sorcerer'), and *trollkollin* ('a hermaphrodite').[55] The last two are particularly interesting, and he records that *trolleman* occurs in a Norn refrain *Trolleman*,

52. Ibid.: 259.
53. Ibid.: 967.
54. Kanerva 2013: 15.
55. Jakobsen 1985: 967–968.

trolleman tak vara! ('Wizard beware!'). Unfortunately, he does not provide any further detail about its providence.

He is surely correct in claiming that *trollkollin* comes from *trollkerling* ('female troll'), hinting that there was something masculine about this female magical being. In the Faroe Islands, Terry Gunnell pointed out that in a description of the traditions on Svínoy by the Faroese author William Heinesen – in his short story 'Grylen' – the female troll or *grylen* sports a large wooden phallus which can bring fertility to barren women.[56] These cases of mixed-gender magical beings might be relevant to a wider discussion around the nature of the *göndull*, the staff employed by magical practitioners – generally female – to send out *gandr* spirits.[57] *Göndull* can also mean 'penis'.

Heide[58] explores 'spirit penises' in *Gand, seid og åndevind*, where he argues that *gandr* might have been seen as a metaphorical 'spiritual penis' sent out to perform a spiritual phallic attack. He relates that southern Sámi shamans, in the eighteenth century, used to contend with each other by sending out magic projectiles called *nåejtiendïrre* against each other. This word literally means '*noaidi's* penis' (the *noaidi* was the shaman). If the *göndull* were seen as a 'spiritual penis', then female practitioners might have been regarded, in a sense, as hermaphrodites or mixed gender. However, one does not want to take speculation too far.

Jakob Jakobsen proclaimed that *Norn var også det sprog som heksene brugte på Shetland og Orknøerne i deres trylleformularer og besværgelserie* ('Norn was also the language that witches used in Shetland and Orkney in their spells and incantations').[59] Clearly, this would have been the case when Norn was still

---

56. Gunnell 2000: 40.
57. Price 2019: 134.
58. Heide 2006a: 274.
59. Jakobsen 1911: 320.

spoken in the islands. Magical practice, spells, and incantations were part of the islands' inherited Norse culture. Like others before me, I have not been immune to the *vam* ('mysterious magical influence') cast by this example of the Northern Isles' intangible cultural heritage. Elsewhere I have argued that Shetland has an 'identifiable Norse folklore dialect'.[60] The rich legacy of dialect words and the evidence from the witch trials indicates this is also the case with regard to witchcraft. Perhaps it was not geography alone which caused James VI to lump the Northern Isles together with Lapland and Finland as centres of witchcraft. It is impressive that so many words with links to Norse magical practice have survived in the dialect, particularly in Shetland. It gives us some insight into what has been lost.

To conclude, I would like to balance the Shetland refrain *Trolleman, trolleman tak vara* with one from Orkney. Jakobsen was told a story about the Rousay witch Kada (Katherine Craigie) by Hugh Marwick. She successfully sank a ship by means of sympathetic magic, agitating a cup, representing the ship, in a tub of water. In exultation, she exclaimed *Ta'r a' gort* ('It's done!').[61] Just like this short chapter.

Bibliography

Árnason, Jón. 1958–61 [1862–64]. *Íslenzkar þjóðsögur og ævintýri. Nýtt safn.* Árni Böðvarsson and Bjarni Vilhjálmsson (eds). Reykjavík: Bókaútgáfan þjóðsaga.

Black, G.F. 1903. *County Folklore Volume III Orkney and Shetland Islands.* London: David Nutt.

Dalyell, John Graham. 1834. *The Darker Superstitions of Scotland.* Edinburgh: Waugh and Innes.

---

60. Jennings 2016: 32.
61. Jakobsen 111: 320.

Dennison, Walter Traill. 1995. *Orkney Folklore and Sea Legends*. Kirkwall: The Orkney Press.

Edmonston, A. 1809. *A View of the Ancient and Present State of the Zetland Islands; Including their Civil, Political and Natural History; Antiquities and An Account of Their Agriculture, Fisheries, Commerce, and the State of Society and Manners*. Edinburgh: John Ballantyne and Co.

Ekrem, I. and Mortensen, L.B. (eds). 2006. *Historia Norwegie*. Copenhagen: Museum Tusculanum Press.

Graham, J. 1979. *The Shetland Dictionary*. Lerwick: The Shetland Times.

Gunnell, T. 2001. 'Grýla, Grýlur, Grøleks And Skeklers: Medieval Disguise Traditions in the North Atlantic'. *Arv* 57, 33–54.

Heide, E. 2006a. 'Gand, seid og åndevind'. PhD thesis. University of Bergen.

———. 2006b. 'Spirits through respiratory passages'. In John McKinnel et al. (eds), *The Fantastic in Old Norse/Icelandic Literature. Sagas and the British Isles. Preprint Papers of the 13th International Saga Conference, Durham and York, 6th–12th August, 2006*. Durham: University of Durham, 350–358

Jakobsen, Jakob. 1911. 'Nordiske minder, især sproglige, på Orknøerne'. *Maal og Minne*, 318–347.

———. 1985. *An Etymological Dictionary of the Norn Language in Shetland*. Lerwick: Shetland Folk Society.

James VI. 1597. *Daemonologie in forme of a Dialogue*. Edinburgh: Robert Waldegrave.

Jennings, A. 2016. 'Memories and Metamorphoses: A Short Introduction to the Supernatural Tales and Beliefs from Fetlar in Shetland'. In T. Kuusela. and G. Maiello (eds), *Folk Belief and Traditions of the Supernatural*. Copenhagen: Beewolf Press, 27–56.

Jónsson, G. (ed.). 1954. *Göngu-Hrólfs saga*. Fornaldarsögur Norðurlanda 3. Reykjavík: Íslendingasagnaútgáfan.

Kanerva, K. 2013. 'Eigi er sá heill, er í augun verkir. Eye Pain in Thirteenth and Fourteenth-Century *Íslendingasögur*'. *Arv* 69, 7–35.

Klintberg, B. 1980. *Svenska trollformler*. Stockholm: FiBs Lyrikklub/ Tidens forlag.

Kvideland, R. and Sehmsdorf, H. 1988. *Scandinavian Folk Belief and Legend*. Minneapolis: University of Minnesota Press.

Lamb, Gregor. 1995. *Orkney Wordbook*. Kirkwall: Byrgisey.

Marwick, E.W. 1975. *Folklore of Orkney and Shetland*. London: Batsford.

Marwick, Hugh. 1929. *The Orkney Norn*. Oxford: Oxford University Press.

Mitchell, Stephen. 2000. 'Learning Magic in the Sagas'. In Geraldine Barnes and Margaret Clunies Ross (eds), *Old Norse myths, literature and society: The proceedings of the 11th International Saga Conference, 2–7 July 2000*. Sydney: Centre for Medieval Studies, University of Sydney, 335–345.

Munch, P.A. 1847. *Den Ældre Edda*. Christiania: P.T. Mallings.

Nicolson, James R. 1981. *Shetland Folklore*. London: Robert Hale Ltd.

Nicolson, John. 1912. 'Some Old-Time Shetland Customs'. *Old-Lore Miscellany* 5:3, 122–125.

Olsen, Magnus. 1916. 'Varðlokur: et bidrag til kundskap om gammelnorsk trolddom'. *Maal og Minne,* 1–22.

Pálsson, Gisli. 1991. 'The Name of the Witch: Sagas, Sorcery and Social Context'. In Ross Samson (ed.), *Social Approaches to Viking Studies*. Glasgow: Cruithne Press, 156–168.

Price, Neil. 2019. *The Viking Way: Magic and Mind in Late Iron Age Scandinavia*. Oxford and Philadelphia: Oxbow Books.

Robertson, J.D.M. 1991. *An Orkney Anthology: The Selected Works of Ernest Walker Marwick*. Edinburgh: Scottish Academic Press.

Saxby, Jessie M.E. 1932. *Shetland Traditional Lore*. London: Simpkin Marshall Ltd.

Siikala, Anna-Leena. 2002. *Mythic Images and Shamanism: A Perspective on Kalevala Poetry*. Helsinki: Academia Scientiarum Fennica.

Spence, J. 1899. *Shetland Folklore*. Lerwick: Johnson & Greig.

Stewart, George. 1877. *Shetland Fireside Tales*. Edinburgh: Edinburgh Publishing Company.

Tolley, Clive. 1995. 'Vorðr and gandr: Helping Spirits in Norse Magic'. *Arkiv för nordisk filologi* 110, 57–75.

Torvanger, M.H. 2016. *Einar Seim - i norske fotepar på Shetland*. Førde: Selja.

· XV ·

Homeward Bound

Hilde Rognskog and Heidi Rognskog Mella

As a greeting from our family and as Arne's holiday-home neighbours, we have had the pleasure of partaking in his knowledge of the Nordic language and history. Arne's academic commitment to our cultural heritage shows us that we are part of a rich language history that binds us together by the sea. The text that follows is written by Hilde Rognskog as a series of associative memories on the journey 'home', to Veiholmen.

* * *

It was the wind. Shouting and screaming at it, 'you can't catch me'. Or leaning your back against it, trusting it to keep you upright. The freedom of it. Usually, it was the opposite. The fear of its force. Its power being so great that it is impossible to move forward or breathe against it. The first nightmare is about the wind. The wind that fills all cavities – throat, nose, armpits, and eyes. Sneaking in all over the place. Hair blowing in all directions, making it hard to see. Never still, never calm. The windswept island with windswept people and the clouds drifting past.

The ferry rocks vigorously. It's not scary. Feeling the impact of the waves. Head moving slowly from side to side. Not unwell, just a wee bit queasy. None of the passengers leave their cars to go up to the lounge for a coffee and a snack. On this late autumn evening, they remain safely cocooned in their separate shells.

It's dark. Markers with reflectors and white stripes on the road edge are all that is visible. Narrow roads. Over narrow bridges. From Edøy island to Kuli. The Kulibrua bridge over the Kulisvaet strait, Dampleibrua bridge over the Dampleia strait. From Kuli over Hestøya island and further out to Lamøya island. Some names are signposted along the way. Others are only mentioned on the map. The fishing boats are gone, and the recreational boats driven away on trailers.

The quickest route is through Frostaheia. Some slack turns and then straight ahead. A meeting place signposted with M. for cars coming in the opposite direction, or to allow cars to overtake. No cars. Straight ahead over the flat marsh. The lowland plains, like the prairie. A generation ago, there were no trees here. You could see for miles in all directions. The flatness beneath you, and the sky above you. Clusters of imported Sitka fir block the view now. Welcome as protection from the wind for some, a plague and nuisance for others. Marsh and bog, poor man's coal, and oil. The wind and rain, lack of sun and evaporation.

There is no consistency in the story. Just fragments. A disparity between mind and body. Where is the connection between the bigger picture and the smaller stories? Moving on, moving on. Over the moor, further out. Way out, towards the outermost reef. It's late and the weather is bad. Past Frostaheia and a right turn towards Sætran. Smooth turns, enjoyable to drive.

Round the church slowly, past Hopen Pier, over Kvalpøystraumen to Kvalpøya island. Pitch-black night. The frantic movement of the windscreen wipers whipping everything away. Names of islands come to mind. Place-names that tell of a property, a quality, a utility. Ausa, Måøya, Svinsylta, Pissarholmen. Like a delightful children's rhyme.

Finally, the bridge over the Verjeskift. Almost home and emotion takes over. The trinity – landscape, home, tears. White foam tops on the reef, turbulent sea and wind. This is Veiholmen, the real Veiholmen. Not summer, calm and idyllic.

Over Haugøya island. The little pine forest. Light brown barn needles, cones, and ants on the ground. The smell of summer. Further on to Hamarøya island. The dream of summer, rarely attainable. It's all about finding the right moment when all the variables align. A warm morning at low tide, just enough to warm up rock and sand. High tide in the afternoon, warm and delightfully free. To dive in and be saturated by the wild Atlantic waters.

The thoughts are interrupted by a gradual realisation. Strolling on the shoreline and climbing the island peaks. Look what I found! A sea urchin shell and a bird's skull. Crab claws coloured pink by the sun. Mussels and razor shells. Lovely clusters of sunburned black tang. Tossed in the middle of the island by storm surge and hurricanes. Look here, a bottle with Russian writing, a fish crate from Scotland! In the beginning a phenomenon, and a fleeting thought about storms at sea and reckless crew. Eventually, there were other things crunching underfoot! Jumbles of nylon nets, plastic bottles in all shapes and colours. Pipes, bags, and polystyrene. Entangled in the heather and becoming overgrown. As if ashamed and sweeping the stranger under the carpet. Until it can't be hidden anymore. So quickly, over so many years.

The car wipers are noisy and are turned off. Moving on, past the fishing co-op and the sports ground, past Stortjønna. Past Varden and Verkjen that provide views of the sea and the mountains, which can be glimpsed towards the mainland.

Flaksbåen rock acts as *mèdast* ('marker') for Veiaflesa in the outermost Langfjellet, and Dyrnestuva on the eastern side of Andholmen. Double Dutch for most people, but fun to recall from *Mål og méd.*[1] Locating the fishing spot requires systematic record taking and experience, local knowledge of weather, wave conditions, the seabed, and tides. The movements of the fish through the seasons are yet another variable. Weather-worn houses, boats, and their usage, all requiring extra care. Repairing fishing nets, mending engines. Take a deep breath and move on. Past Gulltjønna, the graveyard and the turn between the corner houses.

The last stretch across Sementveien, past Samvirken, and parking in Johan Været's living room. The house that once fitted into the row with Øyenhuset, Indre Angelhus, and Tangstad. It's missing. Now it's a parking lot. The house is cold. A glass of wine, a blanket, and out on the terrace. The smell of seaweed, kelp, and the sea. It's windy, but the familiar sounds are easy to call forth. The black-backed gull's wings as it flies close to the house walls, and its rough, easy call – *kaa-ga-ga*. Its sound more complex than the irksome *kija-kija* of the seagull. Its gaze moving on towards the Atlantic.

Remman, a reef strip into the ocean to the north-west, enables people to live out here. A natural barrier to the ocean. Small and large reefs protruding over and under the water. Only the cormorant sits on the clean-cut reefs in the barren and grey winter. With breaking waves, you can't get ashore. In summer, it explodes with dooryard dock, mayweed, viola, and hogweed. Electric green, white, and yellow. Growths cling between cracks and small patches of soil, fertilised with bird excrement. Plants make haste to grow before the autumn

---

1. Triangulation navigation technique using two or three landmarks to get one's bearing. See Kruse, Arne. 2000. *Mål og méd. Målføre og médnamn frå Smøla.* Trondheim: Tapir Akademisk Forlag.

storms set in. Ducks wade past and lose feathers; gulls rest on the wind. The oystercatcher plunges down to defend his nest. Baby seagulls do their best to hide in the rock crevices. But best of all, the kelp forest. Toothed wreck, oar weed, black tang, and dead man's rope. Leaning over the side of the boat, hand in the water, the feeling as fingers slide along dead man's rope, bulging like spaghetti on the surface. Cold, smooth, and slippery.

Several stories can be told about Veiholmen. For example, about stone stacking. Not as in Hamsun's *Growth of the Soil* – a single man's struggle to clear stones to create a living in the barren soil. Rather, the large stacks of stone used as supports under houses and boathouses. The cairn tower with its tarred wide stones, or boulders placed rhythmically over the pier. Buildings that made it possible to not only fish here, but also to live. Cutting, blasting, and moving an infinite amount of stone. Stones must be angular, pointed, and crooked to withstand the waves. Round smooth stones are spineless and slip easily apart. Stones should be entwined and resilient, like the islanders themselves.

Other stories will follow. Not about individuals fighting the forces of nature, but collective efforts and community building. Such as that of the Haugjegla Lighthouse. To stand by its lantern, observing the curvature of the earth, the peace and tranquillity. Tomorrow, the wind will abate.

Bibliography of Arne Kruse
(up to 2022)

Monographs

1983. 'Médnamn frå Smøla'. Cand.philol. thesis. University of Trondheim.

2000. *Mål og méd. Målføre og médnamn frå Smøla.* Trondheim: Tapir Akademisk Forlag.

Edited volumes

1989. *Stadnamn i kystkulturen: rapport frå NORNAs fjortande symposium i Volda 4.-6. mai 1987.* Uppsala: NORNA-förlaget. With Peter Hallaråker and Terje Aarset.

1992. *Minority Languages – The Scandinavian Experience: Papers Read at the Conference in Edinburgh 9–11 November 1990.* Oslo: Nordic Language Secretariat. With Gunilla Blom and Peter Graves.

1998. *Hamsun in Edinburgh: Papers Read at the Conference in Edinburgh 1997.* Hamarøy: Hamsun-selskapet. With Peter Graves.

2006. *Barra and Skye: Two Hebridean Perspectives.* Edinburgh: Scottish Society for Northern Studies.

2007. *Images and Imaginations: Perspectives on Britain and Scandinavia.* Edinburgh: Lockharton Press. With Peter Graves.

Articles

1991a. 'Norske stadnamn i Coon Valley, Wisconsin. Møte mellom to tradisjonar'. In Botolv Helleland (ed.), *Norsk språk i Amerika*. Oslo: Novus, 135–171.

1991b. 'A Few Names in a Vast Land – Scandinavian Place-Names in the Midwest'. *Northern Studies* 28, 25–34.

1996a. 'Scandinavian–American Place-Names as Viewed from the Old World'. In P. Sture Ureland and Iain Clarkson (eds), *Language Contact across the North Atlantic*. Tübingen: Max Niemeyer Verlag, 255–268.

1996b. 'Ivar Aasen and Knud Knudsen: The Centenary and the Legacy'. *Northern Studies* 31, 57–68.

1998a. 'Sjønamn på medfjella'. *Namn og Nemne* 15, 21–31.

1998b. 'Hamsun and Britain'. In Peter Graves and Arne Kruse (eds), *Hamsun in Edinburgh: Papers Read at the Conference in Edinburgh 1997*. Hamarøy: Hamsun-selskapet, 9–17.

2004. 'Norse Topographical Settlement Names on the Western Littoral of Scotland'. In Jonathan Adams and Katherine Holman (eds), *Scandinavia and Europe 800–1350: Contact, Conflict, and Coexistence*. Turnhout: Brepols, 99–109.

2005a. 'An Ethnic Enigma – Norse, Pict and Gael in the Western Isles'. In Andras Mortensen and Símun V. Arge (eds), *Viking and Norse in the North Atlantic: Select Papers from the Proceedings of the Fourteenth Viking Congress, Tórshavn, 19–30 July 2001*. Tórshavn: Føroya Fróðskaparfelag, 284–296. With Andrew Jennings.

2005b. 'Explorers, Raiders and Settlers. The Norse Impact upon Hebridean Place-Names'. In Peder Gammeltoft, Carole Hough, and Doreen Waugh (eds), *Cultural Contacts in the North Atlantic Region: The Evidence of Names*. NORNA, Scottish Place-Name Society, and Society for Name Studies in Britain and Ireland, 141–156.

2007. 'Fashion, Limitation and Nostalgia: Scandinavian Place-Names Abroad'. In Arne Kruse and Peter Graves (eds), *Images and Imaginations: Perspectives on Britain and Scandinavia*. Edinburgh: Lockharton Press, 9–39.

2009a. 'One Coast – Three Peoples: Names and Ethnicity in the Scottish West during the Early Viking Period'. In Alex Woolf (ed.), *Scandinavian*

Scotland – Twenty Years After: The Proceedings of a Day Conference Held on 19th February 2007. St Andrews, 17–40. With Andrew Jennings.

2009b. 'From Dál Riata to the *Gall-Gaidheil*'. *Viking and Medieval Scandinavia* 5, 123–149. With Andrew Jennings.

2011. 'Fair Isle'. *Northern Studies* 42, 17–40.

2012a. '*Christiana* og *Eidswold*: norske namm I den nye verda'. *Norsk Lingvistisk Tidsskrift* 30, 110–124.

2012b. 'Tabu og fiske'. *Smølaminne*, 122–129.

2014a. 'Columba and Jonah – A Motif in the Dispersed Art of Iona'. *Northern Studies* 45, 1–26.

2014b. 'Ordet Ballvollen knytt til transnasjonal overføring av idéar'. *Historisk tidsskrift* 93, 407–423. With Liv Helene Willumsen.

2015. 'Laithlind'. *Namn og Nemne* 32, 49–86.

2016. 'Scots: The Role of Language in Civic Nationalism'. In Guri Ellen Barstad, Arnstein Hjelde, Sigmund Kvam, Anastasia Parianou, and John Todd (eds), *Language and Nation: Crossroads and Connections*. Münster: Waxmann, 241–264.

2017a. 'The Norway to Be: *Laithlind* and Avaldsnes'. In Christian Cooijmans (ed.), *Traversing the Inner Seas: Contacts and Continuity in and around Scotland, the Hebrides, and the North of Ireland*. Edinburgh: Scottish Society for Northern Studies, 198–231.

2017b. '*Laithlind* – Pre-Unified Norway?' *Scottish Place-Name News* 42, 10–12.

2020a. 'On Harbours and Havens: Maritime Strategies in Norway during the Viking Age'. In Anne Pedersen and Søren M. Sindbæk (ed.), *Viking Encounters: Proceedings of the Eighteenth Viking Congress*. Aarhus: Aarhus University Press, 170–185.

2020b. 'Magic Language: The Transmission of an Idea over Geographical Distance and Linguistic Barriers'. *Magic, Ritual, and Witchcraft* 15:1, 1–32. With Liv Helene Willumsen.

2021a. 'På grensa: Kulisteinen som geografisk og kulturell grensemarkør'. In Morten Stige and Ole Risbøl (eds), *Kulisteinen – grensemerke i tid og rom*. Kristiansund: Nordmøre museum, 13–33.

2021b. 'Namnet Møre'. In Morten Stige and Ole Risbøl (eds), *Kulisteinen – grensemerke i tid og rom*. Kristiansund: Nordmøre museum, 34.

2021c. 'Kuli og andre namn i nærområdet'. In Morten Stige and Ole Risbøl (eds), *Kulisteinen – grensemerke i tid og rom*. Kristiansund: Nordmøre museum, 58–63.

2021d. 'Landsnamnet'. In Morten Stige and Ole Risbøl (eds), *Kulisteinen – grensemerke i tid og rom*. Kristiansund: Nordmøre museum, 108–113.

2021e. 'Nokre Smøla-namn'. In Morten Stige and Ole Risbøl (eds), *Kulisteinen – grensemerke i tid og rom*. Kristiansund: Nordmøre museum, 148–151.

2021f. 'Om namnet Smøla og andre øynamn'. *Smølaminne*, 71–79.

2022. 'Tradition and Innovation: The Function of Ambiguity in the Three Scandinavian Runic Conversion Monuments'. In Ian Giles (ed.), *Scandinavia Refracted: A Festschrift in Honour of Bjarne Thorup Thomsen*. Edinburgh: Scottish Society for Northern Studies, 15–44.

Reviews

1995. 'Norwegian Studies: Language'. *The Year's Work in Modern Language Studies* 57, 935–946.

1996. 'Norwegian Studies: Language'. *The Year's Work in Modern Language Studies* 58, 945–955.

1997. 'Norwegian Studies: Language'. *The Year's Work in Modern Language Studies* 59, 881–890.

1998. 'Norwegian Studies: Language'. *The Year's Work in Modern Language Studies* 60, 801–807.

2000. 'Norwegian Studies: Language'. *The Year's Work in Modern Language Studies* 62, 825–832.

2006. '*Skandinavisch-schottische Sprachbeziehungen im Mittelalter: der altnordische Lehneinfluss*. By Susanne Kries'. *Saga-Book* 30, 112–114.

2010. '*Nordiske navnes centralitet og regionalitet*. By Birgit Eggert, Bente Holmberg, and Bent Jørgensen (eds)'. *Scandinavica* 49:2, 91–92.

Other

2008. 'User-Group Identity in Scandinavian Place-Names'. PhD thesis (by research publications). University of Edinburgh.

Notes on Contributors

Christian Cooijmans is a British Academy Postdoctoral Fellow at the University of Liverpool. His research explores the reach and repercussions of viking activity across the Frankish realm, as well as its subsequent, pre-modern historiography. His first monograph, *Monarchs and Hydrarchs*, was published in 2020.

Ryan Foster is an historical and cultural geographer who completed his doctoral study in Scandinavian Studies at the University of Edinburgh. His PhD thesis was an interdisciplinary investigation of Viking shieling names in Scotland.

Peder Gammeltoft is Scientific Manager of the Norwegian Language Collections (*Språksamlingane*) at the University of Bergen, in charge of curating and modernising existing language resources and developing new ones. Previously, he was Associate Professor in Name Research at the University of Copenhagen, focusing on Scandinavian place-names in the British Isles, Normandy, the North Atlantic, and Denmark.

Brigitte Guenier-Kruse is Teaching Fellow in French and Francophone Studies at the University of Edinburgh. Having graduated from the University of Caen Normandy, she taught in the United States (Wisconsin) and Canada (Alberta), where she established numerous student exchanges. She has served as Assistant Professor at Heriot-Watt University, and was Erasmus coordinator and consultant for the Open University and the

SCHOLAR study guide programme. She is an elected Consular Adviser for Français du Monde-ADFE (French Abroad).

Botolv Helleland is Associate Professor (retired) at the Department of Linguistics and Scandinavian Studies at the University of Oslo. He is a former state place-name adviser, and has been member of the United Nations Group of Experts on Geographical Names (UGEGN) and board member of the International Council of Onomastic Sciences (ICOS).

Arnstein Hjelde is a Professor of Norwegian at Østfold University College in Halden, Norway. His main research interest concerns Norwegian as a heritage language in the Americas, on which he has carried out considerable fieldwork and published a number of papers. Most of this work has focused on the Midwest, but the west coast and Canada have also been included. He is currently involved in a research project documenting and investigating the Norwegian Language in Argentina.

Pavel Iosad is Senior Lecturer in Linguistics and English Language at the University of Edinburgh. He has a doctorate from the University of Tromsø – The Arctic University of Norway, and has previously held a lectureship at Ulster University. He is currently completing a monograph on language contact and phonological convergence in northern Europe, with a focus on Fennoscandia, the Baltic region, and Britain and Ireland.

Andrew Jennings lives in Shetland and is Associate Professor in Island Studies at the Institute for Northern Studies, University of the Highlands and Islands. He has a particular research interest in the cultural history of the Scottish Islands, with an emphasis on place-names and the Vikings.

Alan Macniven is Senior Lecturer and Head of Scandinavian Studies at the University of Edinburgh. He is responsible for honours and postgraduate courses in Viking Studies and Old Norse Literature and Culture, and has organised a number of conferences and seminars on related themes. His recent research has focused on Scandinavian place-names in Scotland and their value as indicators of cultural change.

Guy Puzey is Senior Lecturer in Scandinavian Studies at the University of Edinburgh, where he is also currently Head of the Department of European Languages and Cultures. His main research interests are in language policy and sociolinguistics, critical toponomastics, literary translation, connections between Scotland and Norway, and twentieth-century social and cultural history.

Linda Riddell is an independent researcher, who returned to study at the University of Edinburgh after retiring from her career in the oil industry. A native Shetlander, she has published *Shetland and the Great War* (2015), as well as articles on the history of the Islands, Scottish and Nordic history, and World War I.

Heidi Rognskog is educated as a visual artist at Bergen Art Academy, Norway, and Düsseldorf Art Academy, Germany. Today, she is Project Manager for 'Digital dissemination of cultural heritage' at the Gurisenteret cultural and coastal centre in Smøla. She alternates between working at the artist residences at Bøler, Oslo, and the fishing village of Veiholmen, Smøla.

Hilde Rognskog is a visual artist and author educated at the Academy of Fine Arts in Oslo. In recent years, she has worked in Eidsvoll, Norway, where she manages WI Galleri and Studio. As a visual artist, she works with installations and political art, and has exhibited in various places nationally and internationally.

Berit Sandnes wrote her doctoral thesis on Orkney place-names of Old Norse origin, and how these have been adapted in Scots English. She has worked for the Institute for Language and Folklore in Sweden, and currently works for the Norwegian Mapping Authority.

Brian Smith is archivist at the Shetland Museum and Archives. He is the author and editor of articles and books about Shetland and Orkney.

Anke-Beate Stahl wrote her PhD thesis on 'Place-Names of Barra in the Outer Hebrides'. She was Meisterschülerin in Fine Arts at the Hochschule für Bildende Künste Braunschweig, Germany, and now is a painter and freelance curator living in Edinburgh.

Bjarne Thorup Thomsen is an Honorary Fellow and a former Reader in the Scandinavian Studies section of the School of Literatures, Languages and Cultures at the University of Edinburgh.

Liv Helene Willumsen is Professor Emerita of History at the University of Tromsø – The Arctic University of Norway with a PhD in history (University of Edinburgh, 2008) and a PhD in literature (University of Bergen, 2003). Her books include *Witches of the North: Scotland and Finnmark* (2013) and *The Voices of Women in Witchcraft Trials: Northern Europe* (2022). She has written the exhibition texts of Steilneset Memorial, Vardø, Norway. She was awarded the Norwegian King's Medal of Merit in 2019.